WASATCH TOURS

Volume 2

Intermediate and Advanced Ski Touring in the Northern Wasatch Mountains

David Hanscom   and Alexis Kelner

WASATCH TOURS PUBLISHING
Salt Lake City, Utah

Dedicated to Brett and Eric and Greg.

Published by:
WASATCH TOURS PUBLISHING
Salt Lake City, Utah

ISBN 1-884744-03-6

PREFACE

Volume 1 of *Wasatch Tours*, published in December 1993, contains introductory and background information for tourers of all ability levels. Volume 2 provides the details needed by more advanced skiers to ensure enjoyable and safe outings. It covers intermediate and advanced ski touring opportunities in the northern half of the Wasatch Mountains. The area described in the book extends from the peaks southeast of Brigham City to the ridge separating Little Cottonwood Canyon from its southern neighbors.

This book is divided into six chapters, each of which covers one geographic region. In addition to the three major canyons described in the first edition of *Wasatch Tours* (Millcreek, Big Cottonwood, and Little Cottonwood), we discuss skiing possibilities in Parleys and City Creek canyons, among the foothills and side canyons of Salt Lake County, areas east of Bountiful, Francis and Thurston peaks in northern Davis County, the Mount Ogden area, and the Ben Lomond/Willard massif at the north end of the range.

In keeping with the philosophy of providing complete coverage of touring areas and detailed descriptions of touring routes, this volume contains more than 150 aerial photographs and 23 shaded schematic illustrations. The text includes evaluations of avalanche incidents and discussions of other dangers that cross country skiers must understand.

Beyond the detailed coverage of ski touring routes and hazard avoidance, the book contains many historical references, as well as some information for backcountry users who are interested in environmental issues.

We would like to acknowledge and thank a number of individuals who assisted in the preparation of this volume. Larry Swanson's generosity with time and flying skills once again made the aerial photographs possible. Backcountry touring advocates Steve Lewis, Milt Hollander, and Bob Athay never turned down an opportunity to provide valuable information. Karin and Dennis Caldwell and Rolf Doebbelling endured, without complaints, numerous outings planned specifically for photographic purposes. Roly Pearson and Bill Stenquist suffered through many exploratory hikes and ski tours. Jock Glidden and Bob Irvine were extremely helpful with touring information in the Ogden area.

4

Media representatives have been extremely helpful in spreading the word about *Wasatch Tours*. Craig Hansell and Tom Wharton at the *Salt Lake Tribune*, as well as Don Woodward and Ray Grass at the *Deseret News*, have been strong supporters of backcountry skiing for many years. Television coverage provided by KUTV's Reese Stein and KSL's John Hollenhorst was also much appreciated. *Park Record* writer Nan Chalat and *Utah Sports Guide* editor Drew Ross also produced very positive reviews.

Production assistance provided by Joe Zachary with the LaTeX document preparation system is once again greatly appreciated. Ruta Ehlers deserves a special accolade for designing the covers.

These volumes would not have been possible without the patience and understanding of Karla and Mary. We thank them very much.

Dave Hanscom and *Alexis Kelner*
January 1995

5

TABLE OF CONTENTS

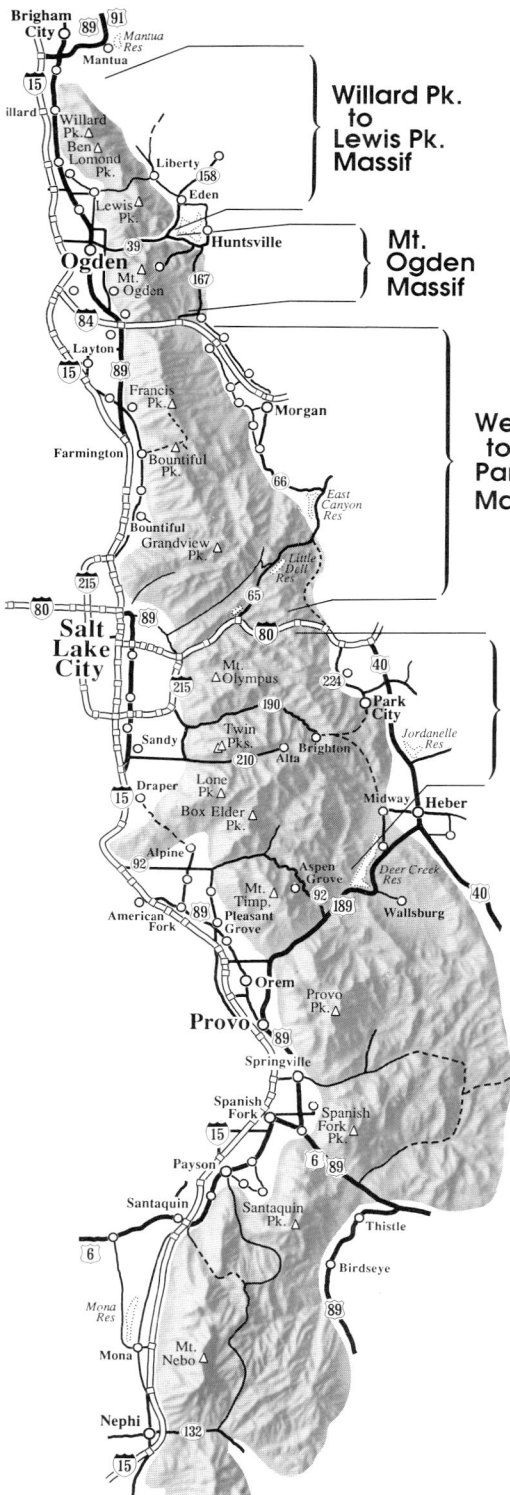

TOURING REGIONS OF THE NORTHERN WASATCH

Willard Pk. to Lewis Pk. Massif

Mt. Ogden Massif

Weber Canyon to Parleys Canyon Massif

Parleys Canyon to Provo Canyon Massif

The Wasatch Range consists of several mountain regions separated by river valleys that serve as major transportation corridors. These corridors provide convenient access for touring and make it possible to ascend any peak or drainage in a single day.

This volume of Wasatch Tours *describes intermediate, advanced, and "super tour" possibilities in the northern Wasatch, the portion of the range north of the Salt Lake/ Utah county boundary.*

Volume 3 will examine touring areas south of that boundary.

6

Chapter 1

INTRODUCTION

The dramatically upthrust chain of peaks known as the Wasatch Mountains has its northern terminus at Box Elder Canyon, near Brigham City and extends southward some 100 miles to Salt Creek Canyon, near the community of Nephi.[1] The Wasatch range is extremely narrow at its northern end, then widens as it approaches the south end of Davis County. Maximum width occurs near the Salt Lake/Utah county divide. The range then gradually narrows as it approaches Salt Creek Canyon. At its northern extreme the major peaks reach elevations of about 9500 feet above sea level. Summit elevations gradually increase as one moves southward. At 11,877 feet, Mount Nebo is the highest and the southernmost summit of the range.

Weather patterns in the Wasatch Mountains are ideal for backcountry skiing. Frequent storms deposit large amounts of light powder snow, and intervening periods are usually dominated by sunshine. Although wind can be a problem on the high ridges, daytime temperatures seldom remain below 10°F. Weather patterns and snow accumulations can be quite different in the northern and southern parts of the Wasatch due to the "lake effect" and the location of the storm track, but snow cover is normally sufficient for enjoyable ski touring in any area during the months of December through March. Another month of touring at the beginning of winter, and two or three months at the end, can be expected at elevations above 9000 feet.

Most of the timbered areas and summits of the Wasatch Mountains are public lands, managed by the U.S. Forest Service. Areas located in,

---

[1]The upthrust actually continues north well into Idaho and south beyond Salt Creek Canyon. The extension immediately north of Box Elder Canyon is known as the Wellsville Mountains; the extension south of Salt Creek is called the San Pitch Mountains.

Figure 1.1   Complex land ownership patterns can adversely affect public access to public lands. Shaded areas represent national forest lands; white areas represent a mix of county, municipal, and private land ownerships.

and north of, Salt Lake County are supervised by the Wasatch-Cache National Forest headquartered in Salt Lake City; areas in and south of Utah County are managed by the Provo-based Uinta National Forest.

The Wasatch foothills, where many access points and formal trailheads are located, have somewhat diverse ownerships. Some parcels are owned by county or municipal governments; others are private. Illustrated in Figure 1.1, the complex "checkerboard" ownership pattern of lands east of Ogden serves as an example; similar ownership patterns exist throughout the range. According to planning documents, officials of the Wasatch-Cache National Forest will attempt to consolidate, by acquisition or by trade, some of the scattered land parcels.

Wasatch Tours is a 3-volume guide for winter users of the backcountry in the Wasatch range. Volume 1, published in 1993, is a general introduction, with emphasis on equipment, mountain hazards, avalanche safety, and beginner tours. This volume details intermediate and advanced ski touring possibilities in the northern Wasatch, the region located between Box Elder Canyon and the southern border of Salt Lake County. Volume 3 will detail touring options in the Wasatch south of Salt Lake County.

Chapter 1 of this volume provides a brief overview of various touring regions and wilderness areas in the northern Wasatch. New sources of backcountry information and recent developments in avalanche search technology are also discussed. Each of the other chapters describes specific ski touring opportunities in one or more of the regions of the northern Wasatch.

TOURING REGIONS

The Wasatch Mountains provide many excellent opportunities for cross country ski touring. Unlike many mountain chains, which consist of a continuous crest sometimes a hundred miles long, the Wasatch is made up of several well-defined massifs,[2] each separated from its neighbor by a major canyon. Each canyon contains a prominent watercourse and serves as a transportation corridor. The map at the beginning of this chapter shows the various massifs described in this volume and the network of roads that separates them.

Proximity to metropolitan areas and their well-developed system of access roads is another characteristic that makes the Wasatch an exceptional area for backcountry winter recreation. Any area in the Wasatch can be toured in a day-long outing. Most peaks can be ascended in a day, although the overall duration of a mountain summit excursion can approach (or exceed) a twenty-four hour period.

The Willard Peak to Lewis Peak Massif

The northernmost massif of the Wasatch Mountains is the land mass located between Brigham City and Ogden Canyon (Figure 1.2). From north to south, it's dominant features are Willard Peak (9764 feet), Ben Lomond Peak (9117 feet) and Lewis Peak (8036 feet). North Ogden Pass, a depression along the main crest, separates Lewis Peak from Ben Lomond. While the three summits are relatively low compared to the 11,000-12,000 foot peaks at the southern end of the range, they rise rather abruptly from the valley floor. Though an occasional well-executed ski track has been observed in the steep couloirs descending from Ben Lomond, the west flank of the massif provides no terrain suitable for "normal" touring.

Most of the practical touring terrain lies along the massif's east side. The best access to the touring areas is from the Ogden Valley, from the community of Mantua, or from North Ogden Pass. Ogden Valley is reached most easily from Ogden Canyon via SR-39 and SR-162, or by way of North Ogden Pass (also SR-162). Mantua is located east of Brigham City along US-89/91.

Intermediate and advanced touring opportunities in the vicinity of Ogden Valley, Mantua, and North Ogden Pass are described in Chapter 2.

---

[2] A *massif* is defined in *The American Heritage Dictionary* to be a "compact group of connected mountains forming an independent portion of a range."

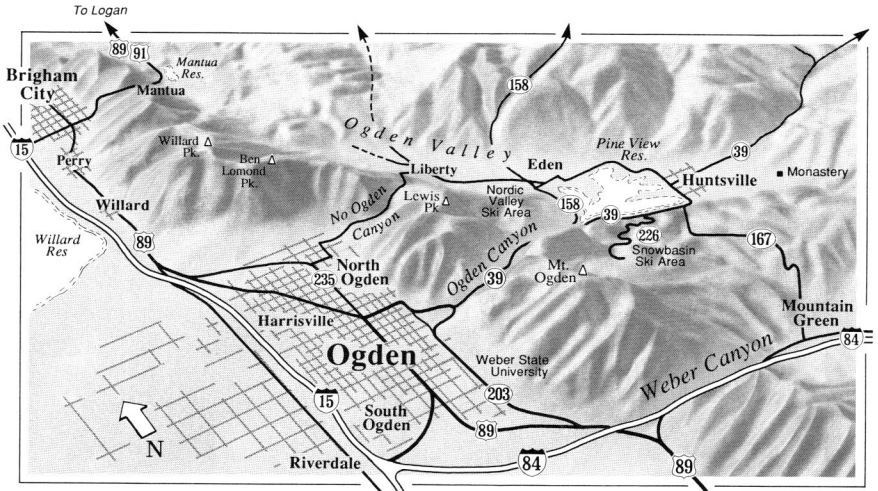

Figure 1.2   Box Elder Canyon (Brigham City) to Weber Canyon—touring areas and access points. The best touring in this region is found along the east slope of the range.

The Mount Ogden Massif

The Mount Ogden massif, also illustrated in Figure 1.2 and described in Chapter 2, rises directly east of Ogden. The massif is dominated by 9572 foot Mount Ogden. Nearly all the canyons that descend the west flank of the massif are steep and narrow. The northernmost of these, privately-owned Taylor Canyon, has been the site of several hiking and climbing fatalities over the years.

The east side of the massif contains Snow Basin and the Snowbasin ski area. A number of tours are possible in and about the area, but due to a recent Forest Service decision to permit transfer of some 700 acres of prime public land to the Sun Valley Corporation, those possibilities may soon vanish.

Snow Basin is accessed from Weber Canyon via the "Trappers Loop Road," SR-167, or from Ogden Canyon.

The Weber Canyon to Parleys Canyon Massif

The Weber Canyon to Parleys Canyon massif is one of the largest in the Wasatch. It commences with Weber Canyon at its northern end and terminates at its southern end with Parleys Canyon. Due to some pronounced geographic dissimilarities, the massif is discussed in two sections, one describing the area in Davis County, and the other describing the area in Salt Lake County.

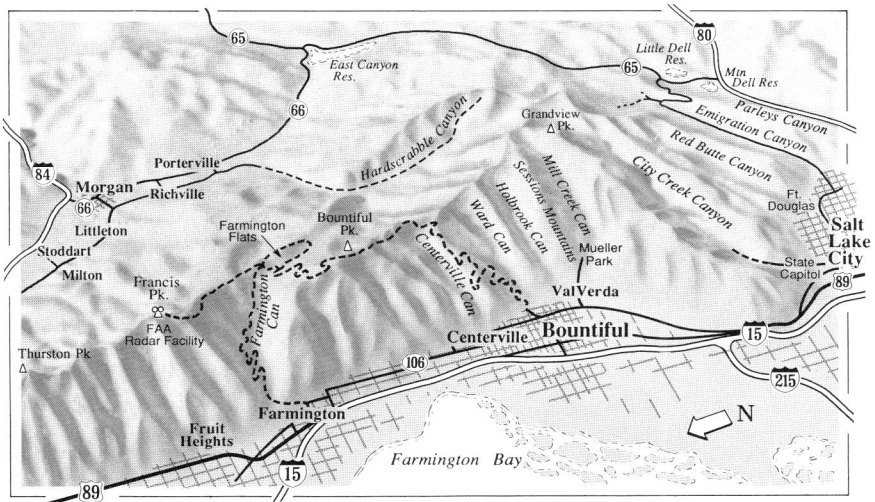

Figure 1.3   Davis County peaks and canyons, located between Weber Canyon and Grandview Peak, are the least accessible of any in the Wasatch. They contain much private land and only two public access roads.

Davis County Area. Illustrated in Figure 1.3, the area of the Wasatch between Weber Canyon and the northern boundary of Salt Lake County is best known for its frequently high canyon winds, sometimes reaching velocities over 80 miles per hour. In this area, the range is relatively narrow and rises very steeply. The west flank is only three miles wide; the east flank is six miles wide. The Federal Aviation Administration's radar domes are highly visible on the 9547 foot summit of Francis Peak. A 9707 foot prominence at the crest's northern end was recently named Thurston Peak, after a Mormon pioneer who explored and helped populate Morgan County. On the east side of the range, a series of small secondary ridges parallels the main crest, forming a high valley suitable for fine touring.

Farmington Canyon nearly bisects the northern part of this massif; it also drains Farmington Flats, a wide, gently-sloped basin just east of the crest. A road, known as "Skyline Drive," ascends Farmington Canyon, follows the ridge southward past Bountiful Peak, then descends westward into Bountiful. Near the southern end of Davis County, an east-west ridge known as the "Sessions Mountains" separates Holbrook Canyon from Mill Creek Canyon. The Davis County portion of the massif ends at 9410 foot Grandview Peak and a ten mile long westward ridge with numerous large gravel pits at its base.

Touring opportunities in the Davis County region of the Weber to

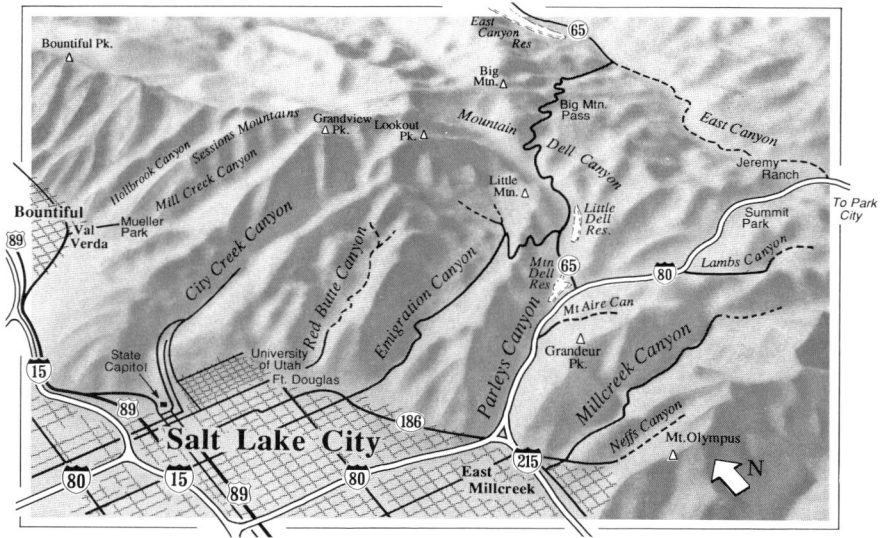

Figure 1.4   Northern Salt Lake County canyons, from City Creek to Parleys, are more accessible to cross country skiers than those in Davis County because most contain roads.

Parleys massif are described in Chapter 2.

Salt Lake County Area. The character of the Wasatch changes radically south of the Davis County/Salt Lake County dividing ridge. The main crest takes an abrupt turn eastward; the west flank canyons, illustrated in Figure 1.4, become longer, deeper, and less steep. Eastwardly descending canyons are generally uninteresting for ski tourers, partly due to the heavily vegetated terrain and partly due to limited public access.

The principal areas described in Chapter 3 drain to the west. City Creek Canyon, the northernmost in Salt Lake County, is eleven miles long. Emigration Canyon is only nine miles from top to bottom. Parleys/Mountain Dell is approximately fourteen miles long. Other canyons, such as Red Butte, terminate west of the main Wasatch ridge and are considerably shorter. The extraordinarily long canyons of northern Salt Lake County contain numerous basins and drainages suitable for excellent intermediate and advanced touring.

The Parleys Canyon to Provo Canyon Massif

The Parleys Canyon to Provo Canyon massif (illustrated partially in Figure 1.5) is the largest land mass in the range. It encompasses portions of

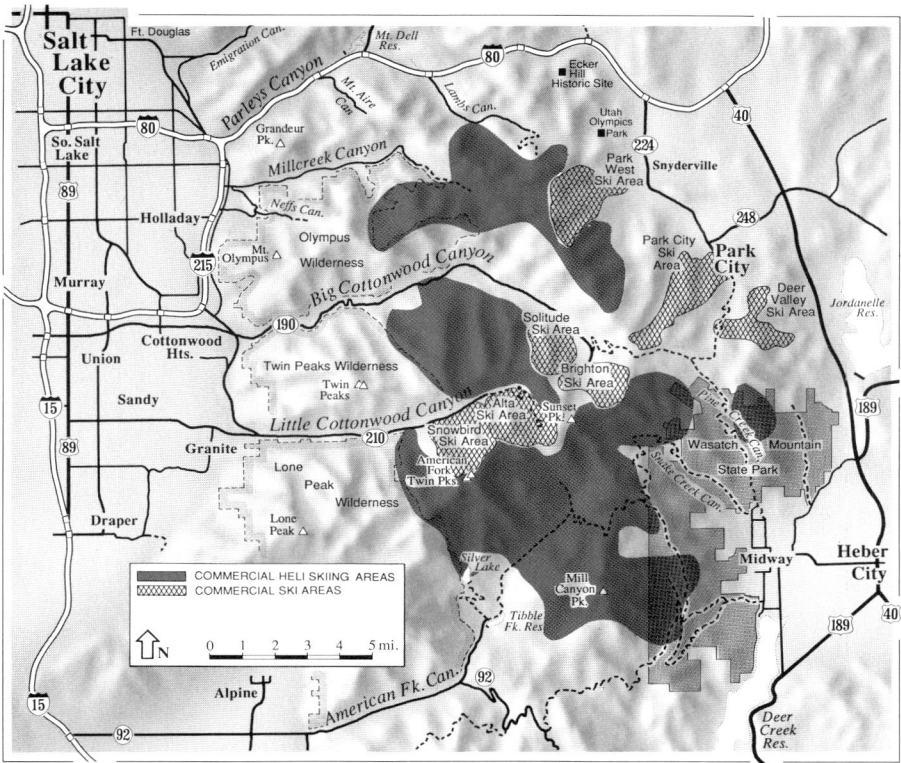

Figure 1.5 The area between Parleys Canyon and American Fork Canyon is the most heavily utilized recreational region in the Wasatch.

four counties and contains four wilderness areas, one state park, one national monument, and eight commercial ski area operations. Four major canyons descend westward into the valleys at the base of the range. Most of these canyons have been extensively glaciated and contain numerous side branches of touring significance.

Commonly referred to as the Central Wasatch,[3] the Parleys to Provo Canyon massif has been subdivided into four parts: (1) the Salt Lake Valley region, (2) Park City and Snyderville Basin, (3) the Utah Valley region, and (4) the Heber-Midway area. Only the Salt Lake Valley and Park City/Snyderville Basin areas will be discussed in this volume.

------

[3] We have chosen to define the Central Wasatch as that area encompassed by Parleys Canyon to the north, Salt Lake and Utah valleys along the west side, Provo Canyon at the southern extreme, and the Heber-Midway-Park City metropolitan area along its eastern flank. Many individuals and agencies define the Central Wasatch differently. The U.S. Forest Service, as an example, defines the Central Wasatch as that area containing only Millcreek, Big, and Little Cottonwood canyons.

Heber Valley
To Midway Mill Canyon Pk
40 248
Park City
Snyderville
Clayton Pk
Brighton Sunset Pk
Brighton Ski Area
Alta Ski Area
224
Solitude Ski Area
Alta Snowbird Ski Area
No. Fk. American Fk. Canyon
American Fork Twin Pks.
Box Elder Pk
80
Mt Raymond
Big Cottonwood Canyon
Twin Pks
210
Lone Pk
Little Cottonwood Canyon
Dry Creek Canyon
Millcreek Canyon
Mt Olympus
FLANK
Bells Canyon
CANYONS
Alpine
Grandeur Pk
Neffs Canyon
WEST
190
"Terra Incognita"
Corner Can
Parleys Canyon
210
Granite
Wasatch Blvd
80
Wasatch
Blvd
Cottonwood Heights
209
Sandy
N
Draper
Salt Lake City
East Millcreek
215
Holladay

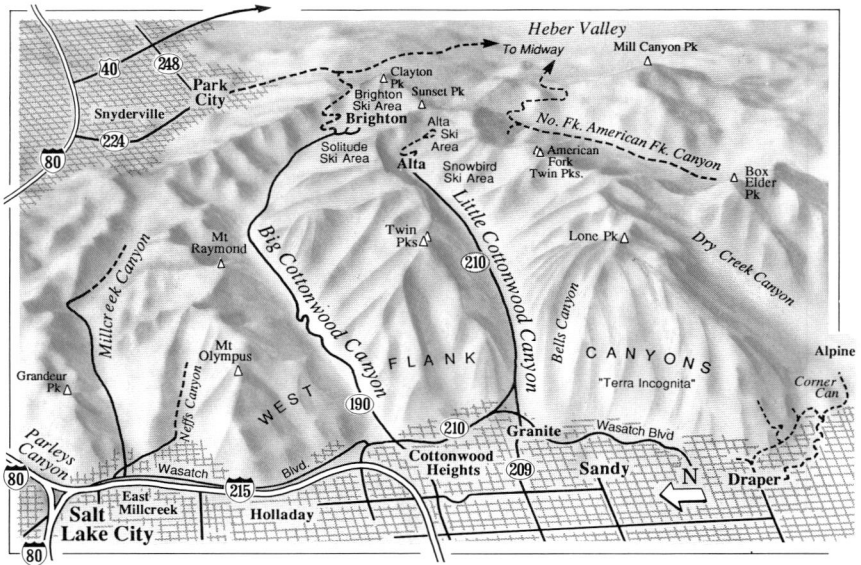

Figure 1.6   The Salt Lake Valley Region of the Central Wasatch includes three major canyons (Millcreek, Big Cottonwood, and Little Cottonwood) that are discussed in separate chapters of this book, A fourth chapter describes touring areas in the smaller, intervening canyons along the west flank of the range.

Salt Lake Valley Region. The area is illustrated in Figure 1.6. Three major canyons, Mill Creek, Big Cottonwood, and Little Cottonwood dominate the area adjacent to the Salt Lake Valley. Several lesser canyons that drain the west flank of the range play significant roles in a number of Wasatch ski tours and will be described later.

Millcreek Canyon. Millcreek Canyon, which joins Salt Lake Valley at 38th South, is the closest *reliable* touring area to Salt Lake City. Mount Raymond (10,241 feet) and adjacent Gobblers Knob (10,246 feet), are the dominant mountain features of this canyon.

Millcreek Canyon is typical of the Wasatch in that the terrain is generally steeper on the north slope of the canyon than on its south. Due partly to steeper slopes and to denser brush that grows at lower elevations, ski touring is also generally more difficult in the side-gulches that are closer to the valley.

The paved Millcreek Canyon road is plowed as far as the Forest Service Guard Station and allows easy access to the snow. In an effort to repair and to rehabilitate many years of land abuse and overuse, the Forest Service, with the cooperation of the Salt Lake County government, has initiated a user fee for recreationists leaving the canyon. Ski touring options in and about Millcreek Canyon are described in Chapter 4.

Big Cottonwood Canyon. The 13-mile long Big Cottonwood Canyon offers the greatest variety of readily-accessible touring terrain in the Wasatch. It has exceptional snow conditions for all levels of skiing ability. The potential for "cross-canyon" touring into adjacent drainages and even into other regions of the massif is also excellent. Ski mountaineering options are plentiful among the 11,000 foot summits of the Twin Peaks Wilderness. Big Cottonwood Canyon is accessed from I-215 via SR-190. Touring opportunities in this canyon are described in Chapter 5.

Little Cottonwood Canyon. Little Cottonwood Canyon is another hub of intermediate and advanced ski touring activity in the Wasatch. Nearby Lone Peak Wilderness provides numerous opportunities for winter mountaineering and extended touring expeditions.

The north wall of Little Cottonwood Canyon is extremely steep and rocky and (generally) does not lend itself to anything but rock climbing and avalanches. The south side of the canyon, however, contains several prominent drainages with some of the best touring terrain and powder snow in the Wasatch. These, as well as several delightful cross-canyon tours into Big Cottonwood Canyon, are described in Chapter 6. Tours into adjacent American Fork Canyon will be discussed in Volume 3.

West Flank Canyons. Originating at the westernmost summits of the Wasatch, several short canyons descend directly into Salt Lake Valley. These canyons are generally quite steep and may have marginal snow cover due to their low elevation and western exposure. The steepness and uncertain snow, however, present irresistible challenges to a growing number of dedicated tourers. Some of these touring routes are described in Chapter 7.

Neffs Canyon. Located between Millcreek and Big Cottonwood, Neffs begins above the Olympus Cove area of Salt Lake City at about 42nd South. Neffs offers a variety of intermediate and advanced terrain to the skier who is willing to take a chance on snow conditions and who is not too faint-hearted to attempt the narrow trail down to the valley. Because the mouth of Neffs Canyon has an elevation of only 5600 feet, the snow there is usually marginal, and the scrub oak beside the trail is impenetrable. The upper part of the canyon, however, has some nice open areas and two large bowls.

Tolcat and Heughs Canyons. These canyons descend westward from the proximity of 9026 foot Mount Olympus. The Mount Olympus trail is located (for most of its length) in Tolcat Canyon, and the highest reaches of Tolcat lead into Neffs Canyon. Heughs Canyon is too rocky to be of any touring interest.

Ferguson Canyon. Located immediately south of Big Cottonwood, Ferguson is a short drainage that originates at Twin Peaks. The canyon is narrow, brushy, rocky, and steep and is generally not suitable for "ordinary" ski touring.

Deaf Smith Canyon. Deaf Smith is another short, steep, rocky, and brushy gulch on the west flank of Twin Peaks. Access to the gulch is complicated by a cantankerous land owner who once threatened to shoot law enforcement officers (who were performing a mountain rescue) for trespassing on his property. The canyon is suited only for experienced tourers outfitted with bullet-proof vests.

Bells Canyon. Bells is a 6-mile long glaciated canyon that drains the north flank of 11,253 foot Lone Peak. It is a popular summer access canyon to the Lone Peak Wilderness. Expert tourers frequently descend the canyon after entering it along its top from either Little Cottonwood or Dry Creek canyon.

"Terra Incognita" Canyons. Several drainages descend the west flank of Lone Peak into the southern end of Salt Lake Valley. These canyons, fondly called Terra Incognita by the authors, are rarely visited, even during summer. Within a few years, however, as Sandy City's and Draper's subdivisions overtake the foothills and as trailheads are developed, these previously "unknown" canyons will become popular among hikers and backcountry tourers.

Corner Canyon. This is the southernmost Wasatch drainage in Salt Lake Valley. Most of its area is privately owned, but long-established public use along specific roadways continues to be permitted by county officials. Several touring and hiking routes into Lone Peak Cirque originate from the canyon's roadways.

Park City/Snyderville Region. The area east of the Wasatch crest and east of the Salt Lake Valley Region (Figure 1.7) also offers many backcountry skiing possibilities. Since most of the touring routes in the region commence on privately-owned land, few are discussed in this book.

The problem of extensive private lands is aggravated by extensive commercial development. The area between the Deer Valley and Park City ski areas has been popular with tourers in past years. Unfortunately, Deer Valley has been expanding toward Park City, and it appears that this trend will continue until both have merged to become a commercial megalopolis that few local skiers will be able to afford.

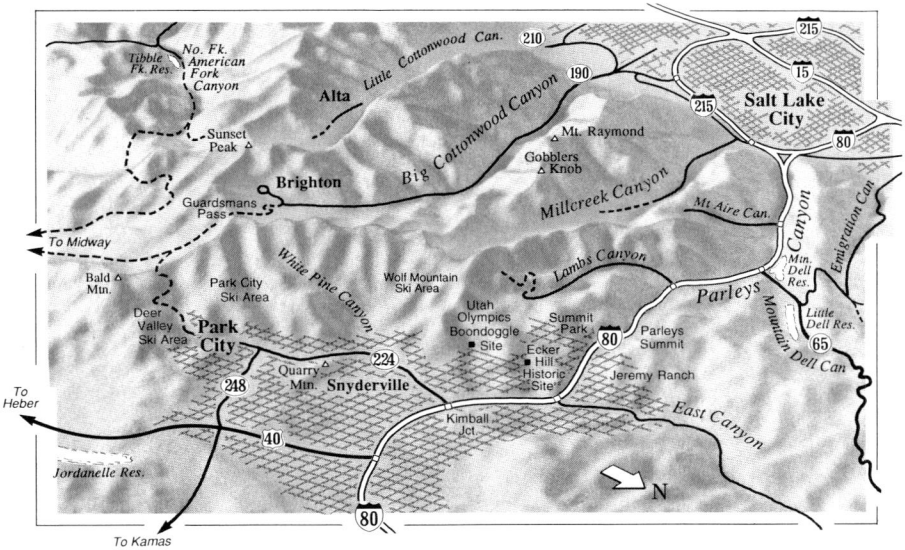

Figure 1.7   The Park City/Snyderville Region of the Central Wasatch receives heavy use by cross country skiers. Most access routes pass over private property, and skiers must get owners' permission before crossing.

WILDERNESS AREAS

Having witnessed development of the Solitude Ski Resort during the late 1950's and Park City's Treasure Mountain Resort early next decade, a group of Salt Lake area skiers, hikers, and mountaineers became concerned about possible commercial exploitation of the wild canyons located west of Alta. There were many reasons for anxiety. Late in the 1950's Forest Service officials recommended construction of four ski lifts in Gad Valley. A proposal to construct a tramway to the summit of the Pfeifferhorn surfaced a few years later.

As the Wilderness Preservation Act neared passage in Congress, University of Utah chemistry Professor J. C. Giddings suggested using the wilderness act to protect Lone Peak and surrounding terrain from commercial development. In a 1965 *Summit Magazine* article titled "Alta—the Hub of Deep Powder Touring," Giddings and co-author A. Kelner[4] reported that the proposal "has been well received" by officials of the Wasatch and Uinta National Forests. The Lone Peak wilderness

---

[4] Giddings' and Kelner's involvement with Lone Peak goes back to the late 1950's. In the summer of 1958 Giddings, Kelner, and Dick Bell made what is recognized today as the first direct ascent of Lone Peak's south face. See *Summit Magazine* (1958) and *Deseret News* (July 10, 1958).

Figure 1.8   Lone Peak. The 30,000 acre Lone Peak Wilderness was the first wilderness area to be established in Utah. Photo by Larry Swanson.

cause was later adopted by the Wasatch Mountain Club, whose members contacted local and national political leaders for sponsorship of legislation. A Lone Peak Wilderness Committee organized a "speakers bureau" to proselytize the wilderness concept, and several conservation organizations stepped in with added support. Despite widespread public acceptance of wilderness designation, nearly ten years of bureaucratically and politically-generated setbacks had to be overcome before the Lone Peak Wilderness finally came to fruition.

Throughout the protracted debate, the main issue revolved around balancing high density (commercial) uses versus low density (backcountry recreational) uses. As expected, the strongest opposition to wilderness came from ski industry, recreational resort, and mountain condominium developers. Support for wilderness was voiced by numerous individuals representing many diverse professions and occupations.

The next major victory for local wilderness came in 1984, when Congress enacted the Utah Wilderness Act. This legislation added over a dozen new wilderness areas within the state, including the Twin Peaks and Mount Olympus areas east of Salt Lake. Much of the lobbying effort to secure the legislation was led by Dick Carter and members of the Utah

Figure 1.9   Dromedary Peak in the Twin Peaks Wilderness. This alpine area was one of several Utah locations to be approved for wilderness designation in 1984.

Wilderness Association.

Due to the ruggedness of the terrain, most of the Mount Olympus, Twin Peaks, and Lone Peak wilderness areas are suitable only for what is generally considered "expert" touring. Specific trailhead and route descriptions for these areas are presented in subsequent chapters.

The Lone Peak Wilderness. Utah's first Congressionally designated wilderness, Lone Peak, encompasses some 30,000 acres of alpine terrain in Salt Lake and Utah counties. About a third of the Wilderness (that portion located in southern Salt Lake County) is described in this volume. Formal trailheads are few, though the Forest Service is planning new ones that will bypass county subdivisions creeping ever closer to the forest boundaries.

The Twin Peaks Wilderness. With a size of only 11,000 acres, the Twin Peaks Wilderness may be the smallest in Utah. The area receives its name from the prominent double summit visible from nearly any point in Salt Lake County. With the exception of a couple of steep gulches, the south side of the wilderness area is too steep and rocky for any kind of touring. West flank access is complicated by private lands.

The Mount Olympus Wilderness. Dominated by the red quartzite faces of Mount Olympus, this 16,000 acre area is the nearest wilderness to Salt Lake City. Most of the terrain located south and south-west of the peak is too rocky and rugged for any kind of cross-country touring, but the part in Neffs Canyon is quite suitable for winter outings. A large amount of the original wilderness proposal was removed from the enabling legislation as a concession to the Wasatch Powderbird Guides heli-skiing operation.

GENERAL INFORMATION

With the continued–and still accelerating–growth of backcountry recreation along the Wasatch Front, it's not unreasonable to expect a proliferation of publications and services that make it easier for people to recreate. A number of books, maps, clubs, classes, and guide services are now available for ski tourers, snowshoers, and winter mountaineers.

Information

Since many of the intermediate and advanced ski touring routes commence at long-established summer trailheads and follow well-worn hiking trails, the more advanced tourer may find useful information in a number of tried-and-true, as well as recently released, hiking guides. The best guidebook for the Wasatch east of Salt Lake City is John Veranth's *Hiking the Wasatch*, published by the Wasatch Mountain Club. Ogden area trails and trailheads are well described in *Outings Guide— Ogden Area*, a pocket-sized booklet published by the Ogden Group of the Sierra Club.

Several maps have been produced by Alpentech's Beat vonAllmen. Each one contains several terrain photographs overprinted with potential touring routes. *Map No. 1* covers terrain from Alta north to Parleys Canyon. *Map No. 2* covers terrain south of Alta. *Map No. 3*, when released in 1995, will cover terrain from Bountiful to Ben Lomond Peak.

A new trail map, *Hiking the Wasatch*, was published jointly by the Wasatch Mountain Club and the University of Utah Press in 1994. Prepared by Dale Green, a long-time hiker who is extremely knowledgeable about hiking trails in the area, the map provides accurate, field-checked, and up-to-date trail information for the tri-canyons area.

The *Central Wasatch Wilderness Atlas*, to be released in 1995 by Alexis Kelner and Larry Swanson, will use numerous high-resolution, low-altitude oblique aerial photographs (summer and winter), as well as

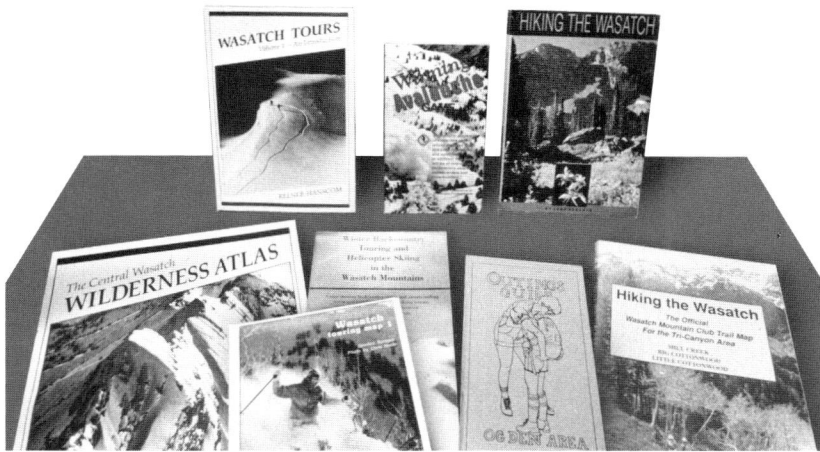

Figure 1.10 The backcountry tourer will find useful information in several excellent hiking guides and trail maps. The *Central Wasatch Wilderness Atlas* will become available in 1995.

4-color maps, to provide a comprehensive "overview" of mountain recreation opportunities in the Mount Olympus, Twin Peaks, Lone Peak, and Mount Timpanogos wilderness areas.

Instruction/Guide Services

As mentioned in Volume 1 of *Wasatch Tours*, instruction in the *basics* of backcountry touring is a buyers' market. Nearly all area universities and colleges have courses designed to acquaint the uninitiated with mountain recreation. Some scouting and church organizations also offer tutoring, depending on availability of experienced instructors at a particular time. Many recreational equipment stores schedule winter seminars in various aspects of cross country skiing equipment and technique. Commercial touring centers offer similar programs.

Wasatch Mountain Club. The Wasatch Mountain Club has a comprehensive program of outings aimed at tourers of all levels of proficiency. Club trips are organized and led by knowledgeable and experienced backcountry tourers. In addition to providing informal clinics dealing with various aspects of touring for its members, the Mountain Club also sponsors an annual, day-long avalanche seminar for members and the public-at-large. The club's annual dues are currently $30.

Commercial Guide Services. Commercial guide services are not new to the backcountry of the Wasatch. The earliest known alpine touring guide service was initiated in 1965 as part of the Alf Engen

Ski School based at Alta. Fifteen alpine ski tours were listed in the advertising brochure titled *Alta Ski-tours*. The tours ranged in difficulty from the easy Alta-Brighton-Alta tour to the 12-mile "Queen of the Wasatch" tour from White Pine Canyon to the community of Granite.[5]

Today, only two guide services are licensed to operate in the Wasatch-Cache National Forest east of Salt Lake County. Both services are being closely monitored by the Forest Service for customer demand and possible impacts on other backcountry users.

Exum Mountain Adventures. Exum Mountain Adventures is licensed by the Wasatch-Cache National Forest to operate on approximately 60,000 acres of terrain in and about Millcreek, Big Cottonwood, and Little Cottonwood canyons. Permitted guiding activities include rock, snow, and ice climbing, as well as ski touring and ski mountaineering. Their winter program includes instruction and guiding for tourers at all levels of proficiency, from rank beginners to skilled mountaineers. To avoid competition (and possible friction) with local backcountry tourers, Ted Wilson,[6] one of the corporate officers, has pledged to operate the guide service with never more than six people in a given drainage. Wilson hopes that Exum Mountain Adventures will become "a quiet recreation alternative to the noisy canyon helicopters."

For information, write to *Exum Mountain Adventures*, 1427 E. Ironwood Ave., Salt Lake City, UT 84121, or call (801)273-1850.

The Snowbird Mountaineering Center. The Snowbird Mountaineering Center offers instruction/guiding in rock climbing, biking, ski mountaineering, and mountain picnics. Anyone desiring to schedule ski tours should contact the Snowbird Activities Center for information.

MOUNTAIN HAZARDS

As backcountry recreation continues its growth along the populated Wasatch Front, more and more individuals are injured or killed in the nearby mountains and canyons. Accidents are most common during the summer and autumn months, with "slip and fall" mishaps being

---

[5]The program was operated by the ski school's Touring Director, Alexis Kelner. Ski touring during the mid-1960's was just commencing its dramatic growth curve. Only a few of Alta's lodge guests (mostly eastern intellectuals and Europeans!) took advantage of the service, and it was discontinued at the end of its first season of operation.

[6]While serving as Mayor of Salt Lake City between 1976 and 1985, Ted Wilson participated actively and effectively in the effort to secure Wilderness Act protection for the Lone Peak, Mount Olympus, and Twin Peaks areas.

Heavy Snow Hampers Search for Alta Skier

Officials Still Seeking Seattle Man After 3 Feet of Fresh Snow

By Mike Gorrell
THE SALT LAKE TRIBUNE

Well-wishers flood hospital with inquiries about Danza

Actor still in intensive care but stable following skiing accident at Deer Valley.

Ogden Hiker Dies in 150-Foot Fall

By Joshua B. Good
THE SALT LAKE TRIBUNE

OGDEN — Brett Cyrus Watkins died Sunday scouting out a

2 Hikers Use Scraps Of Carpet to Survive Overnight Ordeal

By Cornelia deBrun
SPECIAL TO THE TRIBUNE

PROVO — Two hikers who spent a chilly night near Bridal Veil Falls in

Officials Say Seattle Skier May Have Died of Trauma, Not in Avalanche

By Vince Horiuchi
THE SALT LAKE TRIBUNE

Nibley teen in critical condition after breaking neck on ski slope

By Nicole A. Bonham
Deseret News staff writer

Wasatch Mountain Club class surprised by spring avalanche

By Bert Lindler
SPECIAL TO THE TRIBUNE

Body of missing snowmobiler found in a remote area of Weber County

Associated Press

OGDEN — The body of a man who took a snowmobile ride without dressing for cold weather was found Monday in a remote area of Weber County.

Searchers Find Backcountry Skier Killed in Avalanche

Figure 1.11   As popularity of mountain recreation grows along the Wasatch Front, unknowledgeable and unprepared backcountry visitors continue to be injured or killed in the nearby canyons. Preparation for a season of ski touring should include review of avalanche and other mountain hazard related accidents.

the most frequent variety. Death and injury by gunfire may also be expected during autumn, when shoot-happy hunters—mistaking humans, domestic animals, vehicles, and even traffic signs for game—take to the hills. In springtime, as individuals attempt to cross runoff-swollen canyon streams, drownings become common.[7]

The frequency of winter accidents appears to have increased dramatically during the last decade. Snowmobilers, often unequipped and unprepared for winter survival, have died of exposure when their machines have broken down far from help. Out-of-control resort skiers have perished on collision with obstructions so often as to prompt ski industry lobbyists to push (successfully) for legislation that limits resort liabilities. Several backcountry snowboarders and tourers are killed annually by avalanches (see Figure 1.12).

Mountain Hazards Awareness

Several common deficiencies connect most of the mountain mishaps: victims' inexperience, unfamiliarity with terrain, and lack of mountain and avalanche hazards awareness. Familiarity with terrain can be gained by touring with more experienced companions, organized groups, or commercial guides. Hiking along established trails during the snowless sea-

---

[7]The stream in Little Cottonwood Canyon claimed four lives during the 1993 spring runoff; none of the fatalities were related to ski touring.

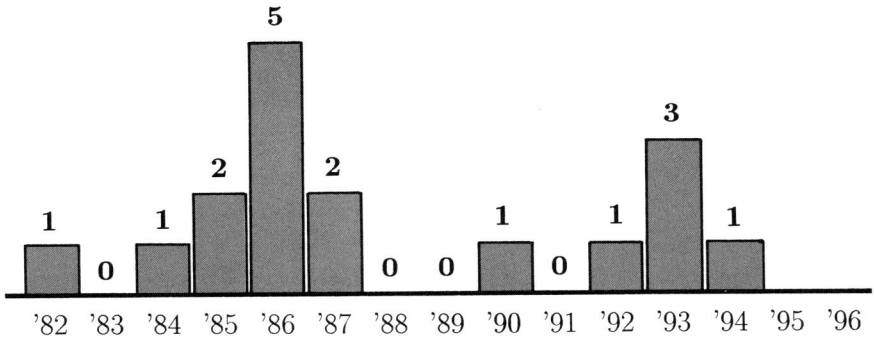

Figure 1.12   Annual avalanche fatalities along the Wasatch Front. Data courtesy of the *Utah Avalanche Forecast Center.*

sons can also familiarize one with the lay of the land. Experience can be obtained by participating in touring classes or attending clinics at commercial touring centers. Backcountry tourers who intend to undertake the intermediate and advanced outings described in this book should participate in an avalanche seminar and regularly practice avalanche search techniques with their touring companions.

Developing a mountain and avalanche hazards consciousness is made easy by two recently released publications. *Wasatch Tours* Volume 1 contains over 50 pages of well-illustrated information related to general mountain hazards; another 50 pages of text and illustrations will acquaint readers with hazards associated with avalanches. *Winning the Avalanche Game*[8] is a 58-minute videotape intended to instill avalanche awareness in the viewer. Besides an "entertaining visual blend of spectacular avalanches," the tape covers topics such as "who gets caught in avalanches and why," "how to read avalanche terrain," and "route finding and safe travel."

In the first volume of *Wasatch Tours* we stated that another means of preparing for a safe season of ski touring was to become familiar with other people's avalanche misfortunes. This advice applies equally well to all types of ski touring accidents. In this volume we've included descriptions and analyses of several avalanche accidents. Each of these is found in a "sidebar" that examines a touring-related tragedy with specific lessons to learn.

---

[8] *Winning the Avalanche Game* is produced by the Wasatch Interpretive Association, a privately operated "auxiliary" of the Wasatch-Cache National Forest. Part of the proceeds from the sale of the video is used to fund winter safety services provided by the Utah Avalanche Forecasting Center.

Safety and Rescue Equipment

Volume 1 of *Wasatch Tours* includes a discussion of items that every tourer or touring party should carry in the backcountry. This section contains descriptions of technological advances that have occurred in the past year and should be used in conjunction with information in the first volume.

Single vs. Dual Frequency Avalanche Beacons. One of the most important pieces of equipment that every backcountry skier should carry is an avalanche rescue beacon. Several years ago the Europeans switched from low frequency beacons that operated at 2.275 Khz to devices that transmit signals at 457 Khz. The higher frequency beacons are technologically superior in two ways. They have a greater range, and they do not require use of an earplug, which was by far the most common source of failure. Americans have used dual frequency devices in recent years, but 1995 is the year when avalanche professionals in this country are scheduled to make the switch.

Tourers who wish to purchase a rescue beacon must decide whether to get the more effective high frequency device, or to buy a dual frequency model that is compatible with both new and old equipment. The decision must be based upon knowledge of *all* touring partners' beacon frequencies.

Cellular Telephones. The cellular phone is potentially the most useful mountain safety device to become available for backcountry recreation since the invention of the avalanche rescue beacon. When it's within range of a repeater station, the telephone can be used to instantly summon searchers and medical personnel to the site of a mountain accident. As a recent example, a victim of a heart attack—on the summit of American Fork Twin Peaks—owes his life to the presence of a cellular phone in a companion's pack.

At present, knowledge of the usefulness of cellular phones from the summits and canyons along the Wasatch Front is limited. The authors have carried a set to the summits of Twin Peaks (above Salt Lake City), Murdock Peak (above Park City), and Lewis Peak (above Ogden). In all three instances, communication capability was excellent. In the basins and canyons below the summits, however, it was either marginal or non-existent.[9] We hope that other backcountry recreationists will help extend the knowledge base of cellular telephone practicalities.

The RECCO Locating System. The Europeans have been using

---

[9] It is expected that coverage will become more universal as satellite technology is developed and implemented.

this system for several years at alpine ski areas, and a number of American resorts (including Alta and Snowbird) are planning to do so this year. It is based upon skiers carrying one or two small, very lightweight "diodes" that reflect a microwave signal produced by a device operated by rescuers. Several manufacturers of downhill ski boots and clothing are designing them into their products, so skiers won't have to remember to put them in their pockets.

Airbags. Another recent European invention is the Avalanche Balloon Securesystem (ABS). Essentially an airbag in a rucksack, it consists of a balloon that inflates when the skier pulls a ring attached to a cord hanging from his chest. The nitrogen-filled bag is intended to make the skier less dense than the surrounding snow in an avalanche, and hopefully to keep him close to the surface. Only available for purchase in Europe at this time, the ABS is becoming more common at alpine ski areas around the world.[10]

CLASSIFICATION OF TOURS

We have chosen to categorize tours principally by their level of difficulty.

Beginner Tours. These range from outings suitable for anyone, to those requiring a reasonable amount of stamina. Most beginner tours are on relatively gentle terrain, so the only required skiing skill is the ability to slow down and/or to stop when necessary.

Intermediate Tours. Tours that have downhill sections steep enough to make it unwise for a novice skier to attempt are classified as intermediate. These typically involve much more climbing, so a higher level of physical conditioning is often required.

Advanced Tours. Both endurance and expert skiing skills are required for outings in the advanced category. All but the most competent and knowledgeable tourer should use mountaineering or downhill equipment on advanced outings.

Super Tours. This label speaks for itself. Anyone who undertakes one of these marathons needs an intimate knowledge of the mountains and weather, the ability to ski any slope under any snow condition, the strength to keep going for a full day or longer, and the willingness to spend a night on the mountain if circumstances dictate.

---

[10]A more advanced and universally applicable version of the airbag is being developed by a vitamin supplement company headquartered in Orem-Provo. Their *Outdoor Recreation Rescue Inflator* (ORRIN) will deploy without use of a pull cord and will require no source of pressurized nitrogen gas. Self-righteous indignation will initiate inflation; pressure will be maintained by rapid political doubletalk.

Volume 1 of *Wasatch Tours* is devoted exclusively to beginner tours. This volume contains descriptions of intermediate, advanced, and super tours in the northern half of the Wasatch Mountains.

In addition to classifying ski tours by level of difficulty, we have labeled many according to existing and potential threats to their continuing availability and enjoyment for human-powered backcountry users. Two labels in *Wasatch Tours* relate to this problem:

- *Rest In Peace*, abbreviated to *R.I.P.*, is a notation used by the authors to describe backcountry touring terrain that has been converted to commercial skiing since the initial publication of *Wasatch Tours* in 1976.

- *Endangered*, abbreviated to *End.*, is a notation used to warn tourers that an area has high potential for being absorbed into a commercial ski area operation.

Helicopter skiing is another major deterrent to enjoyable ski touring in the Wasatch. Most ski tourers, as well as some canyon business and property owners, consider heli-skiing to be a noisy, disruptive, and dangerous form of mountain exploitation.

- *Helicopter Permit Area*, abbreviated as *H.P.A.*, is the notation used by the authors to warn tourers that a particular outing may be affected—or disrupted and endangered—by the presence of the recreational 'copter.

Complaints by backcountry skiers of disruption, endangerment, and harassment by heli-ski copters have become so commonplace that officials of the Wasatch-Cache National Forest (who have the responsibility of regulating the heli-ski concession) have published a map showing terrain and landing sites approved for helicopter skiing. Copies are available free of charge at all Forest Service offices□

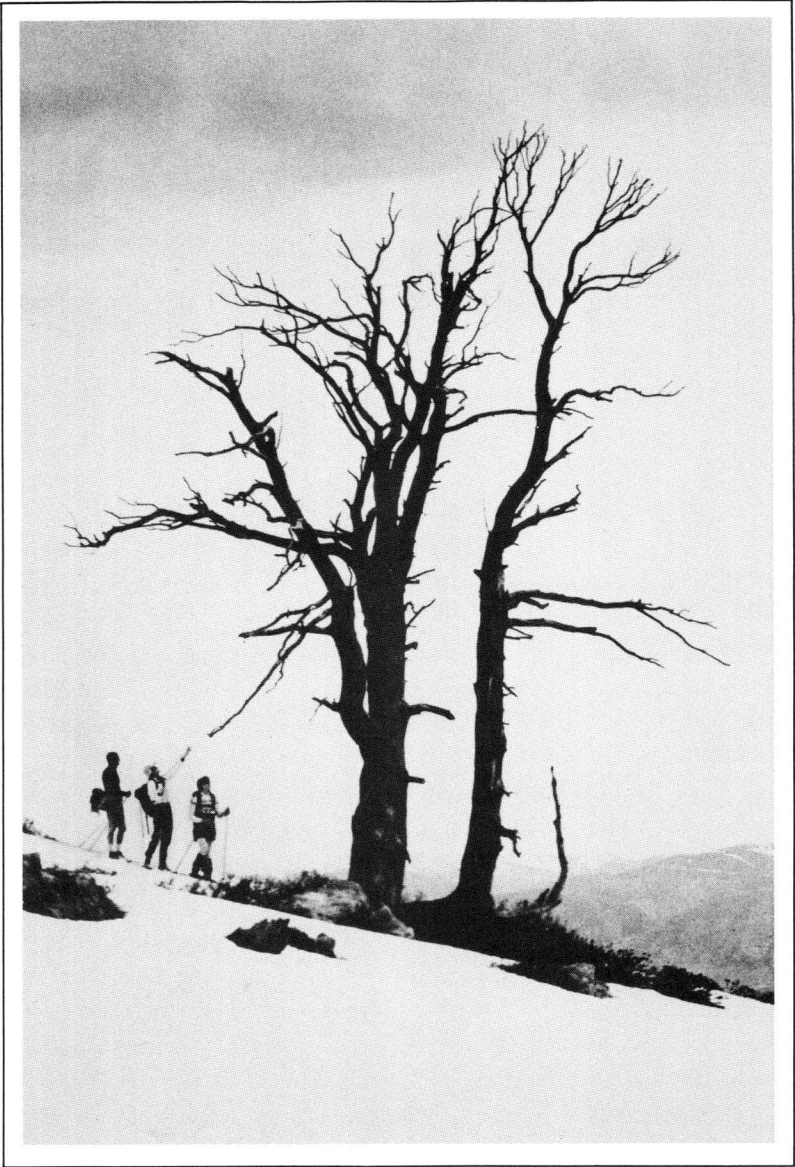

Ogden area ski tourers Jock Glidden and Kathy Edwards speculate with author Dave Hanscom about weather patterns that promoted the growth, and later the demise, of many large trees found along the north ridge of Willard Peak.

Chapter 2

NORTHERN WASATCH MOUNTAINS

Few ski tourers who crowd the canyons of the Central Wasatch each weekend are aware that within less than an hour's drive north of Salt Lake and Summit counties is found some of the most "white and delightsome" touring terrain in the Wasatch Mountains. The terrain is located in the region between Box Elder Canyon, at the extreme north end of the range, and Grandview Peak, a prominent summit at the northern border of Salt Lake County.

The tours described in this chapter are located principally in Weber and Davis counties. Good skiing is also available on the east side of the range in Morgan County, but access is often blocked by a wide belt of ranch land between public highways and the unusually high boundary of the Wasatch-Cache National Forest. A major problem with touring in the northern Wasatch Mountains is the limited number of high elevation access points. Many of the tours described in this chapter require ascent and descent of narrow trails on steep, heavily vegetated terrain. Touring options for those of intermediate skiing ability are quite limited.

The competent and committed tourers who choose to surmount or bypass such obstacles will discover the backcountry of the northern Wasatch to be ideal for all the types of touring found in the canyons of the central Wasatch. Ski mountaineers will delight in ascending the 9000 foot summits of Willard Peak and Ben Lomond. The upper couloirs of Coldwater and Taylor canyons and the headwall above Cutler Basin will challenge the most dedicated of alpine skiers. Tourers of nordic persuasion will appreciate the endless ridges and gentle bowls to be found near Thurston, Francis, and Bountiful peaks. No one will forget the spectacular panorama visible from the summit of Grandview Peak. Since heli-skiing is not permitted in some parts of the northern Wasatch, all tourers who visit there can gain a new respect for the "Heli-Free Wasatch" movement.

The organization of this chapter is geographical (north to south), with no attempt made to separate tours according to their level of difficulty. The descriptions, maps, and photographs should contain sufficient information to help a skier determine if a proposed touring route is suitable for his or her ability. The reader will also notice that some of the descriptions in this chapter are not as detailed as those for the canyons of the Central Wasatch. In these cases, our goal has been the description of general areas for cross country skiing, rather than description of specific routes.

BEN LOMOND/WILLARD PEAK AREA

The northern end of the Wasatch Mountains consists of a massive pair of peaks located between Brigham City and Ogden. Willard Peak and Ben Lomond sit as sentinels with their almost vertical western slopes overlooking Bear River Bay and the many bird refuges that surround it. The two summits are almost as impressive from Pineview Reservoir and the Ogden River Valley to the east. Five ridgecrest prominences— Chilly Peak, Black Mountain, Grizzly Peak, Willard Mountain, and an unnamed 9118 foot rock outcropping—share the northern end of the Wasatch with Willard Peak and Ben Lomond. All possess terrain that's suitable for excellent ski touring.

Ben Lomond and Willard Peaks are separated by a narrow ridge that is frequently buffeted by prevailing winds crossing the Great Salt Lake. Due to the steepness of the west slope, a great deal of snow is often deposited along the leeward east slope by these condensation-laden winds. The summits of both peaks are extremely exposed, so there is no safe way to ascend them when conditions are unstable. Few skiers venture to the top until spring.

The Willard/Ben Lomond land mass is accessed from three of the four compass directions. Access from the north is by way of Mantua, a small community located about four miles east of Brigham City. Access from the south is via North Ogden Pass, just a few miles east of North Ogden. Weber County's North Fork Park, located in the northern reaches of Ogden Valley, provides access from the east. The three access points, *(A)*, *(B)*, and *(C)*, are illustrated in Figure 2.2.

Figure 2.1   Consisting of spectacular cliffbands nearly a thousand feet high, the escarpment that forms the west flank of the Willard Peak/Ben Lomond land mass does not lend itself to any normal ski touring activities.

Tours From Mantua

Mantua is a small town located on US-89/91 about four miles east of Brigham City. This community of 750 was named by Lorenzo Snow, fifth president of the Mormon Church, for his birthplace, which was a town of the same name in Ohio. Mantua is home to a general store, which is open in winter, as well as a reservoir, a fish hatchery, and a National Forest campground for summer visitors.

A gravel road, called the Willard Basin Scenic Backway, goes directly south of Mantua, climbing 3600 vertical feet in 12 miles to end at the Spikecamp Campground in Willard Basin. The campground is less than a mile from Willard Peak's 9764 foot summit. A well-worn hiking trail departs the campground and ascends to a pass just west of the summit.

The lower portion of this road is popular among snowmobilers, who find its gentle grades suitable for their machines. The grades are also ideal for beginning tourers. Despite a low starting elevation, the road-way's northern exposure assures a long season for touring.[1] The terrain around the roadway's upper portions (depicted in Figures 2.4 and 2.5)

---

[1]How far one can drive along the roadway will depend on snow depth at the time of the tour. Late spring is best for these ski tours, since it may be possible to cut four to six miles from the 13-mile skiing distance to Willard Peak.

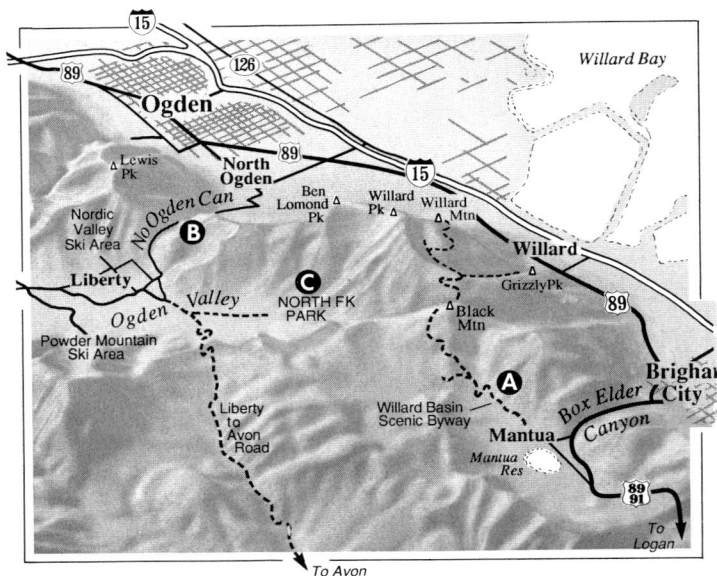

Figure 2.2   The Willard Peak/Ben Lomond land mass is accessed from Mantua (A), North Ogden Pass (B), and northern Ogden Valley (C). The large depression between the two summits is known as Cutler Basin.

makes for excellent intermediate and advanced touring. Three of the best ski tours (Willard Peak, Willard Mountain, and Grizzly Peak) are described in this section.

Perhaps the most unusual feature of the Scenic Backway is its well-apportioned sequence of scenic rest stops. Every two miles, it seems, a new pass is reached, or a new ridge, each with a different panorama of the valleys below. Tourers of different abilities and endurance can use these as convenient turn-around spots. The general topography of the area (along with the road) are illustrated in Figure 2.3.

Willard Peak. The start of the Willard Basin Scenic Backway is easily located. Simply drive south along Mantua's Main Street to a large Mormon stake (meeting) house where Fish Hatchery Road branches diagonally to the left. A Forest Service sign points straight ahead for Dock Flat, Willard Basin, and Inspiration Point. Continue south along the roadway as far as surface conditions permit. (Two forks are encountered along the roadway; in each case the right fork is the one to take.)

The road soon enters (and equally soon leaves) a conifer forest along the east flank of Black Mountain. After a steep sidehill climb the road turns southwestward into a small canyon. About a mile of steady climbing brings one to a ridge, the first of several scenic rest stops. Past the

Figure 2.3   Black Mountain is the northernmost peak in the Wasatch Mountains. The Willard Basin Scenic Backway (A) circles the peak along its east and south sides (out of the photograph) and continues to Willard Basin, at the base of Willard Peak. Route (B) traverses the ridge to Grizzly Peak.

ridge, the road traverses the south shoulder of Black Mountain and gently ascends to the second scenic rest stop, the 7800 foot pass overlooking Perry Reservoir. From the pass the road climbs southward, switchbacking several times along a steep sidehill with numerous signs of severe avalanching.   After nearly two miles of traverses, a broad sparsely-timbered ridge containing a large Forest Service informational sign is reached. The elevation at the sign is about 8800 feet. It's enlightening to read about how the Forest Service, the Soil Conservation Service, and the Civilian Conservation Corps rehabilitated the once overgrazed and abused Willard Basin.

The Willard Basin sign is a good place to ponder where one should go next. Three routes, and several summit options, are depicted in Figure 2.4. The "Roadway Traverse," marked *(A)*, leads into Willard Basin and can be used to ascend the summit of Willard Peak and Willard Mountain. The "North Ridge Route," marked *(B)*, can be used to access the basin and the two summits. Route *(C)* leads to Grizzly Peak.

The Roadway Traverse Route. It's easy to be tempted to continue

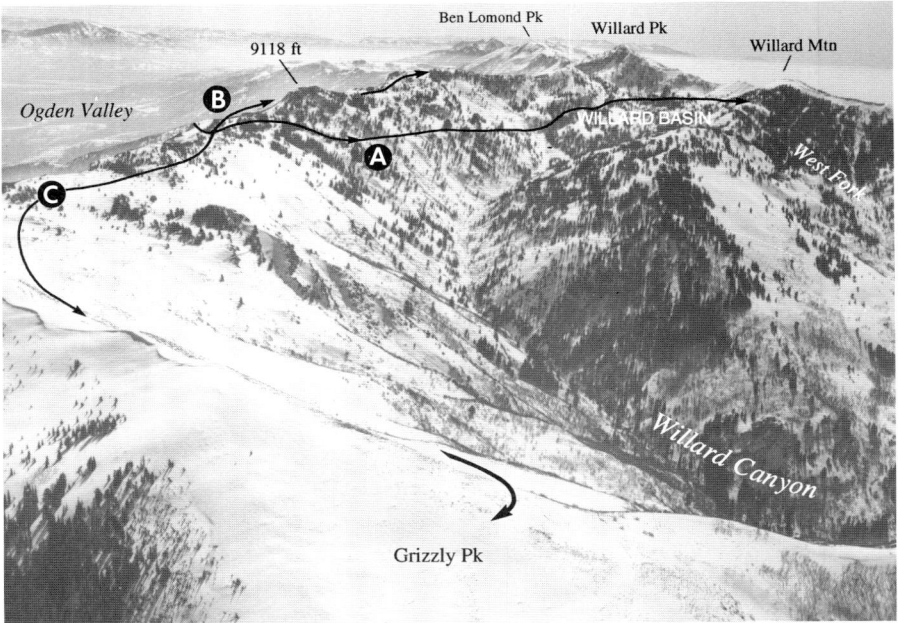

Figure 2.4   Upper Willard Canyon. Three touring options are possible from the Willard Basin informational sign at the ridge crest: (A) roadway traverse to Willard Basin, Willard Peak, and Willard Mountain; (B) continuation along Willard's north ridge to the same destinations; (C) ascent of Grizzly Peak.

following the Scenic Backway into Willard Basin. The roadway, however, traverses approximately two miles of extremely steep, west-facing avalanche slopes. Obviously, the snowpack must be exceptionally stable for this tour to end without tragedy. Dropping into the canyon at this point may appear to be a safer option, but the bottom is a narrow, V-shaped gully that's exposed to the same avalanche paths.

Once in the basin, the pass between Willard Peak and Willard Mountain (Figure 2.5) is easily reached, although avalanches are still possible at and near the headwall. From the ridge, one can turn east to follow the hiking trail route to the summit of Willard Peak.

For a more benign summit ascent, one can turn west at the pass and follow a prominent hiking trail to the top of Willard Mountain. Because Willard Mountain is offset westward from the main Wasatch crest, the panoramas in all compass directions are unsurpassed.

The North Ridge Route. From the informational sign, the simplest and the safest route would be to follow the main crest to the summit. It's not that simple, however, and it's not totally safe. About a quar-

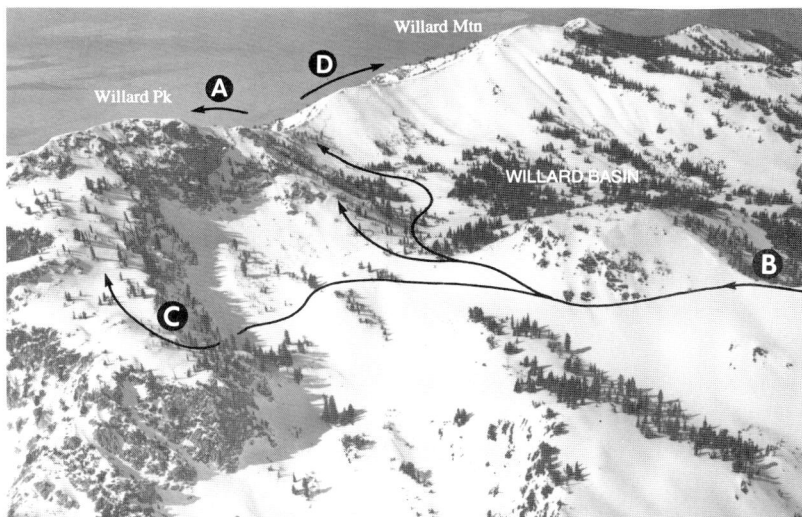

Figure 2.5   The summit of Willard Peak can be reached by several routes: (A) the pass between Willard Peak and Willard Mountain; (B) the north ridge; (C) the east ridge. The two ridge routes to Willard Peak are extremely steep and risky. The pass route, while safer, still has potential for avalanches. Route (D), from the pass to Willard Mountain, follows a wide hiking trail.

ter of the way to the summit, the ridge is blocked by a prominent, and rather precipitous, 9118 foot rock outcropping that must be surmounted or bypassed. Surmounting it requires climbing a very steep (though short and well protected by trees) couloir along the west side of the outcropping. Bypassing the outcropping along its west side entails traversing the top of a very steep avalanche slope.

The ridge widens past the outcropping and makes for excellent touring. Just before the final ascent to the summit of Willard Peak, a rocky dropoff must be negotiated. This can be down-climbed or bypassed on either side. Once again, a tourer may have to traverse a potentially dangerous slope, but the risk factor of such a short traverse is considerably less than the two mile roadway traverse described in the preceding section.

The final climb to the summit of the peak also exposes tourers to a dangerous avalanche slope. Great care should be taken to stay near rock outcroppings and clumps of trees as the ridge is ascended.

Additional options for an approach to Willard Peak from North Fork Park are described in a later section and depicted in additional photographs. All of the routes from the park intersect Willard's north ridge near the rocky dropoff mentioned in the preceding paragraph.

Grizzly Peak. A jeep road leads northwestward from the Willard Basin informational sign. It descends gently to bypass (along its west side) an 8882 foot prominence, then continues traversing westwardly to the summit of 8727 foot Grizzly Peak. The peak is really not a peak in the true sense; it's just a broad summit at the end of a prominent ridge. What makes this "side trip" attractive is the absence of severe avalanche hazard. The only moderate avalanche danger is found along couple of the sidehills. Another feature that makes this side trip inviting is a steep, sparsely-timbered ski slope that descends from the ridge directly into the Perry Reservoir basin. This slope commences among several very dangerous cliff bands, but a careful search along the east side of the rocky prominence (labeled 8816 feet on the topo map) will lead to a continuous descent slope that is uninterrupted by cliffs.

Tours From North Fork Park

North Fork Park is in the Ogden River Valley, not far from Pineview Reservoir. Tourers who drive from areas located south of Weber Canyon should take I-84 to Mountain Green, exit there onto SR-167 (the recently completed "Trappers Loop" road), then follow SR-167 to its junction with SR-39 near Pineview Reservoir. The park is near the community of Liberty, north across the reservoir from the junction and easily reached by driving around either end of the reservoir. Tourers who come from Ogden and its suburbs can get to the area via SR-39 through Ogden Canyon and then across the dam on SR-158 to Liberty.

From the dam, follow SR-158 for 4.3 miles, then turn left on SR-162 toward the Nordic Valley ski area. Continue on SR-162 through Liberty, where the road turns sharply to the left (west) and heads for North Ogden Pass. Just beyond (west of) town, turn right and go north on a road that follows the river. Stay left at the road fork about 1.4 miles north of Liberty and continue to one of the three park entrances. The middle and upper park entrances are on this road, 1.9 and 2.6 miles, respectively, from the fork. To get to the lower park entrance, turn left on a side road 1.0 mile north of the fork and drive 0.9 mile to the gate.

All three entrances are closed in winter, so skiers must park beside the road. At the upper entrance, the best parking is up the road near the Camp Utaba gate where the snow plows stop. The lower entrance is on a dead end road, so there is room to park where the plows turn around.

Tours for Beginners and Intermediates. The North Fork area is typical of the terrain throughout the northern Wasatch Mountains.

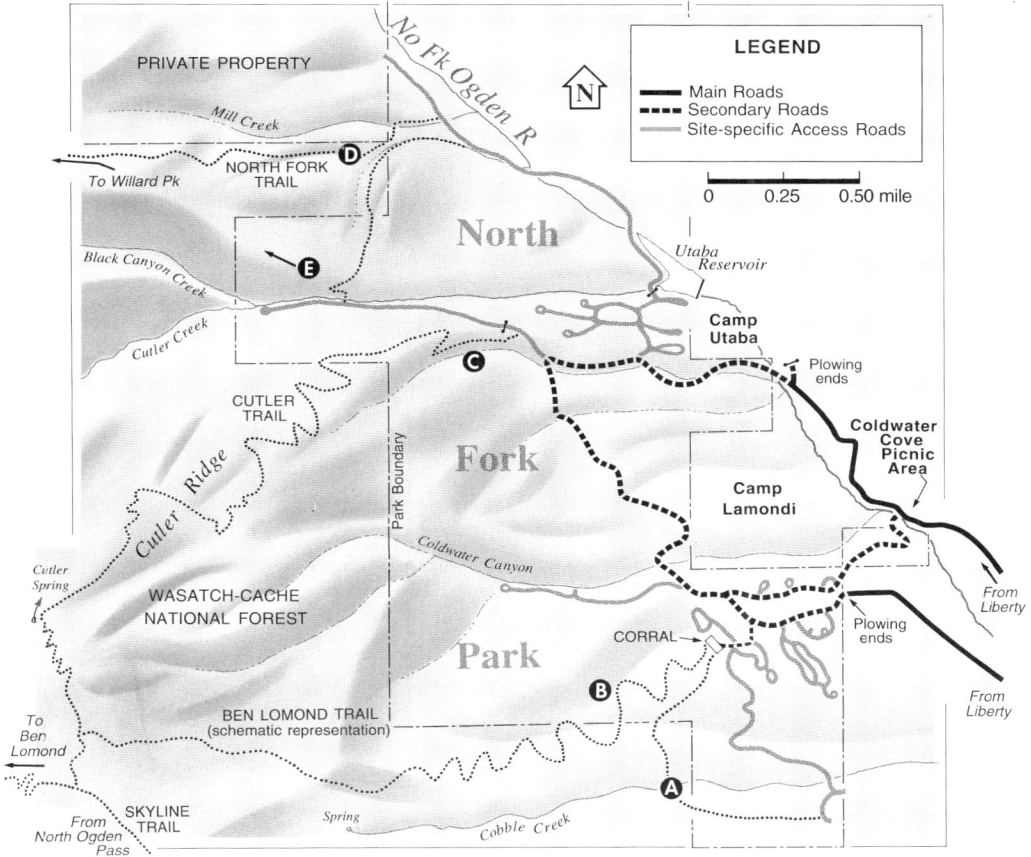

Figure 2.6 Weber County's North Fork Park provides opportunities for outdoor recreationists in all seasons. Cross country skiers can stay on park roads for easy tours or follow the hiking and equestrian trails to more difficult terrain at higher elevations. Labeled routes, also shown in the next photo, are intermediate tours described in the text.

High elevation slopes are extremely steep and prone to avalanche. Less skilled skiers are limited to the foothills, most of which are covered with closely-spaced trees and bushes. Intermediate tourers typically wait until mid and late winter—when the snow is deep enough to cover the underbrush and stable enough to minimize the avalanche hazard—and climb up the trails as far as their skiing skills allow.

Volume 1 of *Wasatch Tours* describes the possibilities for beginners, who enjoy the many miles of unplowed roads that wind through North Fork Park. (See Figure 2.6.) This volume outlines a few possibilities for intermediate skiers who wish to follow the trails that ascend from the park to slopes where they can find lighter snow and open areas among the trees.

Two trails are most easily accessed from the lower park entrance.

Cobble Creek Trail. About 0.4 mile into the park, the road bends to the right (northwest). Just beyond that bend, another road goes left (southwest) to "Horse Stalls and Camping Area." This road enters a large meadow with a corral and trailhead for summer hikers and horseback riders. At the south end of the meadow, a trail climbs fairly steeply up a gully and bends south into Cobble Creek. This trail, labeled *(A)* in Figures 2.6 and 2.7, intersects a park road that leads back to the corral area. Distance around this loop is about two miles.

Ben Lomond Trail. At the north end of the meadow near the corral, the Ben Lomond trail begins its ascent of the ridge between Cold Canyon[2] and Cobble Creek. This trail, *(B)* in the two figures, makes numerous gradual switchbacks as it gains elevation. Tourers must be careful to avoid the steep rocky faces and gullies in upper Cobble Creek.

Two other trails suitable for intermediate skiers can be found near the upper North Fork Park entrance.

Cutler Ridge Trail. A hiking trail follows the ridge that separates Cutler Creek from Cold Canyon. From the park gate, the tour follows a road across the river and up the hill for about 0.8 mile to a fork. (Be sure not to take the right turn to Cutler Flats.) Bear right at the fork and continue climbing for about 0.2 mile to where the road levels off. (If you come to a gate, you have gone about 100 yards too far.) A trail, labeled *(C)* in Figures 2.6, 2.7, and 2.8, climbs through the trees along the ridge. No sign marks the start of the trail, but a vehicle barrier can be seen there if the snow isn't too deep.

North Fork Trail. One other possibility for intermediates is to follow the main drainage of the North Fork of the Ogden River to the park boundary and ski up a trail that climbs toward Willard Peak. From the upper North Fork Park entrance, stay on the park road for 0.6 mile and then turn right and ski to Cutler Flats. Go directly across the large open area and find the road that drops down into Cutler Creek. Follow it (after going around the gate) across the bridge over the creek. The road then traverses around the bottom end of the ridge separating Cutler Creek from the North Fork, just above Utaba Reservoir, and enters the North Fork drainage. (See Figure 2.6.)

After crossing the river twice (no culverts), the road passes through

---

[2]This canyon is called Coldwater on some maps and Cold on others. We have chosen the latter term, since that is used on U.S.G.S. maps.

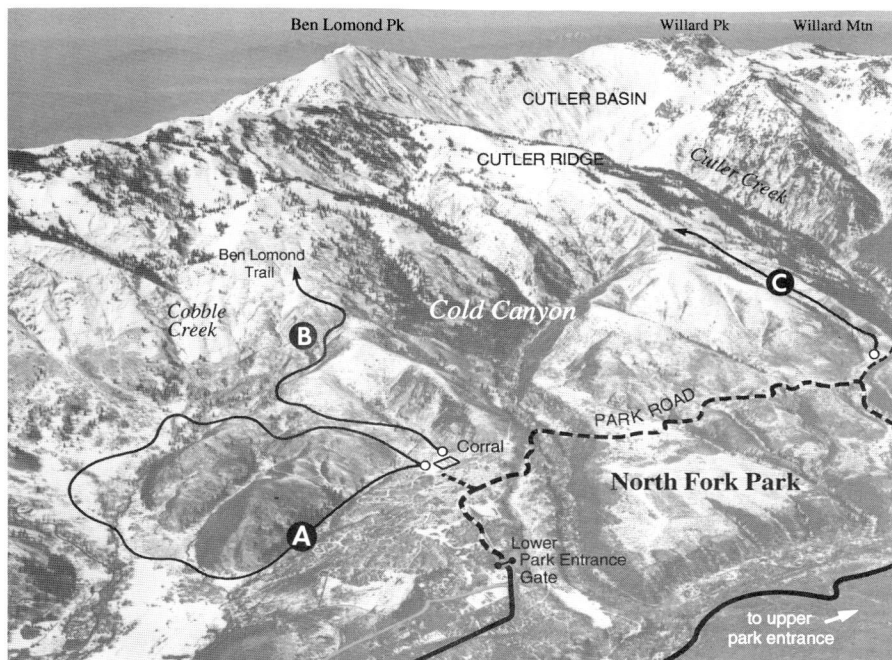

Figure 2.7   North Fork Park is a good access point for tours to Ben Lomond and Willard Peak. Intermediate skiers can enjoy the Cobble Creek Trail (A) and the Ben Lomond Trail (B), both of which commence at the stable area near the lower park entrance, as well as the Cutler Ridge Trail (C), which is most easily accessed from the upper entrance.

a large meadow. A trail goes left through this meadow to a saddle and drops down to Cutler Creek. Tourers interested in a four mile loop could follow that trail to the Cutler Ridge trailhead described above and then ski back to the car. A more challenging alternative is to continue on the North Fork road through the meadow and take the next left turn. This trail ascends a side drainage toward the main Wasatch ridge, marked (D) in Figures 2.6 and 2.9.

Ben Lomond. The southern-most peak adjacent to North Fork Park is Ben Lomond, named after the mountain that it resembles in Scotland. Its 9712 foot summit is 5100 vertical feet above North Ogden to the west, and 4600 feet above Liberty to the east. The best route to the summit involves climbing from North Fork Park. Relative to the alternative from North Ogden Pass (described in a later section), this is a shorter but steeper route with more vertical gain. Since the difference is less than 500 feet, an approach from North Fork Park is significantly faster. If your interest is to get to the powder as soon as possible, and you don't mind missing out on the westerly view, this is the place to start. Also, the best downhill routes all end up at the park, so it eliminates a car shuttle.

There are two good routes to the summit of Ben Lomond from North Fork Park. Labeled *(B)* in Figures 2.6, 2.7, and 2.8, the first route basically follows the Ben Lomond Trail that switchbacks up the wide ridge between Cold Canyon and Cobble Creek described in the preceding section. Near the top of the ridge, the trail bends north through a saddle and traverses through the trees across the top of Cold Canyon. This slope is quite steep and should not be crossed unless the avalanche hazard is minimal. As shown in Figure 2.8, the trail intercepts Cutler Ridge, which can be followed to the main Wasatch crest. Total distance of this part of the ascent is 3000 vertical feet over about seven miles.

Most tourers will terminate their climb at this point. An ascent of the summit of Ben Lomond involves an additional 1000 feet of elevation gain on a slope exposed to high winds and direct sun. Compacted snow, usually quite unpleasant for both ascent and descent, should be anticipated.

The other possibility for a winter ascent of Ben Lomond from North Fork Park is to follow the Cutler Ridge Trail described in the preceding section and labeled *(C)* in the figures. This route is steeper but more direct. It may also be safer, since it avoids the requirement to ski across the top of Cold Canyon. The distance from the upper North Fork Park entrance to the ridge overlooking the Great Salt Lake and Ogden is about five miles, with a vertical gain of 2700 feet.

Descent. Skiing possibilities from the top of the main ridge are numerous. Several good routes can be seen in Figures 2.7 and 2.8 for a descent into Cutler Creek or Cold Canyon. Tourers should seek the security of the many subridges and trees found on northerly and easterly slopes that lead back to North Fork Park. Cutler Bowl, the steep basin bordered by the face of Ben Lomond and the ridge between Ben Lomond and Willard Peak, is very steep and has extreme avalanche hazard.

Willard Peak. Willard Peak lies directly north of Ben Lomond on the main Wasatch ridge. Access from the north via Mantua is described in the previous section and illustrated in Figure 2.5. It can be reached more directly from the south and/or east via North Fork Park, but the climb is steeper and more prone to avalanche hazard than the Mantua routes.

South Ridge. One alternative for an approach to Willard Peak is to traverse the ridge from Ben Lomond. This is an advanced outing

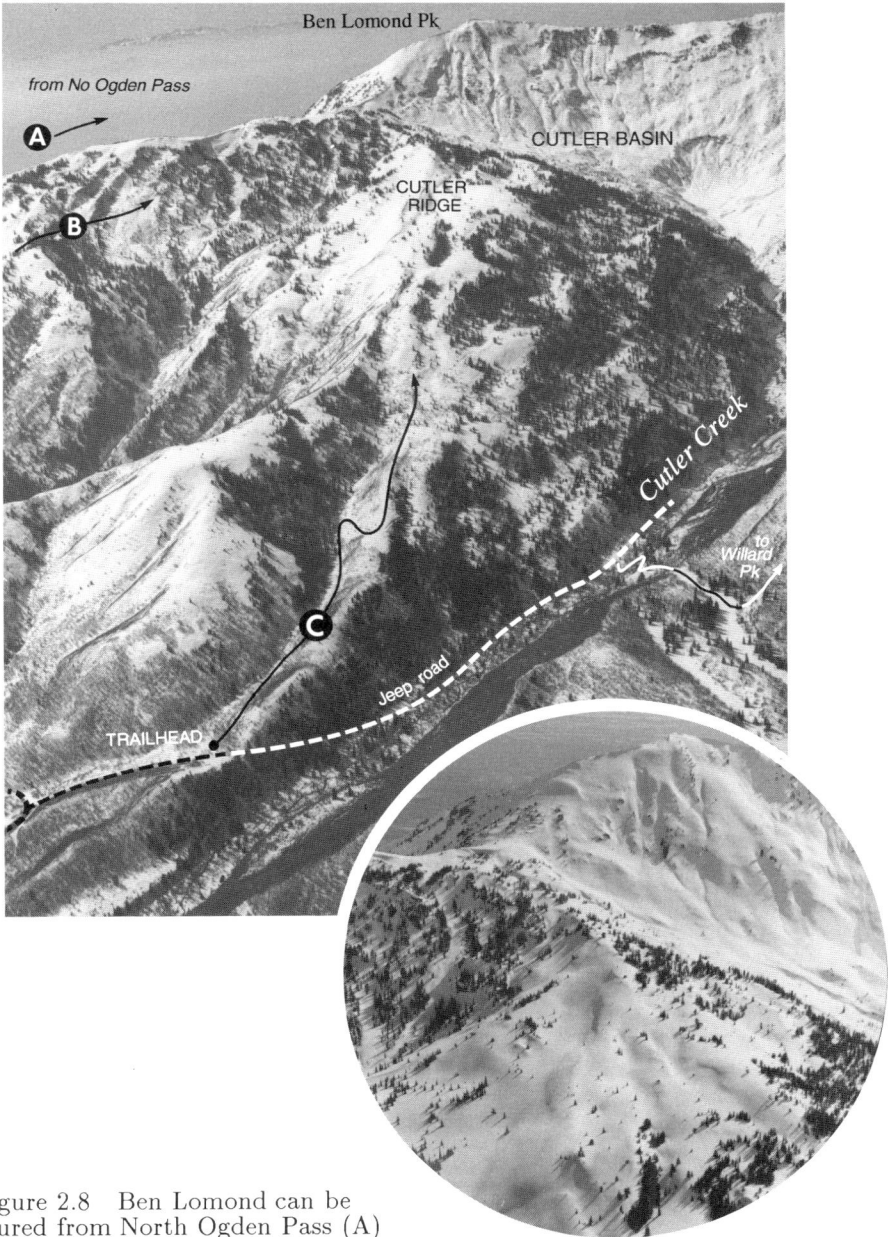

Figure 2.8   Ben Lomond can be toured from North Ogden Pass (A) and from North Fork Park via the Ben Lomond Trail (B) or Cutler Ridge Trail (C).
Inset: Upper Cutler Ridge. On January 15, 1995, two snowmobilers died in Cutler Basin when one driver released a massive avalanche onto the other. Neither snowmobiler carried an avalanche beacon.

that should be attempted only in stable conditions by those with ski mountaineering experience. The ridge is susceptible to high wind velocities and is very narrow with steep dropoffs on both sides. The ridge is clearly visible in several of the photographs in this chapter and is labeled *(A)* in Figure 2.9.

North Ridge. A safer possibility is to connect with the north ridge route from Mantua, shown as *(B)* in Figures 2.4 and 2.5. This ridge is accessed via a subridge that intersects the main Wasatch crest near the second rock outcropping described in the Mantua section.

Two variations are practical for the lower part of the ascent route from North Fork Park. The first is a continuation of the North Fork Trail tour described earlier and shown as *(D)* in Figure 2.9. This trail follows a gully that parallels the park and National Forest boundary westward toward the peak. Terrain at the upper end of this ascent is extremely steep and should be avoided when there is any danger of avalanches.

A second alternative for accessing the north ridge of Willard Peak is to follow the park road for 1.1 miles from the upper entrance to the gate near the bottom of the Cutler Ridge Trail described earlier. A jeep road continues through the gate and parallels Cutler Creek. About 0.5 mile from the gate, a trail goes right, crosses the creek, and climbs the north side of the drainage to a low saddle. Ski tourers must leave the trail at this point and climb straight up the ridge. (See *(E)* in the upper photo of Figure 2.9.) It's pretty heavily vegetated for the first half mile,[3] but quite open and skiable above that. (The best place to start up the ridge is the grove of conifers about 100 yards beyond the high point in the trail.)

East Ridge. The final route to the summit of Willard Peak, also suggested by Jock Glidden, is a variation of the north ridge route. Labeled *(C)* in Figures 2.5 and 2.9, the ascent departs from the North Fork Park subridge at a point just below the upper cirque. A short traverse across the base of the cirque gets a tourer to the east ridge, which can be followed to the summit. It should be emphasized that avalanche prediction and mountaineering skills are a prerequisite for anyone attempting the east ridge of Willard.

Descent. There are several options for the return trip from Willard Peak. The most direct and least prone to avalanche hazard is the north

---

[3]This route was suggested by Dr. Jocelyn Glidden, Weber State University philosophy professor and holder of the "World's Greatest Bushwacker" award. Jock's friends have been known to get on their hands and knees trying to follow him through undergrowth in summer.

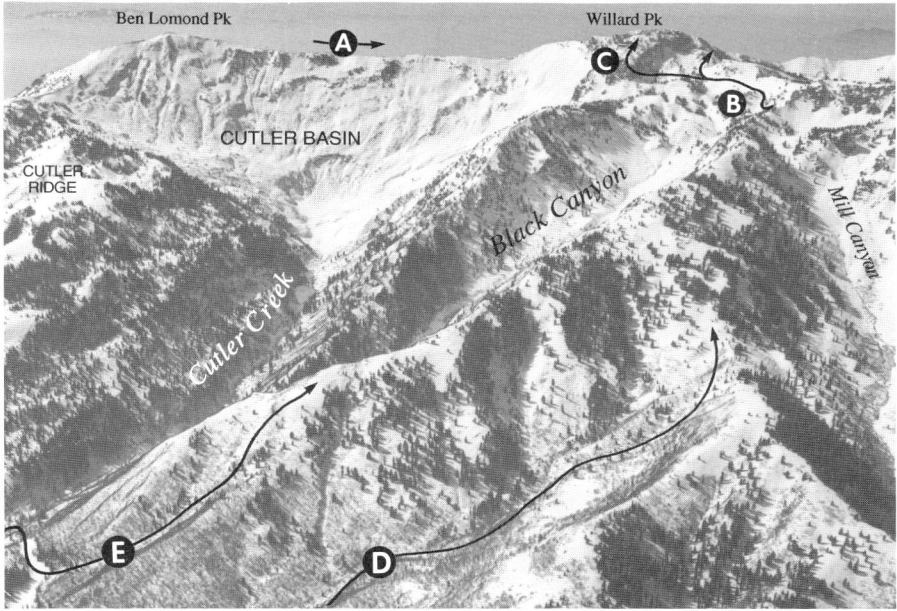

Figure 2.9   Willard Peak approachs from Ben Lomond (A), from the north ridge (B), and via the east ridge (C). The two routes from North Fork Park are the North Fork Trail (D) and the Glidden Ridge Variation (E).

Figure 2.10   The south ridge of Ben Lomond, with Willard Peak in the background, is noteworthy for the dearth of snow on the south-facing slopes above North Ogden Pass.

ridge. The north side of the subridge into North Fork Park has lots of powder shots all the way down. (See Figure 2.9.) All routes have some avalanche danger, and all have steep sections. Particular caution is urged in the upper bowls. The greatest hazard at lower elevations is the thick vegetation, so it is best to check the snow depth on the way up and plan a suitable escape route.

Ben Lomond from North Ogden Pass

One other possibility for accessing Ben Lomond is a northward traverse along the Skyline Trail from SR-162 at North Ogden Pass. A point to point tour from the pass to North Fork Park is an excellent alternative. The ridge has a southern exposure, so it is most pleasant for early morning climbing, and the slopes that drop into the park are sheltered from the sun and are ideal for the descent.

The hike from North Ogden Pass to Ben Lomond is about seven miles, with a total elevation gain of almost 3500 feet. After a steep beginning, the ridge levels out and is generally quite a gentle climb for four or five miles. (See Figure 2.10.) The last 0.8 mile to the summit becomes steep again, as mentioned in an earlier section and illustrated in Figure 2.8.

Later in the spring it is often possible to walk up the south-facing switchbacks of the Skyline Trail and then put the skis on for the rest of the tour. The view from this ridge is spectacular in all directions. On a clear day one can see all of the Great Salt Lake and beyond to the west and south, Idaho to the north, and Wyoming to the east.

Descent. All of the suggested ski descent routes from the summit of Ben Lomond terminate in North Fork Park, as described in previous sections. The trail from North Ogden Pass is seldom suitable for down-hill skiing. The snow is usually quite wind-blown and crusty, and the steep section near the pass is exposed to the sun most of the day.

LEWIS PEAK

The Lewis Peak massif lies between Ogden Canyon and North Ogden Pass on SR-162. The mountain is accessible from the north via the Skyline Trail, which was recently adopted into the Great Western Trail system, from North Ogden Pass. The same trail can be used to get to the summit from the south by starting at the Pineview Reservoir boat dock, about a mile northeast of the dam. The peak was named after Lewis Shurtliff, the local postmaster in the late 19th century, who claimed to be among the first group to get to its summit. This must have been quite a feat, considering the density of the oak brush at lower elevations!

Thanks to an elevation of just over 8000 feet and a "lakeside" location, Lewis Peak is not known for steep open bowls and light powder snow. In fact, it is included in *Wasatch Tours* as much for completeness as for its desirability as a touring destination. Despite limited downhill skiing possibilities, however, the nice rolling terrain along the ridge is suitable for intermediate skiers, and a beautiful view from the top makes a winter visit worth the hike required to get there.

The shortest route to Lewis Peak follows the Great Western Trail southward from North Ogden Pass. This involves a 1.4 mile climb of 1200 vertical feet from the pass in quite steep terrain, followed by 1.6 miles with much more gradual changes in elevation to a fork. The left fork is a continuation of the Great Western Trail to Pineview Reservoir; this is not recommended for skiers due to its southern exposure and low elevation. The right fork is a spur trail that traverses upward in a westerly direction for about 2.2 miles to the summit of Lewis Peak.

Figure 2.11   This view of Lewis Peak shows the Great Western Trail as it traverses along the east side of the massif, as well as other trails in the vicinity of Nordic Valley. *Inset:* The summit of the peak is a spiderlike series of ridges.

Descent. One possibility for the descent is to return via the same route to the starting point, but the trail is very steep and surrounding terrain is too brushy to be enjoyable. A better alternative for skiing this area involves a car shuttle. After touring around the upper elevations, possibly taking the side trip to the peak, one can descend the east-facing slopes near the Nordic Valley Ski Area.

Even a cursory look at Figure 2.11 should make it obvious that a great deal of thick vegetation will be encountered at lower elevations. The descent is certainly not for the unskilled skier. In addition, most of the land along the east side of the massif is privately owned. Fortunately, a 400-acre strip of land about a mile wide between the ski area on the north, Pole Canyon on the south, and the National Forest on the west is owned by Nordic Valley operators, and they don't object to ski tourers enjoying their mountainside.[4]

The best alternatives for a descent of the east side of the Lewis Peak massif are the north sides of the subridges where the brush is less dense. The ridge directly above Nordic Valley is not recommended, due to the density of trees and bushes, but that would be an ideal access point if the ski area ever extends its lifts higher on the mountain. It is also possible to ski down Pine Creek or Union Creek and traverse to the ski area if the snow is particularly deep. Pole Canyon has a very steep hiking/equestrian trail that would work for ascent and/or descent, but there is little room in the scrub oak for making turns in the lower elevation section.

The ridge that descends southeastward from the summit to Pineview Reservoir has the least amount of vegetation, but tourers must realize that much of this route is on private land, so they must get permission from owners before crossing.

All descent routes between Pole Canyon and Nordic Valley terminate at a jeep road/trail that traverses the base of the mountain and intersects the ski area about half way up its southern boundary. This trail is entirely on Nordic Valley property, and ski tourers are welcome to use it. The trail is a nice beginner tour in its own right.

MOUNT OGDEN AREA

Only three rivers have succeeded in cutting a channel all the way through the mountains in the northern part of the Wasatch Range. The Ogden and Weber are separated by only seven miles, and the Provo is more than fifty miles to the south. The eastern backdrop for the city of Ogden is the series of peaks that lie between Ogden and Weber canyons.

The summits that make up this block include (from north to south) Sardine Peak, Allen Peak, Mount Ogden, DeMoisy Peak, and Strawberry Peak. Steep dropoffs are found on three sides of the massif, but the east flank is more accessible. The Snowbasin ski area currently includes terrain on the east sides of Mount Ogden and DeMoisy Peak, but they may take "the whole enchilada" when they complete their expansion plans. There are still lots of good alternatives for ski touring, but they are definitely at risk. Hence, all have the "Endangered" label.

Recommended access for all ski tours in this area is SR-226, which

---

[4]Ski area owners have requested that tourers not use the downhill ski trails unless they purchase a lift pass. Their primary concern is liability if a cross country skier were to collide with a downhill skier.

Figure 2.12   These photos of Mount Ogden illustrate the contrast between the wide open bowls on the east side of the range (left photo) and the narrow wooded canyons to the west (right).

leads from Pineview Reservoir to the Snowbasin ski area. The vertical climb from there to the peaks is no more than 3000 feet.

All of these tours are suitable for advanced skiers, although intermediates could handle the lower elevation terrain as long as they don't attempt to go all the way to the main Wasatch ridge.

Tours From Snowbasin Ski Area (End.)

Snowbasin is surrounded by National Forest land which is accessible to cross country skiers from one of the ski area parking lots, from the upper terminals of ski lifts, or from SR-226.

Sardine Peak. The tour with the least climb and the least exposure to avalanche hazard goes to the summit of Sardine Peak, which is about 2.4 miles north of Snowbasin's lower parking lot. Its elevation is only 7485 feet, so the climb is less than 1100 vertical feet. The peak is the northern point in this massif, where one can overlook Ogden Canyon and Pineview Reservoir. Most of the route to Sardine Peak is shown in Figure 2.13, but the peak itself is just out of the picture.

Access to Sardine Peak is via the lower Snowbasin parking area and the Maples Campground, which is on an unplowed Forest Service road about a mile north of the ski area. From the campground, continue north along a service road and then a power line to the ridge. The peak

Figure 2.13   Snow Basin has suffered considerable abuse over the years, not the least of which is currently threatened by the owners of the Snowbasin ski area and SLOBCO, the Salt Lake Olympics Bid Committee.

is less than a mile from that point. The descent route should be selected with snow and avalanche conditions in mind.

Allen Peak and Mount Ogden. These two peaks lie on an extremely exposed ridge with considerable avalanche danger. In fact, two cross country skiers perished in this area in 1958. This is not a tour for parties without mountaineering experience.

The most direct ascent alternative is to start in the Snowbasin ski area and climb or ride to the top of the Porcupine lift. From there, a northward traverse leads to the bowl east of the peaks. The preferred option at that point is to ascend to the saddle just north of Allen Peak. As the reader can see in the bottom photo of Figure 2.14, however, all routes to the summit include very steep and narrow couloirs

It may be preferable to follow the ridge from the north. Go through the Maples Campground from Snowbasin's lower parking lot and head toward Sardine Peak. A westward route to the ridge should be chosen based upon snow and avalanche conditions. (See Figure 2.13.) The most prudent option is to take the long way around and go all the way to the saddle just south of Sardine Peak. Traverse the ridge back to the south to get to Allen Peak.

The terrain is too steep to ski off the summit of either Allen Peak or Mount Ogden, so you must return along the ridge to a point where a route can be found that is safe enough for current avalanche conditions

UPPER
OGDEN BOWL

Descent route

ACTIONS OF
SEARCH PARTIES

Route of two search parties

ACTIONS OF
TOURING PARTY

Route of upper
search party

Upward traverse through
dense woods

Path of initial avalanche

Descent routes
of lower searchers

Descent and search along
avalanche path

Departure to summon help

Location of tourer's body

Avalanche initiated by
lower search party

Position of "forgotten"
searcher at time of
avalanche 4

Location of searcher's body

Injured tourer's route to
summon help

MASS CONFUSION*

Accompanied by strong winds, a "24-hour blizzard" struck Snow Basin
on March 8, 1958. Next morning, with nearly a foot of fresh snow at the
higher peaks, four experienced tourers commenced a ski tour into Easter
Bowl, the northernmost cirque near Mount Ogden. Before departure,
one tourer grew apprehensive over lingering winds, but said nothing to
his companions.

Utilizing ridges, they worked their way towards their destination.
About 100 yards from the crest, the lead tourer felt an extensive settlement of snow under his skis accompanied by an audible "boom." Con-
sequently, the group decided to ski lower Easter Bowl, avoiding slopes
similar to the one that had settled.

---

* Condensed from *The Snowy Torrents*, Dale Gallagher, Editor, Alta Avalanche
Study Center, U. S. Forest Service, 1967.

After several runs in ideal powder, they began traversing out of the area across a steep, densely-wooded slope. The first skier rounded a small ridge and disappeared from view of his companions. Following him around, the others saw his track disappear into the path of a snowslide, *(1)* in the photo, that had released from above. They had heard no sound from the avalanche.

The three called for their companion, but to no avail. They removed skis and descended along the edge of the slide, probing likely burial spots with ski poles as they went. Halfway down, they decided that one of them should leave to summon help.

During his outbound traverse, the tourer going for assistance triggered a large avalanche *(2)* that swept him 500 feet downslope and battered him against a tree. With one eye bruised shut and hobbling on one ski, he reached the edge of the ski area, where his shouts for help were relayed to the area's Snow Ranger.

Two search groups (one with 15-20 persons, the other with 4-5)** arrived *separately* at a ridge *(A)* overlooking the accident site. The large group decided to approach the site from below; the smaller group chose an upper approach.

Enroute to the accident site, some members of the large group triggered avalanche *(3)*. Meanwhile, the smaller rescue party entered the top of a steep gully adjacent to the initial avalanche. On finding its snow to be extremely unstable, they began a retreat. Concurrently, the main group arrived at the bottom of the same gully. Unaware of the upper party, but sensing a possible snowslide from above, the main group crossed carefully, one person at a time. One searcher had crossed the gully, and another was halfway over, when the retreating upper group triggered the snowslide *(4)* all had feared.

One of the upper searchers was swept downslope 1000 feet but was not buried. Most of the lower searchers avoided burial by holding onto trees. Unnoticed by anyone, the person midway across was engulfed and buried. All searchers then moved to the site of the first avalanche. Only later did the rescuers realize that one of their group was missing. The bodies of the tourer and the "forgotten" searcher were located later that evening by probing.

The Forest Service's accident analysis states: "The tourers seriously underestimated avalanche hazard in spite of some obvious warning signs. When any doubt about snow stability exists, *stay off the avalanche paths and especially out of the release zones.*" "Divided authority, uncertain leadership, loss of discipline or control over a large rescue group, can all lead to sudden disaster," was their conclusion with respect to the rescue.

** No one could ever ascertain the exact number of searchers.

Figure 2.14   *Top:* The peaks of the Mount Ogden massif and the Snowbasin ski area. *Bottom:* The south end of Mount Ogden ridge, showing all the great intermediate terrain that is at risk due to Snowbasin's expansion plans.

and moderate enough for one's skiing ability.

DeMoisy Peak and Strawberry Peak. The terrain surrounding the two peaks south of the Snowbasin ski area is similar to Mount Ogden, but not quite as extreme. Unfortunately, the downhill skiers sometimes traverse into this area; fortunately, their range is limited by the necessity to get back to the lifts.

The quickest access for cross country skiers is from the top of the

Middle Bowl ski lift. A less congested touring alternative is to follow a Forest Service road/trail that goes south to Green Pond from the maintenance shed in Snowbasin's upper parking lot. Continue south beyond the boundary of the ski area and climb to the peak via one of the eastern ridges. Again, the long way around is the safest. (See Figure 2.14).

One could return to Snowbasin via a similar route or consider a couple of options for point to point tours. It is usually possible to ski down Dry Creek to the new Trappers Loop road (SR-167). Alternatively, if the snow is particularly deep, one can follow Gordon Creek southeast to the town of Mountain Green on the Weber River. These descents offer 3600 and 4000 vertical feet of downhill skiing, respectively, but require long car shuttles. They also cross some privately-owned land, so be sure to get permission from the owners.

Tours From Ogden

Several hiking trails ascend the Mount Ogden massif from the west. All begin at an elevation of about 5000 feet, which means little snow and lots of brush. All could be used to access the high peaks and bowls on skis during mid-winter weeks or when the skiing is less hazardous in the spring. None would be a pleasant ski descent due to their steepness and narrowness. Tourers may have to remove skis for some sections of the trails.

Taylor Canyon. The northwest slopes of Allen Peak, which stands at the head of the Snowbasin ski area, descend 4600 feet in less than four miles to the city of Ogden. It should be obvious from Figure 2.15 that the top of Taylor Canyon is not for the faint of heart in any season. The lower part of the canyon is even *less* inviting, particularly in winter, since the hiking trail traverses terrain that is much too steep and rocky for skiing. This canyon has been the scene of several very serious and fatal accidents involving skiers and hikers in recent years.

For the extreme skier who wishes to attempt some of the steepest and narrowest couloirs in the Wasatch, upper Taylor Canyon might be an interesting alternative in late winter or early spring when avalanche conditions are most stable. Easiest access is from the Snowbasin ski area, as described in the previous section. Another possibility is to hike up the canyon from Ogden via the trail that starts near the top of 2700 South Street. In either case, a return to the valley will involve a great deal of walking.

One potential problem with Taylor Canyon is that its entire length

Figure 2.15   Upper Taylor Canyon has possibilities for the extreme skier who enjoys steep and narrow couloirs. The canyon is privately owned, so permission to trespass may be required.

is currently in private ownership. So far there has been no attempt to control public access, but the Forest Service is trying to negotiate a land trade with the owner.

Beus Canyon. Another hiking trail ascends the west flank of Mount Ogden via Beus Canyon. A new trailhead is being constructed just north of the Forest Service Insect Control Station at the top of 4600 South Street in Ogden. When completed, the public will be able to access the canyon by making a short traverse to the Shoreline Trail, which ultimately will go along the base of the Wasatch Mountains for the entire length of the city of Ogden. Until the trailhead is finished, it is necessary to cross private land to get from 4600 South up to the Shoreline Trail. The Forest Service facility is about 200 yards north of

Figure 2.16   The Beus Canyon trail provides access to Strawberry Peak and Mount Ogden from the southwest.

the mouth of Beus Canyon.

The trail up the canyon ascends moderately along the stream for about 1.4 miles to a large rock outcropping on the right. From this point, a new trail is being constructed which may be completed in 1995. This new trail traverses to the right (south) around the ridge between Beus and Burch canyons; it then traverses along the south side of that ridge to the main Wasatch crest. An old trail follows the Beus drainage for another half mile by going around the north side of the rock outcropping mentioned above. It then traverses northeastwardly to the top of the mountain. Skiers may prefer to follow the route of the old trail to minimize southern exposures.

The upper bowls of Beus Canyon and its neighbors to the north and south have some excellent skiing possibilities. The slopes are less steep and rocky than those in Taylor Canyon, and the vegetation is sparse. Unfortunately, the lower slopes have the usual problems of marginal snow and little room to make turns. Skiers will have to deal with scrub oak, scrub maple, and scrub just-about-everything-else when descending this canyon; the only redeeming possibility is that they might spot a scrub jay.

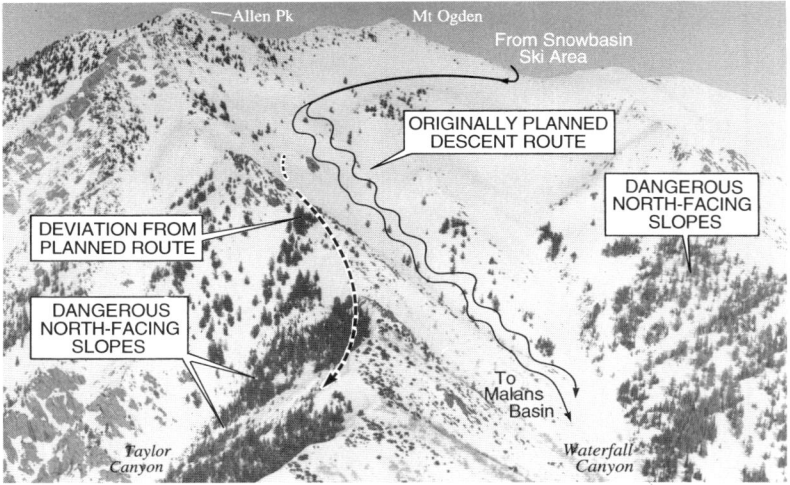

Allen Pk   Mt Ogden

From Snowbasin
Ski Area

ORIGINALLY PLANNED
DESCENT ROUTE

DANGEROUS
NORTH-FACING
SLOPES

DEVIATION FROM
PLANNED ROUTE

DANGEROUS
NORTH-FACING
SLOPES

To
Malans
Basin

Taylor
Canyon

Waterfall
Canyon

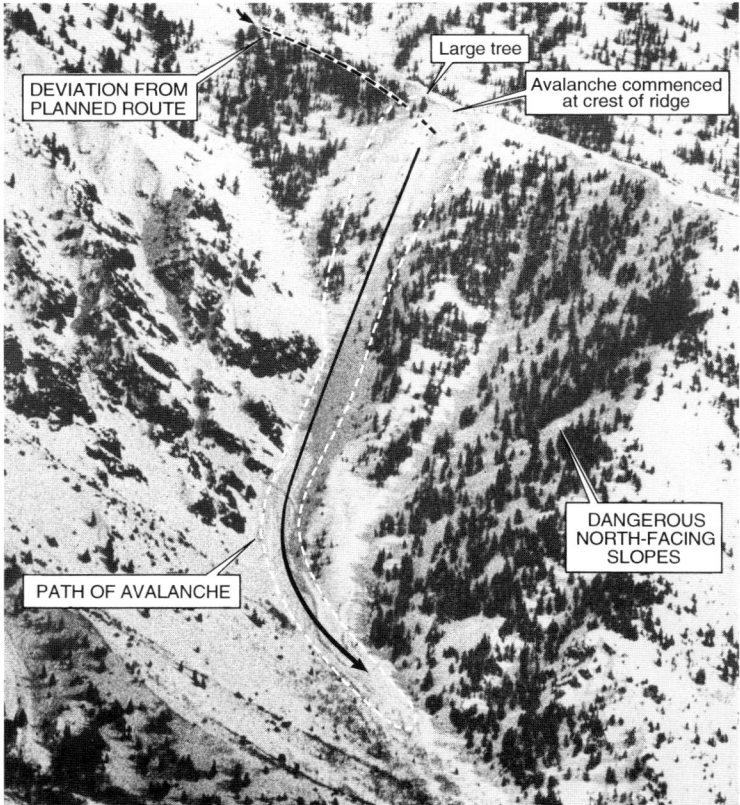

DEVIATION FROM
PLANNED ROUTE

Large tree

Avalanche commenced
at crest of ridge

DANGEROUS
NORTH-FACING
SLOPES

PATH OF AVALANCHE

A CHANGE OF PLANS[*]

On Sunday, March 29, 1964, a doctor (A.R.) and his 14-year old son decided to tour from the Snowbasin ski area into Ogden. The tour would go across the crest of the Wasatch and down Waterfall Canyon into Malans Basin; Ogden would be entered via Taylor Canyon. Two Snow Rangers (L.A.) and (P.J.) were planning a similar tour to evaluate snow stability along the slopes of upper Waterfall Canyon.

Although the four tourers would not travel together, they discussed the route along the south and west-facing slopes of the Waterfall/Taylor divide (top photo), and determined it to be free of hazard *as long as they avoided avalanche-prone north-facing slopes.*

By 4:00 pm A.R. and son had reached the crest of the range and commenced their descent into Ogden. The two rangers traveled considerably behind. On approaching the divide between Waterfall and Taylor canyons, they noticed that the front party had deviated from their stated route and had crossed onto Taylor Canyon's north-facing slopes. The rangers shouted warnings that went unheard. Entering terrain they knew was extremely dangerous, they attempted to overtake the couple. Due to the dense forest below the ridge, the first party had traveled well onto a slide area before they realized the immediacy of danger. The two rangers skied to the protection of a large tree, one stopping above it, the other below. A.R. and son, at this moment, were located just in front and below the rangers. All decided to evacuate the slope by their entry route.

As A.R. was making a kick-turn, Ranger P.J. felt and saw the snow in front and above start to move. "Swim for your lives!" he shouted as he watched A.R. and son become engulfed. As the slide stopped, P.J. could find no trace of his partner. He removed skis and descended the slide-path in search of the others. He found A.R. and son high in the slide area; each had sustained only minor injuries. P.J. moved downslope, checking for clues. A ski was found, then a ski pole, but no ranger. P.J. headed for help after searching for 20 minutes. After fighting a trail heavy with scrub oak thickets, he reached a telephone and notified authorities.

L.A.'s body was located by a probe line the following day. The lethal avalanche had descended 1300 feet over a distance of nearly half a mile. A Forest Service analysis concluded that the first party "seriously erred" in leaving the planned, safe route "without discussion or consent."

Allen Peak was named after Lawrence Allen, the Snow Ranger who lost his life while attempting to direct tourers out of harm's way.

---

[*] Condensed from *The Snowy Torrents*, Dale Gallagher, Editor, Alta Avalanche Study Center, U. S. Forest Service, 1967.

Figure 2.17   The Federal Aviation Agency radar towers demark the north section of Farmington Ridge.

FARMINGTON RIDGE

Farmington Ridge is the name that we have assigned to the part of the Weber Canyon to Parleys Canyon massif that lies north of Bountiful. This ridge is notable for being extremely narrow and steep. Its west side is so steep, in fact, that the suburban neighborhoods and adjacent Great Salt Lake seem but a step away. The contrasting east side drops off more gently to the rural Morgan Valley with its numerous farms and small communities.

The only high-elevation vehicular access to this area in winter is a gravel road up Farmington Canyon maintained by the Federal Aviation Agency (FAA). The road is suitable only for 4-wheel drive vehicles in winter but is popular with skiers and snowmobilers. Farmington Ridge is most noteworthy for Francis Peak, about five miles north of Farmington Canyon, which houses two white FAA radar domes that are visible for miles in all directions.

We have chosen to describe this 13-mile section of the Wasatch

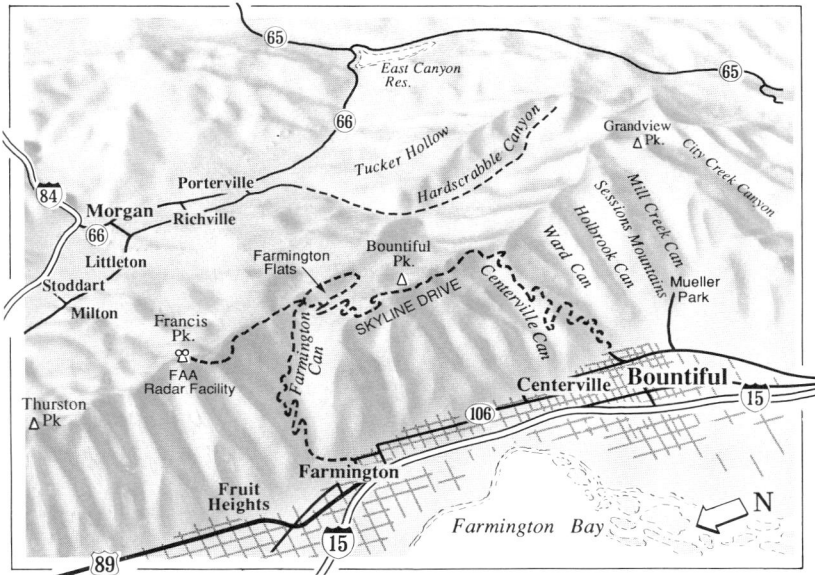

Figure 2.18   The northern part of the Weber Canyon to Parleys Canyon massif lies in Davis County. It includes the Farmington Ridge, which is most easily accessed via the Farmington Canyon road, and the area above Bountiful.

Mountains in three parts. The northern end of the ridge has an elevation that varies between 9000 and 9700 feet, with Thurston Peak as its highest point. The central third lies between Francis Peak and Farmington Canyon. The part south of Farmington Canyon includes Bountiful Peak. Many of these areas are exposed to commercial helicopter skiing and thus are designated *H.P.A.*

Thurston Peak (H.P.A.)

The 9706-foot summit of Thurston Peak is about four miles south of Weber Canyon along the main Wasatch ridge.[5] This mountain was named in honor of Thomas Jefferson Thurston, an early settler of the Morgan Valley. In 1852, the Centerville resident climbed the peak from the west and decided that the valley would be an ideal place for the Mormons to expand their growing empire. After convincing other pioneers to carve a wagon trail through Weber Canyon, he became the founding father of Fort Thurston and the community of Thurstonville, located near the

---

[5]This is the most northerly of the Helicopter Permit Areas. A request was filed for permission to expand helicopter skiing into the Ben Lomond/Willard Peak region, but so far that has not been approved.

current town of Milton. In 1993, citizens of Morgan and Davis counties joined to commemorate Thomas Thurston by placing a monument and plaque in his honor on the summit of the highest peak in both counties.

The northern section of Farmington Ridge is not easily accessed. The three possibilities described in this book are from the west, north, and east. Tourers have also traversed from the south via Farmington Canyon and Francis Peak, but this is usually done as a multi-day outing.

The rewards for those ambitious enough to ascend Thurston Peak from the valley are well worth the effort. In addition to the superb 360-degree view, tourers have below them snow-covered slopes in almost every compass direction. The east-facing bowls are sufficiently steep to challenge even the most expert skier.

Hobbs Canyon Trail. Access from the west is best accomplished via the Forest Service trailhead in Layton. The Hobbs Canyon Trail has undergone significant reconstruction as part of an effort to complete the Great Western Trail along the Wasatch Front. It leads to the first prominence south of Weber Canyon, which is about a mile north of Thurston Peak.

The trailhead is accessed via Valley View Drive, which intersects US-89 between mile posts 340 and 341 in Layton. The intersection is easily recognized by Texaco stations on both sides of Highway 89. Follow Valley View Drive northeast for 0.6 mile, then turn right onto Fernwood Drive, which winds up the hill for 0.7 mile to a Forest Service picnic area. You will certainly notice a nearby house, visible for miles in all directions, that looks like a Bavarian castle. According to a September 1994 *Salt Lake Tribune* article, the inside of the building is even more ornate than the outside, with custom wood carvings, stained-glass windows, and secret passageways.

The Great Western Trail starts at the upper end of the picnic area. It climbs steeply for a short distance, then traverses north (above the castle) and into a canyon. After crossing the stream and going around the next ridge, the trail continues northward, gradually climbing as it crosses a couple more gullies. The lower photo in Figure 2.19 shows the details of the drainages that intersect the valley in this area.

About two miles from the start, the trail heads up a ridge, winding through oak and maple, at a considerably steeper pitch. As you toil upward, don't hesitate to turn around occasionally to enjoy the view as it unfolds below. The Great Salt Lake, with its island mountains, and the Oquirrhs and Stansburys provide a spectacular contrast to the current surroundings.

When one finally breaks out into the upper bowl, an impressive

Figure 2.19 *Top:* Corbett Canyon and the northwest ridge of Thurston Peak, which may offer possibilities for skiers and hikers. *Bottom:* Thurston Peak from the west showing the Great Western Trail access via Hobbs Canyon.

rock formation becomes visible to the right, on the south side of the adjacent canyon; this is fondly called "Chin Scraper" by organizers of the Wasatch Front 100-Mile foot race. The prominence just east of this rock is easily accessed by continuing to climb southeastward. The

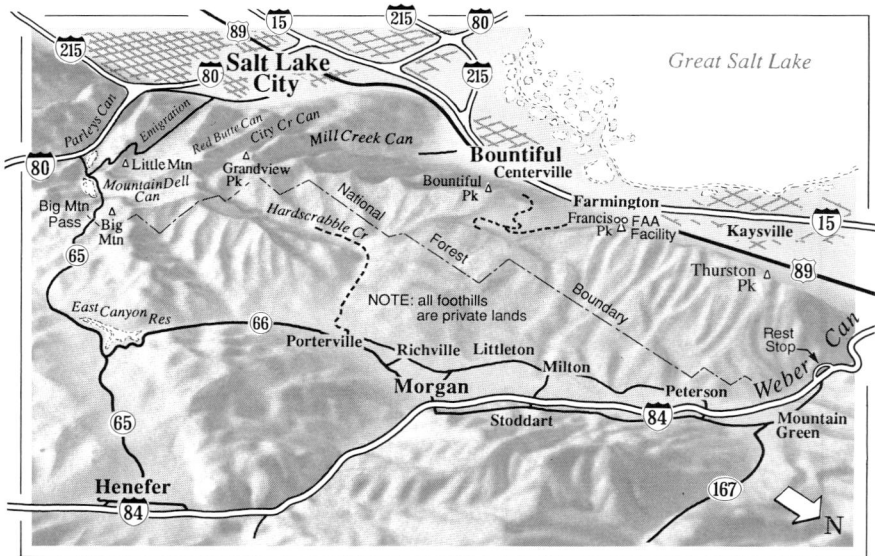

Figure 2.20   The Forest Service boundary along the east side of the Weber Canyon to Parleys Canyon massif is located high on the flank of the mountains. Easy access to the upper basins is blocked by numerous ranches and farms.

summit of Thurston Peak is about a mile farther south on the main Wasatch crest. The total distance of this tour is about seven miles, with an ascent of 4500 vertical feet.

Thurston Peak from Weber Canyon. The north end of the massif climbs extremely precipitously from Weber Canyon. Neither of the authors have attempted a Thurston Peak tour from this direction, but careful study of aerial photographs and several summer visits have convinced us of the feasibility of this tour. A couple of open areas appear to be suitable for skiing descents when low elevation snow is deep enough to cover natural obstacles and when higher elevation avalanche conditions are suitable.

The best route appears to be the northeast ridge, which intercepts the canyon opposite the Rest Area near milepost 91 on I-84. This ridge is almost entirely in the National Forest, but a narrow strip of private land separates it from the highway. To get to the bottom of the ridge, one must follow a gas pipeline that parallels the river on its south side. This pipeline passes very close to the interstate near milepost 90, but parking is not allowed at that point. The pipeline can also be accessed by crossing a bridge and the railroad tracks at the Mountain Green exit at mile 92, but several "No Trespassing" signs are found there. The alternatives are to either find a friend to drop you off on the

Figure 2.21 Thurston Peak and its eastern bowls. The northern route from Weber Canyon is shown, as well as some of the roads that cross private land west of Peterson.

interstate or to get permission from a landowner. It is most definitely *not* recommended to park at the rest area and try to cross the river and railroad tracks or to hike across the freeway overpass to the pipeline!

The ridge suggested for this tour is a steep, north-facing slope with little vegetation other than grass. Skiers should stay very close to the crest of this ridge all the way up to a saddle just below a cliff area. A couple of small groves of trees and rock outcroppings have to be bypassed along the way, but the ridge is almost totally clear. This part of the ascent covers almost 3000 vertical feet in less than two miles. It should not be attempted if avalanche conditions are anything but stable. The elevation at the saddle is 8200 feet.

From there, take a level traverse left (southeast) across the upper ends of two subdrainages through sparse evergreen trees and into the Jacobs Creek drainage, as shown in Figure 2.21. Great care should be taken when crossing these small bowls; they are the most exposed part of this ski tour. When ascending Jacobs Creek, it is best to stay left and go up to its east ridge for the remainder of the climb to the Wasatch crest. The high point at the head of Jacobs is only about a mile north of Thurston Peak. (The last mile of this route is the same as that described in the previous section.) The entire tour has 4500 feet of elevation gain in about six miles.

Thurston Peak from Peterson. Were it not for the fact that so much private land must be traversed, Peterson Creek would certainly be the best alternative for both the ascent and descent of Thurston Peak. Of all of the possibilities discussed, this is the longest route. It is also the safest and gentlest road/trail to follow through the low elevation brush. The rancher who owns the land in this area sells use permits to hunters and would presumably extend the same service to cross country skiers. His residence, as well as the beginning of the jeep road into the Peterson Creek drainage, are near the end of 4000 North in the town of Peterson. The preferred route follows jeep roads southwestward from there, bears left at a couple of forks, and ultimately climbs a trail in the Left Hand Fork of Peterson Creek. See Figure 2.21 for more detail on the terrain near the summit. Extreme care must be exercised by skiers who enter the upper bowls in this area.

Descent of Thurston Peak. Regardless of how one gets to the top of Thurston Peak, and regardless of how easily one masters the steep and deep in the the high bowls, the greatest challenge is still ahead. Skiing back to the valley from the Wasatch crest south of Weber Canyon is not pleasant to contemplate. The first problem to consider is avalanche hazard at high elevations. Both east and west-facing slopes have extremely steep sections with rock outcroppings and dense vegetation. Tourers are encouraged to study Figures 2.19 and 2.21 very carefully while planning their descent route.

Most tourers will choose to follow their ascent path back to their cars. This may involve steep narrow trails in thick brush and marginal snow. It is not uncommon for skiers to put their climbing skins back on to help control their speed while descending such routes.

By far the least complicated exit is to the east. Several jeep roads can be found in the lower parts of canyons that lead to highways where a shuttle car could be parked. All of these roads are on privately owned land and are posted with "No Trespassing" signs, so permission to enter must be obtained from property owners.

Francis Peak (H.P.A.)

With a well maintained road all the way to the summit, Francis Peak is a favorite launching place for hang gliders in the summer. Unfortunately for cross country skiers, the last five miles of the road to the peak is closed to the public in winter, so it is very difficult for them to get to the top. There are jeep roads part way up the east side in Line Creek and Smith Creek out of Milton and Deep Creek out of Littleton. These

Figure 2.22 The east flank of Francis Peak contains many bowls and side canyons. Both Line and Smith creeks enter the Weber River near the town of Milton. The southeast bowl of the peak, barely visible at the top of the lower photo, is at the headwaters of Deep Creek, which drains toward Littleton.

alternatives are are all on private land, however, and the vertical climb is much greater.

The most reasonable winter access is from the head of Farmington

Canyon. Tourers who tackle Francis Peak often walk along the road with skis strapped on their backs. A more ambitious, but more enjoyable, alternative is to repeatedly ski down an inviting bowl to the northeast until the good snow runs out and then climb back to the ridge in a northwesterly direction. The total vertical climb of such a tour is limited only by the strength and endurance of the skier. Refer to the photos in Figure 2.22 for ideas.

The return to the car can be done in the same manner as the ascent, or one can simply ski back along the edge of the roadway.

The road up Farmington Canyon is a continuation of 100 East Street going north out of the town of Farmington. It is paved for 1.5 miles, then dirt for about seven more. The road is quite steep and extremely narrow in some places with severe dropoffs on the downhill side, so it is only recommended for four-wheel drive vehicles with good snow tires and attentive drivers. The gate at the top of the canyon is usually kept closed in winter, so ski tours are described from there. The elevation at the gate is 7250 feet, which is high enough for several months of good powder snow.

Bountiful Peak (H.P.A.)

The next major mountain south of Francis Peak is Bountiful Peak, which is actually located east of Centerville, not Bountiful. Like the peaks to the north, this also has an extremely steep west flank that drops almost to the shore of the Great Salt Lake. The east and north slopes of the peak are among the very few places suitable for intermediate skiers in the northern Wasatch.

The view from the 9260 foot summit of Bountiful Peak is spectacular in all directions. There are lots of summer homes near the peak, so snowmobile traffic is unavoidable. Fortunately, snow machines seldom venture into the steep terrain that skiers enjoy, but the best opportunities for solitude are found on weekdays.

Bountiful Peak is most accessible from the Farmington Canyon road, which enables a skier to drive to 7250 feet elevation. (See the previous section for details.) It is also possible to reach the peak via Skyline Drive, the jeep road that goes up Ward Canyon from the white "B" carved in the foothills above Bountiful, but that would be a long hike in midwinter when the snow is too deep to drive very far out of the valley.

Bountiful Peak can also be approached from the East Canyon side. This would require getting permission to use one of several jeep roads on private land that go up Deep Creek out of Littleton, Taggart Hollow

Figure 2.23   Bountiful Peak from the north. The east flank offers numerous possibilities for intermediate skiers.

out of Richville, and Hardscrabble Canyon out of Porterville.

From Farmington Canyon, park by the gate near the top and follow Skyline Drive, the road that branches off to the south. In about 0.6 mile, Skyline Drive forks. The right fork traverses around the west side of the ridge, eventually climbing almost to the summit of Bountiful Peak before it drops down into Bountiful. The left fork leads to a campground and to Farmington Flats, a relatively level area northeast of the mountain. Both alternatives lead to good ski touring, but less snowmobile traffic will be encountered by turning right and heading for the peak. The best skiing from the summit is in upper Hardscrabble Canyon to the east. The west side of the ridge is exposed to a moist updraft from the lake, which means that the snow there is usually wind packed and crusty, but the eastern slopes collect lots of skiable powder.

The terrain along the ridge south of Bountiful Peak is similar to that around Francis Peak, except that the elevation is not quite as high. The ridge drops to 8000 feet within three miles of the summit, so there is more vegetation along the east side where the skiing is best. This means that avalanches are less frequent, but the downhill runs are not as long.

BOUNTIFUL CANYONS

Three major canyons—Ward, Holbrook, and Mill Creek—rise toward the Wasatch crest from the city of Bountiful. The ridge between Holbrook and Mill Creek terminates in a cluster of peaks called the Sessions Mountains,[6] which wrap around the northeast corner of Mill Creek Canyon. The Great Western Trail winds its way from Skyline Drive, at the upper end of Ward Canyon, along the tops of the upper basins of Holbrook and Mill Creek canyons, and continues in a southerly direction to the heads of City Creek and Mountain Dell canyons in Salt Lake County.

Few tours in the area are suitable for intermediates. The upper bowls have slopes that could be enjoyed by less advanced skiers, but access is a problem. Most require ascent and descent of steep, narrow, low-elevation trails through brushy terrain. Also, the good skiing is a long distance, both horizontally and vertically, from the valley trailheads.

The easiest access to all of the Bountiful canyons is via Exit 318 of I-15 between Bountiful and Woods Cross. Go east at that interchange and follow 2600 South Street up the hill to its merger with Orchard Drive. Continue on Orchard beyond where it bends to the north, and turn right (east) on 1800 South Street. If Mueller Park is your destination, continue to the end of 1800 South. If you are looking for the Ward Canyon road or one of the Holbrook ridges, turn left (north) on Bountiful Boulevard, which is at 1650 East. To get to North Canyon, turn right (south) on Bountiful Boulevard. The elevation at this intersection is 5100 feet.

Ward Canyon

Clearly visible in Figure 2.24, Skyline Drive goes from Bountiful's east bench to the Wasatch crest. The road then continues north along the west side of Bountiful Peak to Farmington Canyon and Francis Peak, as described in previous sections. The Great Western Trail, which intersects Skyline Drive at the crest, follows a jeep road south along the east side of the ridge around the heads of Ward and Holbrook canyons.

Previously known as Stone Canyon, the area has been called Ward Canyon since the early Mormon settlers realized the importance of its water and timber and decided that its ownership (and fate) should be

---

[6]The U.S.G.S. topographical maps call this area the *Sessions Mountains*; many local users call it *Sessions Mountain*. We have chosen to use the former term in this volume.

controlled by the church, rather than private individuals. Although some would frown on this action as compromising the free enterprise system, it is one of many examples of environmental awareness displayed by Brigham Young and his associates, whose foresight can be thanked for much of the land along the Wasatch Front that is currently available for public use today.

Skyline Drive starts near the large **B** on the mountain, about a mile north of the new L.D.S. Temple. Simply follow the general directions to the Bountiful Canyons listed in the introductory paragraph. At the top of 1800 South Street, turn left (north) on Bountiful Boulevard (1650 East) and continue beyond the temple until the road bends west and drops down the hill. Park at that point and walk or ski north on a dirt road to get to the mouth of Ward Canyon.[7]

Skyline Drive is not plowed and therefore is popular with walkers, ski tourers, and snowmobilers. Depending on temperatures and snow depth, the Forest Service sometimes opens the gate to allow people to drive part or all the way up the road. Tourers of all ability levels can enjoy skiing on this road, but they should be aware that low elevation snow often thaws during mid-day and freezes at night. Care should be taken to return to the car early.

Skyline Drive climbs 2900 vertical feet in 8.2 miles from the **B** to the top of the Wasatch crest. At that point skiers can continue along the road to the north, or go south on the Great Western Trail. Both are extremely scenic and are suitable for tourers of all ability levels. The southern alternative is commonly used to access the upper bowls of Holbrook Canyon, the Sessions Mountains, and (for the truly ambitious) Grandview Peak, as described in later sections.

Two other alternatives, labeled *(B)* and *(C)* in Figure 2.24, exist for cross country skiers who wish to explore Ward Canyon. These options are less suitable for novices, but they also are less likely to be used by noisy snow machines. The most inviting tour is to follow a trail that stays in the bottom of the canyon.

The canyon bottom trail *(B)* begins as a jeep road that parallels the stream on its north side for about 0.5 mile from the parking area.

---

[7]It should be noted that the Bountiful foothills are in the midst of an incredible building boom. New housing developments may preclude this access route in the near future. The official public right-of-way to the mouth of Ward Canyon is Skyline Drive. Follow 1300 East Street north to about 700 North, where it bends sharply to the right (southeast), climbs through a new subdivision, and becomes Skyline Drive. The large flat area just below the **B** is a convenient place to park if the snow isn't too deep.

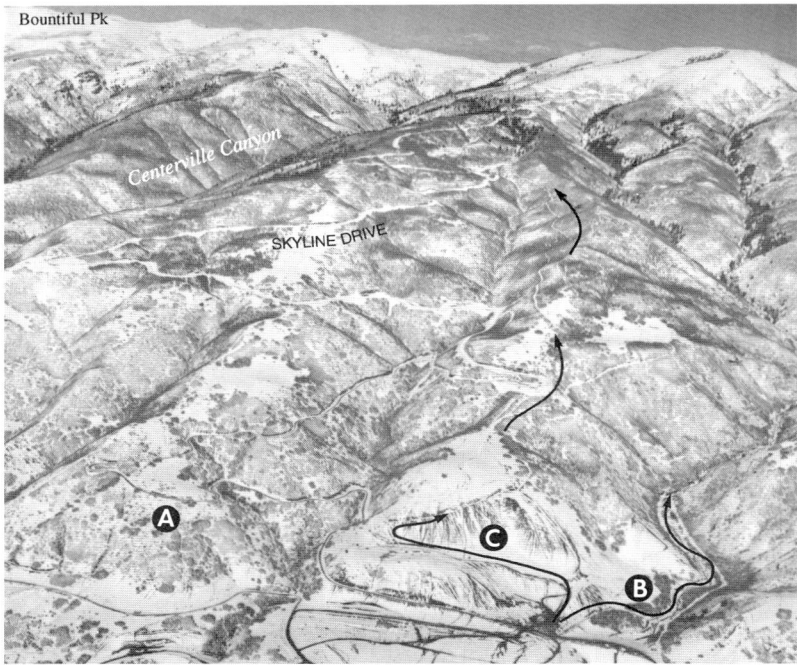

Figure 2.24   Skyline Drive (A) leads faithful backcountry tourers from the new L.D.S. Temple in Bountiful to celestial skiing in the bowls high above the city. Other touring routes in Ward Canyon are (B) the trail in the canyon bottom and (C) the Old Ward Canyon Road. The old road is a favorite play area for ORV's in summer.

When the road crosses the stream, tourers should bear left on a trail that makes a short switchback up the side of the canyon to get around a gravel bank that appears to have been caused by spring runoff. The trail continues along the stream for another mile or two, crossing back and forth several times and finally petering out in dense brush. This trail is not very well maintained and requires considerable snow cover to be an enjoyable option for tourers.

The lower part of Ward Canyon can also be accessed by cross country skiers via the Old Ward Canyon Road *(C)*. A sign at the parking area marks this jeep road, which is a favorite of the motorcyclists and all terrain vehicle riders in summer. The route climbs quite steeply in spots and generally follows the ridge on the north side of Ward Canyon. It intersects Skyline Drive at Buckland Flat, about 2.7 miles from the parking area. (This is about 2.2 miles shorter than the main road.)

Descent. Tourers who make it to the top of Ward Canyon will find a number of slopes that can provide enjoyable powder skiing opportunities in mid-winter. Unfortunately, it is not possible to ski along the canyon bottom all the way back to the parking area unless the snow is exceptionally deep at low elevations. The most prudent descent route is usually via Skyline Drive.

Holbrook Canyon

This canyon empties into the valley about a mile north of Mueller Park in Bountiful. It was named after Joseph Holbrook, an early resident of the area and Bountiful's first probate judge. Holbrook also built a road up the canyon, but his plan to pay for the road's construction and upkeep with user fees proved to be wishful thinking. Holbrook Canyon, like its neighbors, is very narrow and full of brush at lower elevations, but the upper slopes offer many delightful opportunities for skiers.

To access Holbrook Canyon, simply follow the general directions to the Bountiful Canyons listed in the introductory paragraph. At the top of 1800 South Street, turn left (north) on Bountiful Boulevard (1650 East). The mouth of the canyon is at about 900 South, just south of the temple.

Three alternatives are available for a Holbrook ski tour. Trails ascend the ridges that form the north and south boundaries of the canyon, and another follows the stream in the canyon bottom. Labeled *(A)*, *(B)* and *(C)* in Figure 2.25, they are described in north-to-south order, which is also the order of increasing complexity and difficulty.

North Ridge. The simplest alternative *(A)* is to ascend the ridge that separates Holbrook and Ward canyons. A jeep road and pipeline (shown in Figure 2.25) can be followed all the way from the canyon's mouth at Bountiful Boulevard. The ridge climbs 3600 vertical feet in about four miles to the Wasatch crest. During all but the most ideal conditions, tourers may have to hike the lower part of the trail.

There is currently a chain link fence across the mouth of the canyon at Bountiful Boulevard, but it appears to be in place to prevent vehicular access to the jeep road. Hikers, horses, and mountain bikers have made a well-beaten path around the north end of the fence.[8]

---

[8] The city of Bountiful owns the property at the mouth of Holbrook and plans to build a trailhead in that area. Since most of the land above Bountiful Boulevard is privately owned, it is not clear at this time what routes will be available to the public. If "No Trespassing" signs appear in future years, ski tourers may have to access this ridge from the mouth of Ward Canyon. Just south of the parking area near the **B** is a steep grassy slope that can be followed to the north ridge jeep road and pipeline.

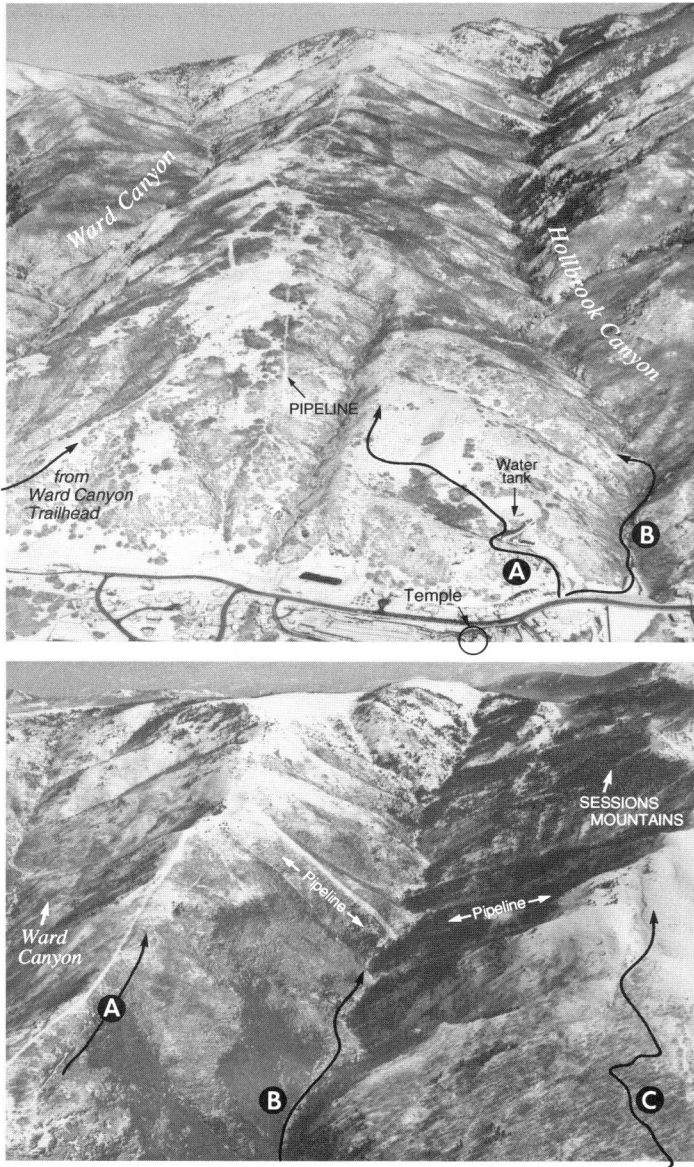

Figure 2.25   Holbrook Canyon is most easily accessed via a jeep road and pipeline on its north ridge (A). Other alternatives are a hiking trail in the canyon bottom (B) and the ridge between Holbrook and Mill Creek (C).

Holbrook Canyon Trail. From the north end of the chain link fence at about 900 South on Bountiful Boulevard, tourers can drop down to the canyon bottom and follow a hiking trail *(B)*.[9] Take the trail that starts along the north side of the stream (rather than the wider one on the south side that soon disappears). Due to the limited amount of space in the bottom of the canyon, the trail crosses the stream many times as it gains elevation. The walls of the canyon are so steep and high that the winter sun hits the trail only where it makes an occasional ascent of the north side to bypass a particularly narrow section.

The slope of the upper Holbrook Canyon trail is quite consistent and quite gentle, so competent tourers will find few spots that cause difficulty on either ascent or descent if the snow is deep enough to cover natural obstacles along the way. The greatest risk results from the canyon's steep sides and narrow bottom. When the gullies on the south slopes avalanche, the deposition is extremely deep due to the confined nature of the runout zone. This could be fatal to a group enjoying a pleasant ski tour on what they believe to be "safe" terrain.

South Ridge. The final alternative for a ski tour in this area *(C)* is a jeep road and trail up the ridge that separates Holbrook Canyon from Mill Creek. The upper part of this ridge is known as the Sessions Mountains, described in the next section. Only the lower part of one access route is covered here.

Stone Ridge Drive climbs in an eastward direction from Bountiful Boulevard at 1500 South. It leads into one of the many new subdivisions that are spreading ever higher into the Wasatch foothills. The trail up the south ridge of Holbrook Canyon starts near a water tank at the top of the subdivision. To get there from the boulevard, simply continue driving uphill and bearing left to the end of Lorien Court. At this time there is plenty of room for cars, but as more houses are built, parking may become a problem.[10]

A jeep road leads from the end of Lorien Court to the water tank, where a large dirt pile blocks further vehicular passage. Foot traffic can simply go around the south side of the tank, over the dirt pile, and continue along the road. The route traverses along the north side of the

---

[9]Considerable construction work was done on this trail in the summer of 1994. As we go to press, the trail has been completed as far as the new pipeline that traverses across Mill Creek and Holbrook canyons. The elevation at the pipeline crossing may not be sufficient for the snow depth to exceed the height of the brush in the canyon bottom, even in late winter. Tourers may want to check if progress has been made on the trail before using this route in future years.

[10]As we go to press in late 1994, there are no signs to indicate that landowners will limit public use of the trail. Like many trailheads along the Wasatch Front, however, access may not last much longer. Tourers are encouraged to respect the rights of property owners and to get permission before crossing private land.

ridge, almost totally sheltered from the sun. After about a mile, the jeep road passes through a tree farm with rows of evenly-spaced spruces and firs. Tourers should turn right (south) off the road just beyond those trees and follow a trail that climbs more steeply up a narrow gully. At the top of the gully, the trail continues on a more gentle traverse for about 1.6 miles along Holbrook's south ridge to the pipeline that crosses over from Mill Creek Canyon. From here skiers can enjoy a superb view of Mill Creek Canyon to the south and the Great Salt Lake and its mountainous islands to the west.

At this point, tourers might be tempted to show their appreciation for the pipeline company's "ski trail" by removing their climbing skins and taking a quick run into Holbrook Canyon. Be forewarned that the slope steepens, and surrounding terrain becomes more wooded as one approaches the canyon bottom, so the return trip to the ridge can be both difficult and dangerous. Anyone caught in an avalanche on this slope would undoubtedly be buried so deeply that the body couldn't be recovered until spring! Also, if the Sessions Mountains are your destination, you still have a *long* way to go!

The next 1.4 miles along the ridge are quite pleasant. The steepness of the trail varies, but is generally suitable for those of intermediate skiing ability. Tourers must be very careful if they choose to go as far as the Sessions Mountains, however. The ridge becomes very narrow with steep dropoffs, so tourers must be careful to look ahead and decide which side of the ridge is safest to traverse. The north side is generally better along the lower (western) part; the south side becomes the preferred alternative at higher elevations.

Descent. The most sensible route back to the valley is via the pipeline/jeep road that follows the ridge north of Holbrook Canyon. Note in Figure 2.25 the numerous open areas along the north side of the ridge that allow skiers more room to make turns and control their speed on the way down. Another alternative for times of heavy snow cover is to follow the canyon trail down to Bountiful Boulevard.

Sessions Mountains (H.P.A.)

Contrary to popular belief, the mountains above Bountiful do not include Bountiful Peak. Rather, a cluster of 9000 foot peaks called the Sessions Mountains lie at the head of the ridge separating Mill Creek and Holbrook canyons. They are bordered on the east by Hardscrabble Canyon, which drains east into Morgan County. The mountains consist of ridges covered with large conifers interspersed with steep north

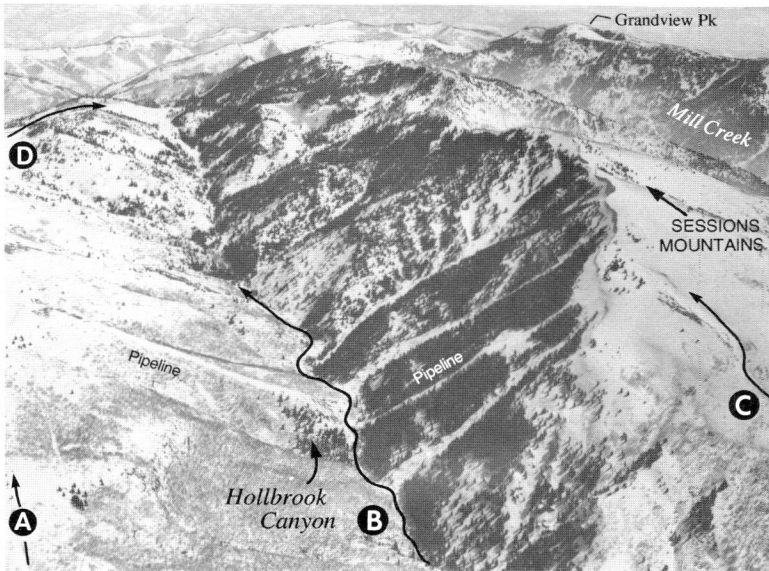

Figure 2.26   The Sessions Mountains can be accessed via the ridge between Ward and Holbrook (A), the Holbrook Canyon trail (B), the ridge between Holbrook and Mill Creek (C), and Ward Canyon (D).

and east-facing gullies and bowls that provide good opportunities for advanced backcountry skiers.

Southern Davis County was initially settled by Perrigrine Sessions and his family, along with a few other Mormon pioneers. In those days, the area at the base of the Wasatch was known as Sessions Settlement. It wasn't until 1855 that the current name of "Bountiful" was agreed upon, and soon thereafter the highest peaks in the adjacent mountains were named for one of the area's first settlers.

The Sessions Mountains are not easily accessed from any direction, either in summer or winter, which probably explains why they display so few ski tracks. When the snow is gone, one can reach the Sessions with a four-wheel drive vehicle via Skyline Drive from Bountiful. In winter, a vehicle can sometimes be used for part of the climb, but the remaining 10-15 miles is more than most skiers are willing to attempt. Another alternative, described in the previous section, is to follow the ridge between Ward and Holbrook canyons or the hiking trail in the bottom of Holbrook. These provide a good compromise for tourers who wish to avoid steep slopes and potential avalanche danger. The most direct route to the Sessions Mountains is via the trail that ascends the ridge between Holbrook and Mill Creek canyons. These possibilities are all shown in Figure 2.26.

The photograph also shows the many open slopes and gullies along the north and east faces of the mountains that are tempting to back-country skiers. Many of those are steep enough to present considerable avalanche danger, so great care should be taken.

Mill Creek Canyon

Mueller Park, a Forest Service picnic area, is located in the mouth of Mill Creek Canyon, which is at the east end of 1800 South Street in Bountiful. (See the introduction to the Bountiful Canyons for more detailed information on how to get there.) The land for the park was donated to Salt Lake City by the Mueller family in 1927, and ownership was transferred to the Forest Service in 1940. This area is extremely popular with local hikers, mountain bikers, and fishermen, who enjoy the stream, picnic facilities, and several miles of trails that are immediately adjacent to the city. The elevation at the park entrance is 5200 feet.

The lower part of the canyon is so narrow, brushy, and steep-sided that there is little room for skiers or hikers to pass. Its heavily wooded slopes were the source of a great deal of timber used by the early Mormon pioneers, and Heber C. Kimball had a lumber mill at its mouth in the mid 1800's. The upper bowl is bordered on the north by the Sessions Mountains and on the south by Grandview Peak. These large prominences offer superb skiing possibilities, particularly on the north and east slopes of Grandview. (See Figure 2.27.)

Access to upper Mill Creek Canyon can be accomplished in several ways. The previous section describes four alternatives for touring to the Sessions Mountains. All of these possibilities can be used to get in and out of Mill Creek. From the Sessions it is best to follow the gently-sloping east ridge to the head of the canyon. Alternatively, if snow conditions and skiing ability allow, it is possible to ski down the steep south-facing slope of the Sessions directly into the main bowl of Mill Creek. One other access route is described in a later paragraph on the Rudys Flat trail.

Options for the descent from upper Mill Creek are few. One can use the same route that was followed on the ascent, probably via upper Holbrook Canyon. Alternatively, a point to point tour into City Creek Canyon is a possibility, but it requires a significant amount of planning due to car shuttling and other transportation problems to be described in the next chapter.

Skiers who don't wish to venture to the top of Mill Creek Canyon

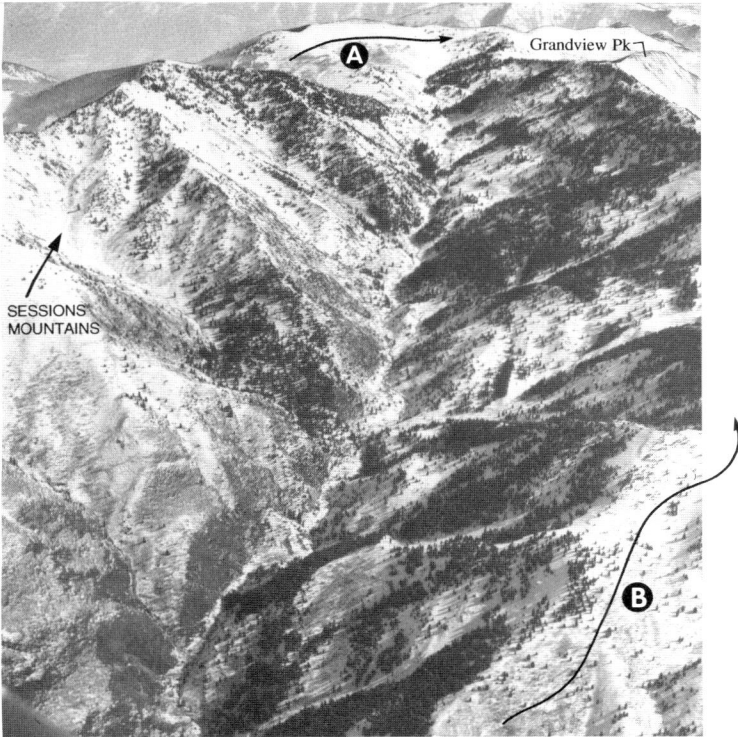

Figure 2.27   Upper Mill Creek Canyon is bordered by the Sessions Mountains and Grandview Peak. Two possible access routes to Grandview are (A) the east ridge and (B) the west ridge.

may prefer to stay on the trails that start at Mueller Park at the mouth of the canyon. The Kenney Creek trail goes to the north, and the Rudys Flat trail goes to the south from Mueller Park. Either could be used as access to upper Mill Creek by advanced tourers, and the latter is popular for shorter tours by those of intermediate skiing ability. The Rudys Flat trailhead is just outside the park gate on the right (south); the trail crosses a bridge over Mill Creek from a small parking area. About 0.1 mile beyond the gate is a larger parking area on the right; the Kenney Creek trailhead is just beyond that on the left side of the road. Both of these are described in later sections.

One other alternative for less skilled skiers in Mill Creek Canyon is to stay on the park road that continues about 0.3 mile beyond the Kenney Creek trailhead to another gate. If snow depth is sufficient, it is possible to tour for another 0.6 mile, just beyond where the pipeline crosses the canyon, before the trail disappears in impenetrable brush.

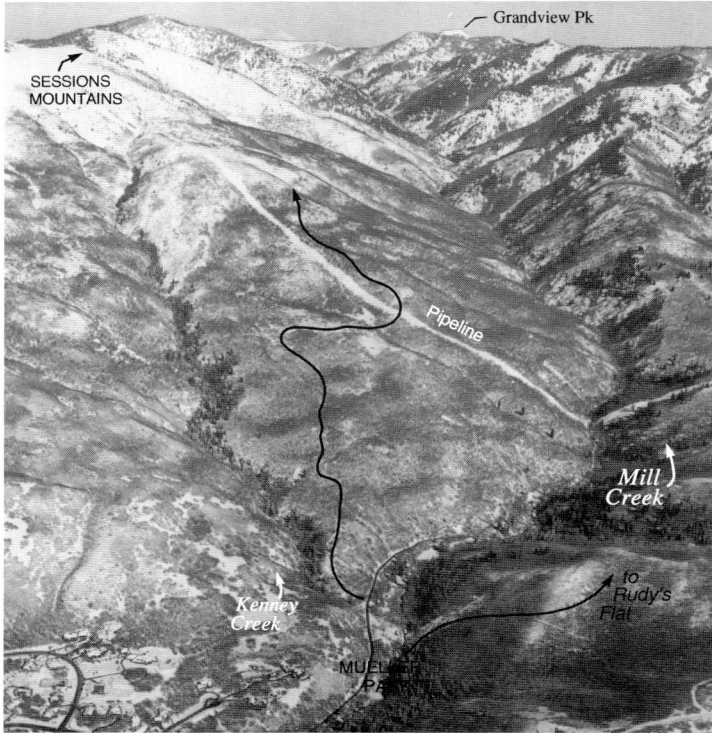

Figure 2.28   The Sessions Mountains can be accessed from Mueller Park in lower Mill Creek Canyon via Kenney Creek and the pipeline. The Rudys Flat Trail traverses to the south from Mueller Park to the ridge overlooking City Creek Canyon.

Kenney Creek Trail. The trail up Kenney Creek to the north climbs to a plateau about 800 feet above the canyon bottom and then traverses for a mile or two before dropping back down to Mill Creek and disappearing. The Forest Service plans to rebuild this trail and to connect it to the Holbrook Ridge trail that leads to the Sessions Mountains, but the schedule for that project has yet to be established. Ski touring possibilities on this trail are currently limited to periods of heavy snow at low elevations.

The Kenney Creek trail starts in a northeasterly direction, climbing for about a mile through scrub oak and maple, to the ridge between Kenney and the main Mill Creek drainage. It then bears east through more open terrain and crosses the pipeline that is clearly visible in Figure 2.28. Tourers should be sure to enjoy the view to the west from this part of the trail; if the refineries aren't putting out too much smoke, the

Great Salt Lake and Antelope Island are indeed a beautiful sight. The trail continues upward along the side of the canyon, but soon steepens and narrows, becoming more difficult to follow. It eventually passes an old mining cabin and tailings pile before dropping down toward the canyon bottom. Tourers can continue along this trail or traverse toward the upper part of Mill Creek. Unfortunately, the steepness of some of the slopes that must be crossed, as well as the direct exposure to sun, often lead to hazardous skiing conditions.

Rudys Flat Trail.[11] The trail on the south side of Mill Creek Canyon out of Mueller Park is a much better alternative for less skilled cross country skiers. Reconstructed for mountain bikers in recent years, the trail climbs gradually, traversing back and forth across the thickly wooded slopes for about seven miles to Rudys Flat, which is a small, relatively level area at an elevation of 7200 feet on the ridge overlooking City Creek Canyon. Most of the trail from Mueller Park is completely sheltered from the winter sun, so snow quality is more consistent than one might expect at such a low elevation.

Four trails, all heavily used in summer, come together at Rudys Flat. The trail out of Mueller Park is most suitable for cross country skiers due to its gentle grade and northern exposure. The trail to the south drops rather steeply into Rotary Park in City Creek Canyon and is seldom used in winter. The trail to Rudys Flat from the west, described in the next section, passes through North Canyon in Bountiful. To the east is one of the routes to Grandview Peak discussed in the final section of this chapter.

North Canyon

This short canyon is a popular access for Rudys Flat. The route starts out as a jeep road in the lower two miles then narrows to a trail for the remaining three miles to Rudys Flat. It is relatively steep in spots and might not be a pleasant descent on skis unless the snow is quite deep and untracked. North Canyon is the shortest and easiest route to the flat if one is headed for Grandview Peak. A nice ski tour is to ascend this route and descend along the more gentle trail to Mueller Park. (Mountain bikers prefer to do the trail in the opposite direction so they don't have to climb the steeper slopes.)

[11]The sign at the bottom of this trail calls it the Mueller Park Trail. We have chosen to use the "Rudys Flat Trail" terminology to differentiate it from the Kenney Creek Trail, which also starts in Mueller Park.

Figure 2.29   Grandview Peak from the northeast, showing upper Mill Creek Canyon and skiing possibilities on the north slopes of the peak.

To access the trailhead, simply follow the directions in the introduction to the Bountiful Canyons listed earlier. At the top of 1800 South Street, turn right (south) on Bountiful Boulevard (1650 East) and follow it for about two miles, past the golf course, to Canyon Creek Drive (3400 South). Turn left (east) and drive to the end of the pavement. Elevation at the trailhead is about 5500 feet.

Grandview Peak (H.P.A.)

This pyramid-shaped mountain is the high point on the ridge between Mill Creek and City Creek canyons. The origin of Grandview's name is obvious. The mountain is visible from just about everywhere, which means that the view is exceptional from the top. At least 10 miles from a road in winter, the peak is not easily accessed from any direction. It has justifiably been said about Grandview Peak that "you just can't get there from here."

The five possible places to start a Grandview Peak tour are (1) Ward Canyon or a Holbrook ridge in Bountiful, (2) Mueller Park, (3) City Creek Canyon, (4) Emigration Canyon, and (5) Mountain Dell Canyon. All routes are difficult, and all are long. They are not quite "super tours," but close. Only the first two are described in this section. The others are covered in Chapter 3.

Grandview from Ward and Holbrook Canyons. All routes to Grandview Peak from the north involve crossing over the Sessions Mountains and then skiing either around or across the large basins at the head of Mill Creek Canyon. The preceding two sections describe a number of options for these tours.

Grandview from Mueller Park. The most direct, but least desirable, option for a Grandview Peak tour is to follow the hiking trail that ascends in an easterly direction along the ridge from Rudys Flat. The trail is very steep for the first mile as it climbs through thickly vegetated terrain. After a more gradual section in somewhat open terrain, the trail makes a traverse to the right through another section of oak brush and then disappears. At that point, one should follow a minor drainage up through a grove of large aspen and fir trees to get back on the ridge. The rest of the tour is like the ridge west of the Sessions Mountains; it is steep-sided in many places, but passable on one side or the other. About two miles of such exposed touring is required to reach the summit of Grandview Peak.

Descent. Having ascended Grandview, tourers should first congratulate themselves on joining a very select group of people with the persistence and endurance to surmount the obstacles required to get there in winter. Before attempting a descent of the peak, be sure to take time to enjoy the view in all directions and to study the text and photographs in Chapter 3.

The first decision to be made is that a descent along the west ridge is not a reasonable option. In all other cases, one can return by the route that was followed on the way up. The simplest alternative is to ski down into City Creek Canyon. (Details on that option are found in the next chapter.) Regardless of the route chosen, tourers may want to take a run or two down the north slopes of the peak into upper Mill Creek Canyon before returning to the car□

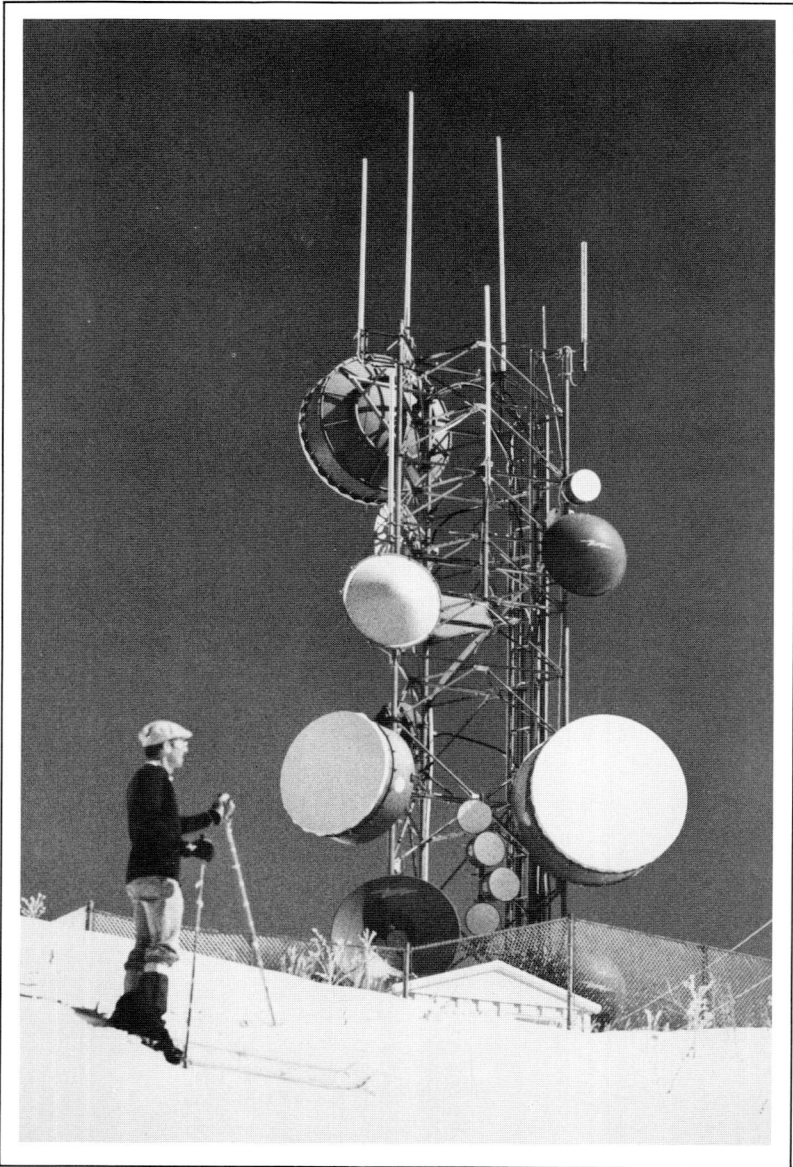

Communications towers dominate the north ridge of City Creek Canyon. Tourers with pacemakers may want to consult with their physicians before exposing themselves to the microwave beams.

Chapter 3

NORTHERN SALT LAKE COUNTY

This chapter includes a description of ski tours between the Davis/Salt Lake county boundary and the ridge north of Millcreek Canyon. In this area, three major drainages empty into Salt Lake Valley. The northernmost is City Creek Canyon, which supplies a large portion of Salt Lake City's drinking water. Next is Emigration Canyon, route to the Wasatch Front and points west for early pioneers. Parleys Canyon, used almost exclusively as a transportation corridor today (for I-80, one of the nation's busiest east-west highways), is the third canyon to be examined. All three of these canyons terminate at the crest of the Wasatch Mountains, and all have upper basins with excellent opportunities for ski tourers.

Also described in this chapter are possibilities for touring in the Dry Creek drainage and among the foothills above Salt Lake City, as well as along the ridges north and south of City Creek Canyon. Although it is closed to public access, a brief description of Red Butte Canyon is included for completeness.

FOOTHILL TOURS

The foothills above Salt Lake City played an important role in the history of Utah skiing. Many of the early inhabitants of Salt Lake Valley were of Scandinavian heritage and brought a love of competitive ski jumping to their new home. Jumps were constructed in several locations along the Wasatch Front, including one near the current location of the University of Utah Medical Center. Skiers and spectators frequently

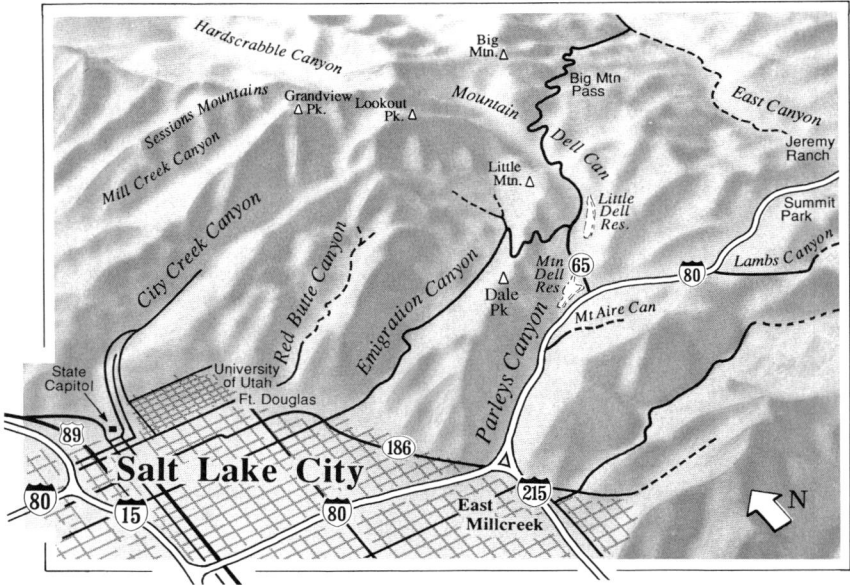

Figure 3.1   Despite a maximum elevation of only 9400 feet, the Wasatch Mountains in northern Salt Lake County provide many ski touring opportunities.

gathered at these sites to enjoy an exciting day in the snow.

In recent years, the foothills have become less inviting to skiers. The character of the area has degenerated as massive housing developments have crept higher and higher, covering and blocking access to the snow-covered mountains. Little restraint is placed on those who would build their grandiose castles on the side of the mountains for all to see and envy.

Fortunately, some foothill terrain remains in public ownership. Many of the ridges that rise eastward between the Capitol and the University of Utah have little vegetation at low elevations. Immediately following a storm, these grass-covered slopes provide excellent opportunities for tourers who want a "quick fix" without taking time to travel to higher locations.

Unfortunately, at this elevation the quality of the snow deteriorates quite rapidly when the sun comes out and causes the snow to consolidate. Tourers are advised to explore these areas either during or immediately following a storm. North facing slopes are preferable, since snow quality is generally better, and it remains that way for a longer time. A few possibilities for foothill tours are described in the sections that follow. Most are of intermediate difficulty.

Figure 3.2   A jeep road along the north ridge of City Creek Canyon services several sets of microwave antennas and provides easy access for hikers and tourers.

North Ridge of City Creek

The ridge north of City Creek Canyon houses several communications towers and antennas visible from the city below. (One set of these is shown in the photograph at the beginning of this chapter.) A jeep road and trail provide access to these facilities and beyond. Unfortunately, the trail does not continue as far east as Rudys Flat, described in the Mill Creek section of Chapter 2, so it is not feasible to ski the entire length of the ridge. One can easily tour for a total of 5.5 miles, however, without encountering terrain that is too steep for those of intermediate ability. The elevation change in that distance is 2300 feet.

The jeep road that provides access to the north ridge of City Creek Canyon starts at the end of Dorchester Drive. To get to the trailhead, ascend East Capitol Boulevard and turn left on Braewick Road. At the stop sign, turn left again on Dorchester and follow it to its end.[1]

Descent. Few opportunities exist for skiing off the ridge in either direction, so it is best to follow the trail back to the car. One possibility is to bear northwest from the lower antenna to the new subdivisions in the foothills adjacent to North Salt Lake, but the required car shuttle is probably not worth the effort.

---

[1]The Forest Service is planning to develop a trailhead in this area, so another access point may exist in future years. Parking is currently quite limited.

South Ridge of City Creek

The ridge south of City Creek Canyon also has a jeep road and trail that is used by hikers and mountain bikers in summer and (less frequently) by ski tourers in winter. The trailhead is at the end of Terrace Hills Drive, which climbs in a northward direction from 11th Avenue above the City Cemetery. Other access points are possible, but all require climbing (and possibly descending) low elevation south-facing slopes.

The first mile of the jeep road leads up a gully and along a subridge to a low saddle (with pipeline warning signs) overlooking City Creek Canyon. From the saddle, the jeep road follows the ridge southward and then eastward toward Black Mountain. A mile past the saddle, at *(A)* in Figure 3.3, the road forks. One can turn right (west) and go a few hundred yards to Twin Peaks, a double prominence just off the main ridge, and enjoy a nice view of downtown Salt Lake City and the University of Utah.

Alternatively, one can go left (east) at the road fork and continue along the main ridge as it rolls gently upward for 1.7 miles to the base of Black Mountain. From there the terrain becomes much steeper, and only advanced skiers should venture farther. Total vertical gain from Terrace Hills Drive is about 1500 feet.

Descent. Most people return the way they came. The dense brush at lower elevations makes a descent into either City Creek or Dry Creek impractical without careful exploration of the selected route in summer. A couple of open areas can be found on the north side of the ridge, but neither is pleasant all the way to the road. The Dry Creek side is more open and provides better descent possibilities if snow conditions allow skiing the south-facing slopes.

Black Mountain. For those who wish a more challenging tour, it is possible to continue eastward beyond the relatively gentle portion of City Creek's south ridge. The jeep road becomes extremely steep for about a mile before terminating along the summit ridge. The ridge can be followed for another mile, but after that it becomes too rocky for skiing. This area, called "The Crags" by organizers of the Wasatch Steeplechase mountain running race, must be bypassed along its south side in order to continue farther east to the 8200 foot summit of Black Mountain. The north slope drops very precipitously into City Creek and is not a safe place for skiers. This was the location of a mid-nineteenth century snowslide that killed four lumberjacks who were felling trees for a sawmill owned by Brigham Young.

Descent. Few tourers will choose to return via the jeep road. Its

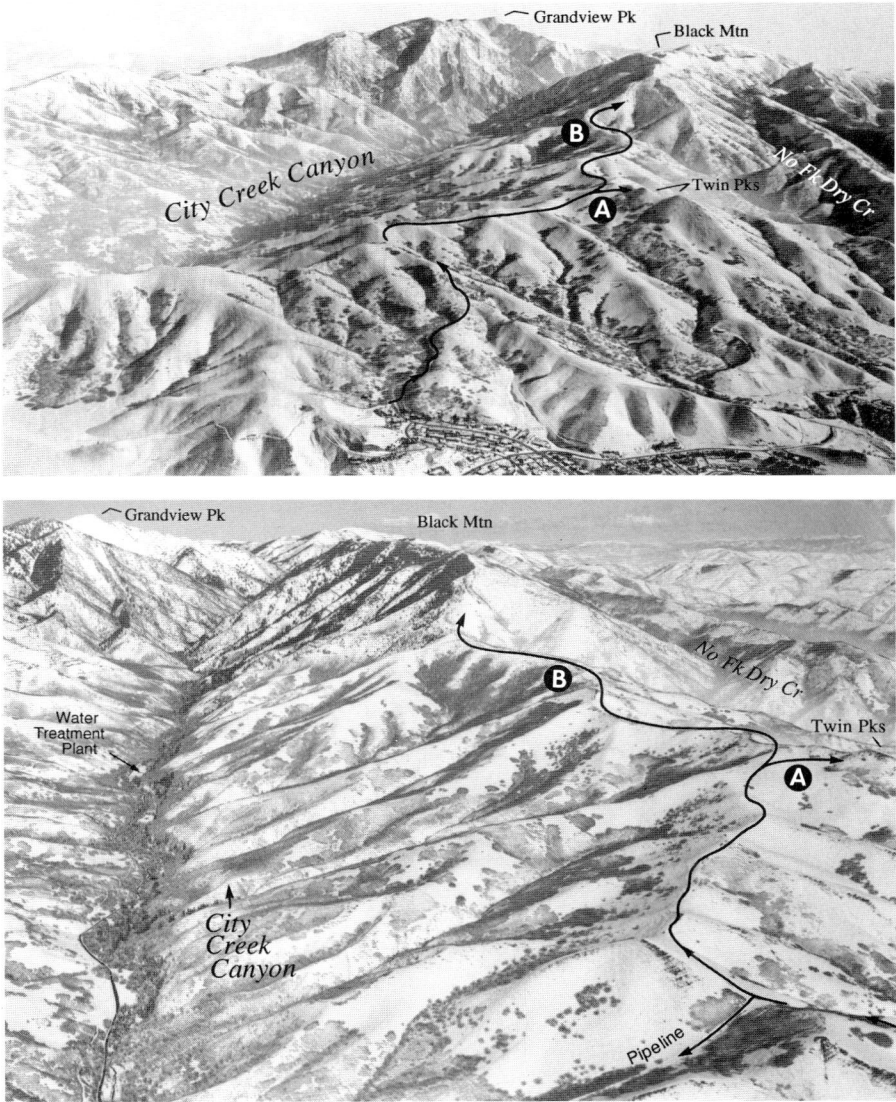

Figure 3.3 City Creek's south ridge is accessed via a jeep road that leads to (A) Twin Peaks and (B) Black Mountain.

steep section is much too narrow to allow skiers to make enough turns to control their speed. The best alternative when conditions allow is to ski down into the north fork of Dry Creek to the University. More details on this route are found in the next section.

It is also possible to continue eastward along the ridge to the pass just beyond Black Mountain summit. A trail drops down quite steeply, switching back and forth across a narrow gully, all the way to the creek. Much of the terrain is open enough for an expert skier to handle when snow depth is sufficient to cover the undergrowth. The road and hiking trail, described in the City Creek section, can be followed back to the valley.

More ambitious tourers may continue along the ridge to upper City Creek and enjoy its steeper, higher elevation slopes.

University of Utah/Dry Creek

Skiing the hillsides east of the University of Utah is reasonable only when conditions are right, but it's really popular among frustrated students who need to catch a couple of powder runs between classes on days when they don't have time for a trip to Alta. The best snow is usually found on the north sides of the ridges right after a storm.

To access terrain above the university, start at the upper University Hospital parking lot. The terrain southward to Red Butte Canyon is all public, so skiers are free to go where the snow is best. The bottom photo of Figure 3.4 shows some of the treeless slopes in the area.

The terrain north of the university is equally inviting. Skiers usually follow the trail to the block **U** on the mountain or hike up one of the gullies that separate the nearby subdivisions. The center photo of Figure 3.4 shows this area. As more houses are built in the neighborhood, access may become more complicated.

Dry Creek. The canyon that enters the valley between the block **U** and the University Hospital is Dry Creek. A gated dirt road goes north from the upper hospital parking lot to the mouth of the canyon, and a trail continues up the drainage from there. The canyon has two main forks, with a trail in each. The north fork ends at the City Creek ridge. The south fork terminates at a ridge overlooking Red Butte Canyon.

North Fork. The slopes of the north fork of Dry Creek are mostly south-facing, so the skiing there is seldom worth while after the sun has done its work. It can be great right after (or during) a storm, however, as long as the route is chosen carefully. The brush is quite thick along the trail in the canyon bottom, but several open spots allow a skier to get to and from the less densely vegetated slopes above.

The north fork can be approached from the trail or from the south ridge of City Creek, as described in an earlier section. The trail route is quite simple—bear left at every fork until a side canyon is reached that leads up to the ridge.

Figure 3.4   When conditions are right, ski touring opportunities abound in the foothills above Salt Lake City. The bottom two photos show terrain north and east of the University of Utah. The top photo shows the beginning of the road up City Creek's north ridge.

In addition to the Dry Creek drainage itself, possible return routes include the west and south slopes of Twin Peaks and the ridge above the block U.

South Fork. The south fork of Dry Creek is used primarily for accessing higher elevation terrain, such as Black Mountain and upper City Creek. The vegetation is generally too thick to allow an enjoyable descent. Tourers should bear right at the first trail fork and follow that to the end. Continue climbing eastward along the ridge that separates Dry Creek from Red Butte Canyon. The nice slopes that drop into upper Red Butte may look inviting, but the canyon is off limits, so don't even think about it. The ridge bends to the north and climbs more steeply to the summit of Black Mountain.

Red Butte Canyon

From the early days of the pioneers, Red Butte Canyon was a source of important raw materials for the residents of Salt Lake City. Its timber was used for poles and fencing. Its rock went into buildings and the making of lime. Its water provided for drinking and irrigation. The rock quarry was sufficiently important that a railroad was build from the city to allow its valuable red sandstone to be removed and transported more efficiently.

For many years, Red Butte was the principal water source for Fort Douglas and hence was closed to the public. The fort has been decommissioned and turned over to the University of Utah, but the canyon remains closed. Since it has always been kept free of grazing, farming, and other human-impact activities, the Wasatch-Cache National Forest has designated Red Butte as a Research Natural Area. The public is allowed only in the lower half mile of the canyon. Today, the Red Butte name is probably better known for its association with the garden and the arboretum, rather than the canyon.[2]

Skiers and hikers may never be allowed in upper Red Butte, but we include a photo (Figure 3.5) just in case the policy changes. The canyon roads are suitable for skiing, but heavy vegetation along each side would prevent much deviation. The area is certainly not worth the effort for powder skiers, but it would be a nice intermediate outing. It would also be a good descent route for point to point tours commencing in City Creek, Emigration, and Mountain Dell canyons.

Many trails have been developed for hikers and mountain bikers in the foothills above the University of Utah Research Park. Some are a bit steep for the low elevation snow conditions, but others are suitable for cross country skiing. The gentlest trail follows a pipeline for about 1.5 miles between the arboretum and This Is The Place State Park. Unfortunately, this is used quite heavily by runners and mountain bikers, even when the snow is relatively deep, so the snow becomes packed and rutted fairly quickly after a storm.

The trail system in lower Red Butte is most easily accessed from the

---

[2]In 1994, Red Butte Garden and Arboretum completed the first phase of a controversial development project that included a multistory building, a huge parking lot, and an unsightly chain link fence that blocks wildlife migration paths—all in the name of environmental education.

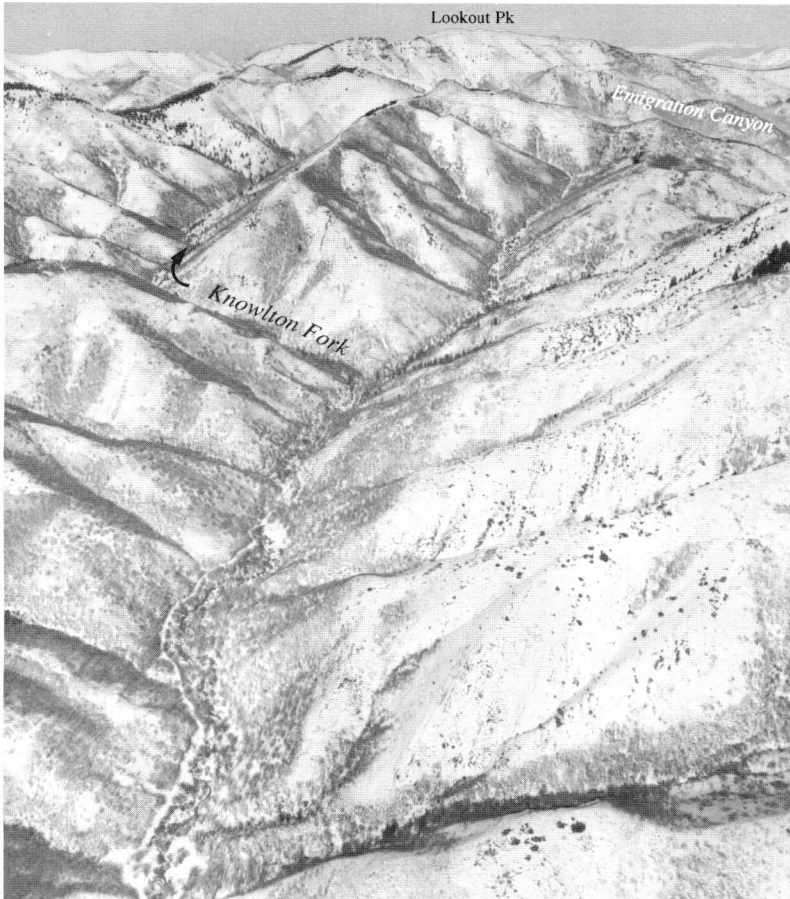

Figure 3.5 Although closed to the public at present, the roads in Red Butte Canyon would make an easy descent route for tourers entering from any direction.

arboretum. Go east into Fort Douglas from the intersection of South Campus Drive and Wasatch Drive at the University of Utah. Cross Fort Douglas Boulevard and continue east another 0.2 mile to the parking lot.

CITY CREEK CANYON

City Creek Canyon empties directly into the heart of Salt Lake City and has been an important part of the city's history for a century and a half. The saw mills and grist mills that formerly dotted its banks no longer exist, but a large percentage of the city's water supply still comes from the canyon.

Today, City Creek is most heavily used for non-motorized recreation. Hundreds of runners and bikers follow the paved road that winds from Bonneville Boulevard for 6.2 miles to the Upper Rotary Park picnic area. A dirt trail parallels the road for its lower 3.5 miles, and another continues from the end of the pavement for 4.8 miles to the main Wasatch crest.

Access to City Creek is controlled to prevent the overuse problems that have plagued other Wasatch Front canyons. Cars are allowed *by permit only* on even-numbered days during the summer months. Bicyclists may use the canyon on odd-numbered days in summer and any day in winter. Snow removal (or lack thereof) presents another limitation to canyon access in winter. Salt Lake City plows the canyon road only as far as the water treatment plant, about 3.7 miles from the gate. This means that would-be City Creek tourers must ascend 2.5 miles of unplowed road to reach the Rotary Park trailhead.

The photos in Figure 3.3 show the lower canyon, and Figure 3.6 includes a picture of its upper basin.

Lower City Creek

The hiking trail along the north side of the road can be an excellent tour for anyone with advanced beginner skiing abilities when there is enough snow at low elevations to cover the rocks. It is accessed from the gate above Bonneville Boulevard by walking a short distance up the pavement and then bearing left on the trail marked "Hiking Trail - Foot Traffic Only." Alternatively, one could climb up to the trail from the boulevard just north of the mouth of the canyon. The trail parallels the road for 3.5 miles and ends about a quarter mile below the water treatment plant. To go farther, just walk up the road (or ski beside it) to the end of the plowing and ski from there. The road continues for another 2.5 miles. The upper section is quite sheltered from the sun, so the snow should last a long time after a storm.

Upper City Creek (H.P.A.)

From the end of the pavement at Rotary Park, the trail is easily followed all the way to the upper end of City Creek, a total distance of 4.8 miles. It starts out as a jeep road that crosses the stream three times and soon narrows to a foot trail along its north side.

Figure 3.6   Upper City Creek Canyon is a delightful, but somewhat inaccessible destination for ski tourers. Note the large cliff band on the north side of the canyon just below the summit of Grandview Peak. *Inset:* Cottonwood Gulch, the southeast bowl of Grandview, can be skiable when conditions are safe.

Most of the canyon is very narrow with extremely steep sides covered with dense trees. The vegetation becomes more sparse, however, as one reaches higher elevations. Notice in Figures 3.6 and 3.7 the many touring options in the upper part of the canyon. On the south side are some steep slopes that drop from the shoulder of Lookout Peak. At the head of the canyon are a number of more gentle west-facing options from the ridge overlooking the town of Morgan and the Weber River valley. On the north side are open bowls along the flanks of Grandview Peak. (See Figure 3.8 for a better photo of the latter options.)

It is also possible to access upper City Creek from the north or

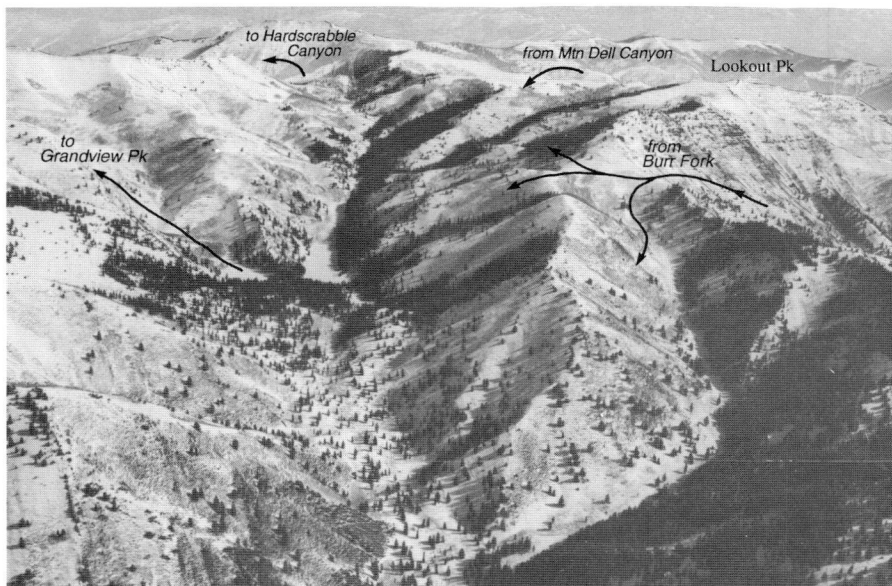

Figure 3.7   This view of upper City Creek Canyon shows the north-facing slopes on the side of Lookout Peak.

from the south. Holbrook and Mill Creek canyons (in Davis County) require really long hikes but allow a side trip to the Sessions Mountains, where one could enjoy a few powder runs. Burr Fork in Emigration has the advantage of being the shortest access route, but it's very steep and south-facing. Ascending upper Mountain Dell Canyon may be the best compromise. More details on the last option are found in the next section.

Descent. The most obvious descent possibility is to return by whatever route one follows on the way up. Regardless of ascent route, a return via City Creek might take as long as the climb. The lower part of the canyon is quite flat and snow is often marginal. Many deadfalls that cross the upper part of the trail, however, can add an element of challenge to an otherwise long and boring trek. An interesting possibility involving a car shuttle would be to go up City Creek and down Emigration or Mountain Dell.

In order to make the run back to Salt Lake City more pleasant and less time consuming, tourers might want to consider doing this as a "biathlon tour." The biathlon event for cross country skiers normally involves use of skis and a rifle, but we recommend a bicycle as the second item of equipment. One might be able to use the gun to hijack a Salt

Lake Water Department truck, but biking is preferred as an aerobic activity. On a dry day, it would be easy to ride a bicycle to the end of the pavement and leave it at the water treatment plant. One could ski from there to the upper part of the canyon, enjoy a day in the powder, and return the same way.

Many variations exist for the biathlon tour. An easier alternative would be to enter the upper bowl from another canyon and return to the valley via City Creek. In this case, the bike would have to be parked at the treatment plant the day before the tour, and the run back to the car would serve as a warmup for the next day's outing.[3]

Grandview Peak. At 9410 feet, Grandview is the highest peak between Francis Peak and Gobblers Knob. The origin of its name is obvious to anyone who has stood on its summit. The view includes most of the Wasatch Range between Ben Lomond and Lone Peak, downtown Salt Lake City, the Oquirrhs and Deseret Peak to the west, Lewis Peak in Coalville and the Uintas to the east, Mountain Dell and I-80, Summit Park and Park City.

Access to the peak is best accomplished along its east ridge, which separates City Creek from Mill Creek Canyon. From upper City Creek, the route to the summit is best seen in Figure 3.8. The steep slopes on the south side should be avoided during the ascent. Rather, tourers should use the gentler terrain southeast of the peak to get to the east ridge. Several options for a Grandview tour from the north were discussed in Chapter 2.

Descent. The safest descent alternative is the southeast bowl. Skiers who decide to descend the steeper slopes on the south side of the peak must be careful of a very dramatic 300-foot limestone cliff band, visible in Figures 3.6 and 3.8. They should stay east of the ridge to avoid the mother of all gelande jumps. Once below the open areas, the remainder of the descent to the trail has less avalanche danger.

Cottonwood Gulch. The most direct route to Grandview Peak is also the least safe. The steep southwest bowl shown in Figure 3.6 drops 2000 vertical feet from the summit in about a mile. This is obviously not a place to be when avalanche conditions are at all threatening.

To access Cottonwood Gulch from the City Creek trail, bear left

---

[3]Pam Wells, Steve Pace, and Alexis Kelner pioneered an excellent "super tour" variation for City Creek Canyon. Their springtime outing commenced from the foothills above Bountiful, followed the serpentine Wasatch crest southward to Grandview Peak, and descended City Creek Canyon. Mountain bikes, planted along the City Creek road the previous evening, provided transportation to the home of one of the tourers.

Figure 3.8   Upper City Creek can be accessed from the south, via Emigration or Mountain Dell canyons, as well as from the north. The safest route to the summit of Grandview Peak is its east ridge.

(north) in a grove of large trees about 1.4 miles from the end of the pavement at Rotary Park. *This is not an obvious turn.* Tourers must be observant and watch for the drainage coming in from the left. Follow a narrow trail on the right (east) side of the stream to the Treasure Box Mine. From there the trail becomes less distinct. It is best to stay on the left side of the stream most of the way. The brush becomes too thick to ski through within a half mile unless the snow is very deep, so tourers may be forced to break one of the prime rules of avalanche safety and hike up the narrow gully cut by the stream.

Descent. Skiing Cottonwood Gulch from the summit of Grandview Peak is tempting for expert skiers who enjoy steep slopes, but it can be extremely hazardous. In addition, it is seldom the best exposure for snow quality, and the brush in the bottom of the gulch can be awful! The only time of year Cottonwood might be both passable and safe is early spring.

Lookout Peak. The best skiing in upper City Creek is usually found on the north slopes of Lookout Peak. A large grove of fir trees, visible in Figure 3.7, keeps the snow dry and helps reduce the avalanche danger. Easiest access to Lookout is from upper Emigration or Mountain Dell, as described in a later section. The side drainage visible in the lower right corner of the photo is a good route for an Emigration to City Creek tour.

EMIGRATION CANYON

The early history of Emigration Canyon is summarized by its name. The Donner Party crossed over Little Mountain Pass from Mountain Dell in 1846 and cut a road through the impenetrable brush of the lower canyon. Mormon pioneers followed their route a year later. Their final rest stop before entry into Salt Lake Valley was Last Camp, near where Crompton's Restaurant is today. From there it was all downhill to Zion.

At first, Emigration Canyon was primarily a farming community, but over the years it became the source of many raw materials needed by the growing population of Salt Lake Valley. The canyon provided water for drinking, sandstone for buildings, limestone for the smelter, and wood for lumber and fuel.

Emigration was also the source of important *processed* materials. Started in 1864 and reportedly the first brewery west of the Mississippi, the Wagner Brewery stood at the mouth of the canyon. Late in the 19th century, a dance pavilion and amusement park were built nearby. On weekends and holidays, crowds of people arrived from the city to enjoy the facilities. Many used the spur of the Salt Lake & Fort Douglas Railroad that serviced the brewery, while others came by horse and buggy.

Another railroad, for hauling sandstone from near the headwaters of Emigration Creek, was built in the canyon in 1907. The railroad, according to Ernest D. Kimball in *Treasures of Pioneer History*, went out of business in less than ten years. It was only operated for three months each year, and "passenger service was only incidental, used mostly by the few people who had summer homes in the canyon, and also by campers and tourists." One unique aspect of this railroad was that it was powered by electricity. Due to the heavy vegetation in the canyon and the extremely dry conditions in summer, the builders feared that sparks from a steam locomotive might start a forest fire.

This fear was not unfounded. In the summer of 1988, a careless picnicker at Affleck Park let a campfire get out of control. It quickly spread down Mountain Dell Canyon and crossed the ridge into Emigration. The wind finally turned around just in time to save the homes built high in the canyon. Although new growth began sprouting from the ashes the following summer, the effects of this near disaster are still visible during all seasons of the year.

The drainages in upper Emigration Canyon are connected like the fingers of an open hand. Killyon Canyon corresponds to a thumb point-

Figure 3.9   Pinecrest Resort was a popular gathering place for 1920's era skiers and hikers belonging to the Wasatch Mountain Club. Since the Emigration Canyon road remained closed during winter, access was generally by horse-drawn sleighs furnished by the Wagner Brewery, located at the mouth of the canyon. Photo by W. H. Hopkins, courtesy of the Wasatch Mountain Club.

ing to the east, with Birch Springs Pass at its tip. The four fingers aim north toward Lookout Peak. (See Figure 3.10.) The little finger is Brigham Fork, the ring finger is Burr Fork, with Pinecrest at its first knuckle, and the other two fingers are Killyon side canyons. The best skiing is found in the upper end of these drainages, but all are steep enough to require intermediate or advanced skiing skills for a safe descent. Some people enjoy touring the pipeline that traverses along the north side of Emigration Canyon, but it is on a south-facing slope and access is increasingly difficult as more homes are constructed.

Emigration Canyon is a good example of the checkerboard land ownership pattern in the Wasatch. In the upper part of the canyon, lands controlled by the Wasatch-Cache National Forest are interspersed with privately-owned areas. At this time, land owners allow public access in Killyon Canyon, but the main trail up Burr Fork has been gated off. Other access routes into upper Burr are available for hikers and tourers, but they are much less convenient. It is unlikely that this situation will improve in the near future.

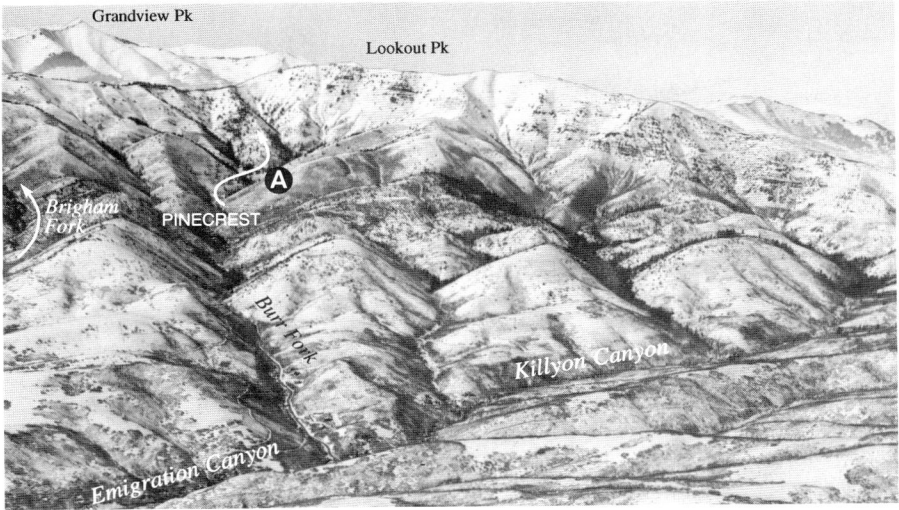

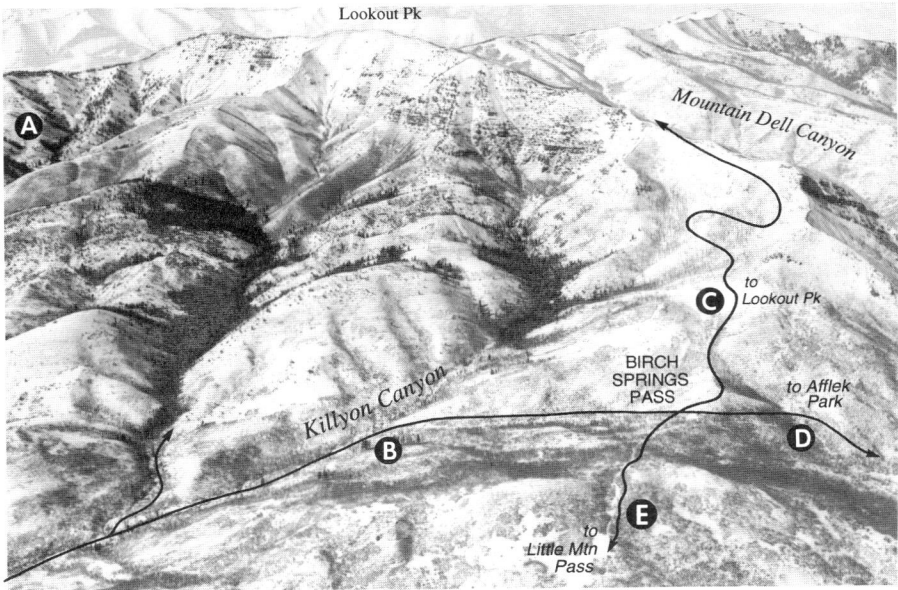

Figure 3.10   *Upper:* The north side of Emigration Canyon contains four forks that terminate near the summit of Lookout Peak. *Lower:* The easternmost point in Emigration is Birch Springs Pass. Touring routes shown in the photos are (A) Burr Fork to City Creek Canyon, (B) Killyon Canyon to Birch Springs Pass, (C) Birch Springs Pass to Lookout Peak, (D) Birch Springs Pass to Affleck Park, and (E) Birch Springs Pass to Little Mountain Pass.

Burr Fork

Early development in upper Emigration Canyon was due in large part to the railroad built to service sandstone quarries in Burr Fork and in adjacent Brigham Canyon. The railroad cutback is still visible on the west side of the road just above the Killyon turnoff; it can also be seen about a mile beyond that where it returns to the canyon bottom. Several summer homes were built there in the early part of the twentieth century, along with the Pinecrest Resort, shown in Figure 3.9. The resort operated off and on for about fifty years and was eventually torn down in about 1950. The homes have multiplied and are now occupied year around.

Despite the generally south-facing aspect of Burr Fork, it has become popular with ski tourers. It provides quick access to Lookout Peak and upper City Creek, which usually have better snow due to northern exposure and higher elevation. Also, the east sides of some of Burr's high ridges have steep open slopes that are less exposed to the sun and quite nice for skiing.

The road up Emigration Canyon ends in the Pinecrest home area at an elevation of about 6700 feet. The upper end of the road is too narrow to allow parking in winter. Also, homeowners in the area have blocked access to some of the public lands in the upper part of the fork. The Forest Service may some day work out an agreement for developing a trailhead in the area, but until that happens, tourers should get permission before touring in Burr Fork.

A dirt road, presently blocked by a gate and "No Trespassing" signs, continues beyond the pavement in Burr Fork along the east side of the stream to a large spring. At that point the road crosses the stream and a trail continues north up the drainage. The canyon becomes extremely narrow, so the bottom is not a good place to be when there is danger of avalanche. A safer climbing route is the ridge on the west side of the fork, which ends at an 8700 foot saddle overlooking City Creek Canyon. Total distance from the end of the road is 2.4 miles. The summit of Lookout Peak is an easy 250 vertical foot climb to the east as shown in Figure 3.10.

Descent. Much of the terrain in upper Burr Fork is extremely steep and south-facing.[4] The snow is usually more pleasant on the slopes that

---

[4] Burr Fork was the scene of a 1992 fatality. Two skiers had made four runs from the top and decided to go for "just one more." The fifth run was on a slope just a couple of degrees steeper than the others. A small avalanche released and caught the first skier, sweeping him into the narrow gully and burying him. By the time his

face more to east than those in the center of the fork. It is possible to follow the ridge on the west side of the fork and find open areas to ski along its side. A better alternative is to ski the ridge on the east side of Burr, then traverse across another ridge to a trail that follows the next drainage into Killyon Canyon. Not only does this route avoid the access problem, it has 700 additional vertical feet of skiing.

Another descent possibility is to ski the north-facing slopes of Lookout Peak that were described previously. Returning via City Creek is a much longer tour that requires a car shuttle, so tourers may prefer to climb Lookout Peak and continue eastward into Mountain Dell Canyon as discussed in a later section.

Killyon Canyon

Despite its gentler terrain, Killyon Canyon has not received the development pressure seen in Burr Fork. The road in the lower part of the canyon provides access to only a few residences. A popular hiking, equestrian, and mountain biking trail follows the drainage to its end at Birch Springs Pass.

The trailhead in Killyon is accessed by driving up Emigration Canyon and continuing straight where the main road turns sharply right toward Little Mountain Pass. Go straight again in 0.2 mile where the main road bears left into Burr Fork. Follow a narrow road for 0.5 mile to the snowplow turnaround. A few people live higher in the canyon, so the road is plowed for another quarter of a mile, but no public parking exists beyond the turnaround. It's a short walk up the canyon to where you can put on your skis.

The trail starts as a jeep road that is blocked by a dirt pile. It follows the stream, crossing it several times. A couple of washouts are bypassed on the south side of the canyon, but the trail has no steep sections. This tour is suitable for advanced beginners. The tour up the drainage to Birch Springs Pass is about 800 feet in 1.6 miles.

From the pass, trails going in all four compass directions provide a variety of touring alternatives. One can follow the ascent route back down Killyon Canyon. Another trail heads south along the Little Mountain ridge. Continuing in an easterly direction takes a skier down to Affleck Park in the Mountain Dell drainage. The latter two options, both possibilities for point to point tours, are described in more detail in later sections.

companion had located the victim with his beacon and dug him out, a period of only about 20 minutes, it was too late.

Advanced skiers will probably choose the north trail from Birch Springs Pass and head for the summit of Lookout Peak. This 8954 foot mass of rock common to Emigration, Mountain Dell, and City Creek canyons is recommended only for advanced skiers with excellent avalanche training. The route from the pass to the peak follows the ridge separating Emigration and Mountain Dell canyons and then bears west toward the summit.

Another Killyon Canyon alternative is to follow a trail that bears left (north) just 0.8 mile upcanyon from the houses. This trail begins near several large cottonwood trees that were burned in the fire, but are still standing. It terminates in 1.4 miles at an elevation of about 7200 feet at the base of Lookout Peak, as shown in Figure 3.10. Using the hand analogy from the introduction to this section, this is the "first finger tour." This fork can also be used for ascent and/or descent of upper Burr Fork as mentioned previously.

Little Mountain

Little Mountain Pass is the point where the highway crosses between Mountain Dell and Emigration canyons. Volume 1 of *Wasatch Tours* describes the first two miles of the ridge east of the pass as suitable for beginners. More advanced tourers might enjoy continuing along the ridge to Little Mountain or following the trail to Birch Springs Pass.

The snow plows usually leave plenty of room for people to park at the pass. From there, simply ski along the ridge in an eastward direction, following the trail in areas where the trees are too thick to penetrate. Near the summit of Little Mountain, the trail bears north and descends into Emigration, where it traverses to the head of Killyon Canyon. The trail has a couple of steep spots, but it climbs a total of only 600 feet in three miles. This tour is best right after a storm, before the snow becomes windblown or sun-crusted. Views in all directions are superb.

A point-to-point tour between Little Mountain Pass and the gate across SR-65, via Affleck Park, is a nice alternative. It can be done in either direction with a car shuttle of only about three miles. Total skiing distance is 5.9 miles. More details on the route to Affleck Park are in a later section.

Dale Peak

Dale Peak is on the ridge west of Little Mountain Pass. Its 7376 foot summit overlooks the new Emigration Place subdivision, and I-80 ap-

Figure 3.11   The trail along Little Mountain ridge leads to Birch Springs Pass at the head of Killyon Canyon.

pears to be just a short leap in the other direction. The top of Dale is much more inviting as a hike than as a tour, but all skiers can enjoy the first mile or so of the ridge when snow conditions are good. Most of the slopes around the peak are covered with thick oak brush, but its northeast bowl has good potential for downhill skiing, as shown in Figure 3.12.

Only one reasonable route exists for a winter ascent of Dale Peak. Simply follow the ridge west from Little Mountain Pass for 2.6 miles. The road goes through two gates and passes a pipeline pumping facility. Bear left at the road fork just beyond that and continue along the ridge crest. Just east of the first steep section, the road crosses a pipeline. This should be a decision point. The practical alternative is to ski down the pipeline into Emigration. More adventuresome tourers will continue westward to the peak.

From the pipeline, the road alternately steepens and flattens for about a mile before ending. A trail continues along the ridge from

Figure 3.12   Dale Peak is on the ridge west of Little Mountain Pass. The insert shows Steve Lewis pondering whether to attempt a summit ascent on skis or to wait until summer when the scrub oak is less intimidating.

there to the peak. A total climb of only 1150 vertical feet is required, but much of that has dense brush on each side. The ascent is not a problem, but returning to the car might not be as pleasant. A couple of ridges that descend northward into Emigration appear to allow skiing all the way to the canyon bottom, but tourers are advised not to be tempted without very carefully checking their routes in summer. Most descents will end in the back yards of private homes and/or in thick groves of scrub oak.

PARLEYS CANYON

Early explorers checked out Parleys Canyon as a possible route for crossing the Wasatch Mountains, since it has the lowest pass between Weber and Provo canyons. Due to the difficulty of the lower part of the canyon, the pioneers selected a different route via Lost Creek to East Canyon, then up Little Emigration Canyon to Big Mountain, down Mountain

Dell Canyon and over Little Mountain Pass into Emigration Canyon.

The canyon was named in honor of Parley Pratt, who succeeded in building a road from the valley to the current location of the Mountain Dell Golf Course in 1849-50. His "Golden Pass Toll Road" allowed travelers to bypass Little Mountain and Emigration Canyon. The road over the top part of the canyon was improved a few years later.

In 1900, the Rio Grande & Western Railroad built a track up Parleys Canyon to haul coal from Summit County. In service until 1946, the train was also used by skiers to get to the Park City area. Travelers can still see the old railroad bed along the north side of I-80 near the summit.

Parleys has two main side canyons, Mountain Dell and Lambs. The former branches to the northeast just above the reservoir adjacent to I-80. It terminates at the main Wasatch ridge above East Canyon, and one of its forks leads to Big Mountain Pass from the Affleck Park picnic area. Lambs Canyon branches to the south and ends near Wolf Mountain Ski Area and upper Millcreek Canyon.

Mountain Dell Canyon

The road that turns off I-80 at Exit 134 follows the Mountain Dell drainage for about five miles before it bears east and ascends several steep switchbacks to Big Mountain Pass. This road, SR-65, is plowed for only about three miles to a gate that is kept closed in winter, so the remainder is frequently used by skiers, walkers, and snowmobilers.

The upper basins of the canyon are accessible from the road and contain some excellent intermediate skiing. The starting elevation for Mountain Dell tours is only about 6000 feet, however, so the skiing is best when the snow is deep and cold. The view from the high ridges is spectacular.

All tours in Mountain Dell Canyon follow the highway for two miles beyond the gate to the Affleck Park picnic area, which is nestled along the stream among huge cottonwoods and imposing cliffs at an elevation of 6100 feet. This is a nice lunch stop, as well as a decision point. Beginners might want to turn around here, but a number of options exist for more advanced skiers. Three are shown in Figure 3.14 and described below.

Big Mountain Pass. From Affleck Park, one can continue up the highway for another 3.5 miles to 7420 foot Big Mountain Pass, which overlooks East Canyon. Shown as route *(C)* in the photograph, much of this road is on the sunny side of the drainage, so the snow is often

Figure 3.13   The train up Parley's Canyon was used by Salt Lake area skiers to access the terrain at Parleys Summit, the Rasmussen Ranch area east of the summit, and Park City. Photo by S. Dean Green.

less than ideal. From the pass, ambitious tourers can continue to the east along the highway, or turn right and ski south along the ridge. The latter option follows a jeep road which provides superb views of the main Wasatch peaks east of Salt Lake. Another very nice tour, which involves a long car shuttle, would be to continue down the Mormon Pioneer Trail described in Volume 1.

Big Mountain. An additional two mile hike northward from Big Mountain Pass takes a skier to the peak that gave the pass its name. Total climb from the pass is about 1100 vertical feet. Alternatives for a descent are the north side of Big Mountain into Mountain Dell Canyon and the east side of the mountain back to the highway.

Upper Mountain Dell Canyon. A second alternative from Affleck Park, labeled *(B)* in the photo, is to follow a trail north up the Mountain Dell drainage from the picnic area into the upper basins of the canyon. This is not recommended unless the snow is very deep, since some parts of the canyon are very narrow and brushy. The trail above Affleck Park was a nicer tour before sections of it were washed out by the floods of 1983. Total distance to the ridge from the highway

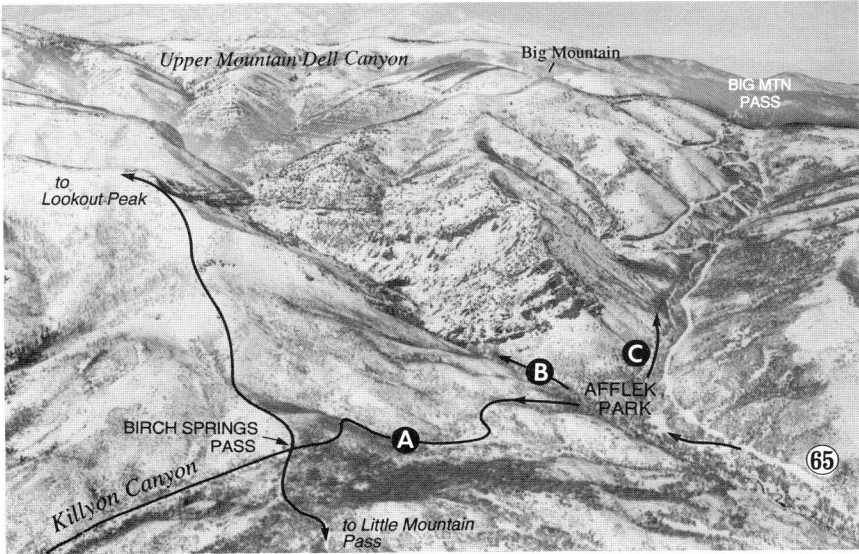

Figure 3.14   Upper Mountain Dell Canyon is home to Big Mountain and the Affleck Park picnic area. Tours shown are (A) Birch Springs Pass, (B) upper Mountain Dell bowls, and (C) the highway to East Canyon.

gate is 5.8 miles, with a total vertical gain of 2400 feet.

Birch Springs Pass. The easiest tour from Affleck Park is to turn left at the upper end of the picnic area and follow a jeep road that climbs in a westerly direction for 0.9 mile to the ridge. This is Birch Springs Pass at the head of the Killyon branch of Emigration Canyon. Total vertical is just 800 feet. Options from this point are to ski down into Emigration or to traverse south and west to Little Mountain Pass, as previously described.

In most snow conditions, the preferred route into upper Mountain Dell Canyon is to follow the ridge north from Birch Springs Pass toward Lookout Peak, rather than following the canyon bottom. This adds about a mile to the tour, but it avoids the brush.

Descent. If there was enough snow in the lower part of the canyon to use it as an ascent route, the return trip from the head of Mountain Dell will be a breeze. From the Lookout Peak ridge, it is possible to drop into the canyon at any point that looks inviting and take the low route home. Several nice bowls provide good alternatives for powder lovers. The steepest slopes and the driest snow are found in the west fork, but there is significant avalanche danger in this area.

Alternative return routes include Big Mountain and Birch Springs

Figure 3.15   The west bowl of Mountain Dell Canyon, adjacent to Lookout Peak, usually has the best snow, but it also has the most avalanche hazard. The preferred route into City Creek crosses the ridge in the upper part of Mountain Dell.

Pass. If your endurance is up to it, another possibility is City Creek. As described in a previous section, this canyon has some excellent intermediate terrain, but it would be a long day on the skis. Figure 3.15 shows the pass between the two canyons.

Lambs Canyon (H. P. A.)

Abel Lamb brought his family to Utah from Nauvoo in 1847. He and his sons started a barrel-making business in Salt Lake Valley and were the first to build a road into the canyon that bears their name. They built a home there and used wood from the nearby forest to make barrels, tubs, churns, and washboards. In later years, a sawmill was built at the head of the canyon, and a toll gate was set up to collect a fee from users of the road.

Today the road is public for 4.6 miles to a gate, with a summer home area above that. None of the road is plowed in winter, so tourers and snowmobilers often enjoy its easy access from I-80. Skiers should respect the privacy of the home owners and stay on the roads and trails

Figure 3.16   Murdock Peak is at the head of Lambs and Millcreek canyons. Upper Lambs is also accessible from the Pinebrook subdivision via a private trail in Toll Canyon.

when skiing in or passing through this area.

Lower Lambs Canyon. Lambs has tours for skiers of all ability levels. Beginners can hike up the road from the Interstate, and go back the same way. Intermediates can climb as far as their confidence allows, either into the upper end of the main drainage or into one of the side canyons.

One tour that has little avalanche hazard but reasonable skiing is the trail to Millcreek, which intersects the road 1.8 miles from I-80. When the terrain steepens near the top, it is possible to bear left and ski through fir trees to a ridge that parallels the canyon. Alternatively, another ridge to the right has slopes with enough room to ski between the aspens.

Elbow Fork Trail. A nice day tour is to ski from Millcreek to Lambs. The best route is the foot trail that starts at "the elbow" in Millcreek and drops into Lambs as described in the preceding paragraph. The trail is quite steep at the top, but there is plenty of room to traverse and kick turn if the snow is deep enough to cover the underbrush.

Ski up Millcreek Canyon 1.4 miles from the gate to the point where the road turns sharply right. A trail goes left at that point and ascends a side canyon. About 0.3 mile from the road, the trail forks. The left fork goes to Mount Aire (described in the next section), and the right fork goes to Lambs. The latter trail switchbacks for 1.4 miles and 1400 vertical feet to the pass. The easiest alternative is to drop into Lambs at that point, but other descent routes are possible, as mentioned previously.

Murdock Peak. This peak is at the head of both Lambs and Millcreek canyons and is very close to the top of Wolf Mountain Ski Area. It has the best powder of any tour in Lambs, but also the most avalanche danger.[5]

The shortest approach to the summit with the least vertical is from Wolf Mountain. Be sure to check with the Ski Patrol before leaving the ski area, but the ridge from the top of the uppermost lift to the top of Murdock is usually open if avalanche conditions allow.

Descent. Many options exist for skiing down Murdock Peak. The most inviting are the steep chutes on the north side of the summit, but these are often very hazardous and are recommended only for those with advanced skiing and avalanche avoidance skills. The safest route is to follow one of the ridges and enter Lambs Canyon below the upper bowls. The west slopes of the peak also provide access to upper Millcreek Canyon.

Mount Aire

One of the most accessible options for advanced skiers is Mount Aire, an 8621 foot peak between Millcreek and Parleys canyons that overlooks the Mountain Dell Golf Course. While traveling east on I-80 in Parleys Canyon, one would never guess that the mountain has some great powder shots. From that perspective, the only visible features are hillsides covered with scrub oak that look totally uninviting. The view of westbound drivers, however, is completely different. Above all the dense vegetation are a couple of bowls that beckon Park City commuters as they head for work on winter mornings. The northeast and the north slopes of the mountain are very steep and have little vegetation to impede a skier's progress (or the rapid movement of avalanche snow).

---

[5]Murdock was the site of a fatality in March 1982. Two skiers had toured up to the peak from Park West and were enjoying some good skiing when an avalanche broke loose. Both were buried, but one skier was able to free himself and locate the other with his beacon within a few minutes. *The tragedy of this event was that neither skier had a shovel.* It took so long to dig the victim out of the hardened snow that he had run out of air and could not be revived.

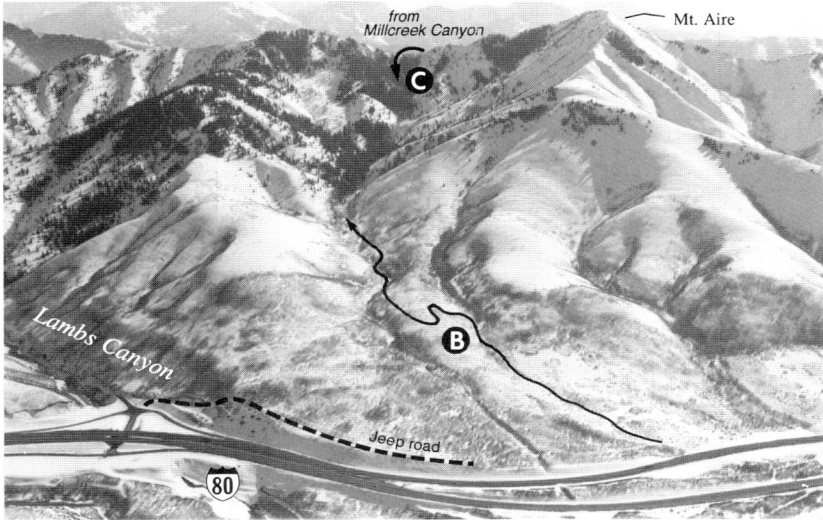

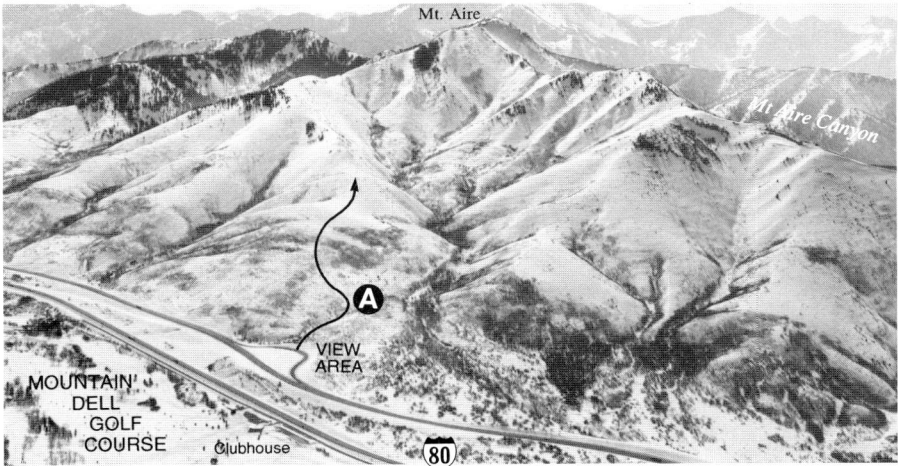

Figure 3.17   Mount Aire from the north showing (A) the north ridge from the I-80 View Area, (B) the northeast bowl, and (C) the trail from Millcreek.

The snowpack on Mount Aire isn't quite as deep as that in the Cottonwood canyons, and the runs aren't as long, but there aren't as many tracks. The reason for this absence is that few people have learned how to reach the powder from the road. Two very nice routes provide access from the north, neither of which is obvious from the highway. Another route exists from the south, but it is quite long and requires a car shuttle.

North Ridge. The most direct route, *(A)* in Figure 3.17, starts at

the "View Area" on I-80 at mile 135.5 just east of the Mountain Dell
exit. This is the best approach to the summit of the mountain and its
north bowl. A foot trail leads south from the middle of the View Area
into a drainage, and the north ridge of Mount Aire is just to the left
(east) of that drainage. A tourer can either follow the drainage for a
half mile or so and then climb up to the north ridge, or immediately
bear left and follow a narrow brushy trail that intersects the lower end
of the ridge. The former option is easier to find in winter, but the latter
is less exposed to the steep slopes near the summit that are more prone
to avalanche. Once on the ridge, skiers can continue to the summit for a
fine view of Gobblers Knob and other points to the south. Total vertical
is 2620 feet over about 2.3 miles.

Northeast Bowl. A less convenient but easier route up Mount Aire
is a jeep road, popular with hunters, that intersects the eastbound lane
of I-80 at mile 136.3, half way between the View Area and the Lambs
Canyon exit. This road leads directly into Mount Aire's northeast bowl.
The first issue that must be considered is where to park. Although
the interstate is well maintained and visibility for oncoming traffic is
good at that point, parking on the highway is not permitted. The
Lambs Canyon exit is the suggested parking spot for tours to or from
the northeast bowl. It requires a hike of about a half mile parallel to
the freeway, but this may be less inconvenient than a parking ticket or
an impounded vehicle.

From the mouth of Lambs, a jeep road climbs gradually westward
parallel to the I-80 off ramp. It disappears in dense scrub oak after
about a half mile, but one can continue skiing parallel to the interstate
for another quarter mile to the jeep road that climbs from the highway
into the northeast bowl. This road starts in an eastward direction, then
bends to the north and climbs quite steeply for about a quarter mile. It
again bears eastward and drops into the canyon bottom. From there the
road follows the creek for about a mile to the base of the upper bowl.
The best route to the top at that point is to climb eastward through
the conifers to a ridge that leads to the summit.

Elbow Fork. A third possibility for climbing Mount Aire is to hike
up Millcreek to "the elbow," where the road bends sharply to the right.
A trail follows the side canyon northward for about 0.3 mile before
splitting. The left branch goes to Mount Aire and the other goes to
Lambs Canyon (described in the previous section). The Mount Aire
trail climbs quite steeply to a pass overlooking the Mount Aire summer
home area and then switchbacks up the south slope of the peak to a
saddle just east of the summit. This is the top of the northeast bowl,

which is the recommended descent route. To access the north bowl, continue up the trail to the top of Mount Aire. Total distance of this tour is 3.8 miles, and the climb is 2500 vertical feet.

Descent. Several descent routes are possible from the summit of Mount Aire. All are very steep and exposed to avalanche danger at the top. The safest alternative is to stay on the north ridge, but the bowls are more sheltered from the wind, usually have better snow, and are more tempting. To get to the north bowl, follow the north ridge down for about 0.1 mile to a lower peak at the head of the bowl. This route follows the drainage that ends near the I-80 View Area. It is extremely narrow in the bottom, so it should not be entered unless the snow is completely stable. The northeast bowl is just as steep but has some trees to offer shelter in more hazardous conditions□

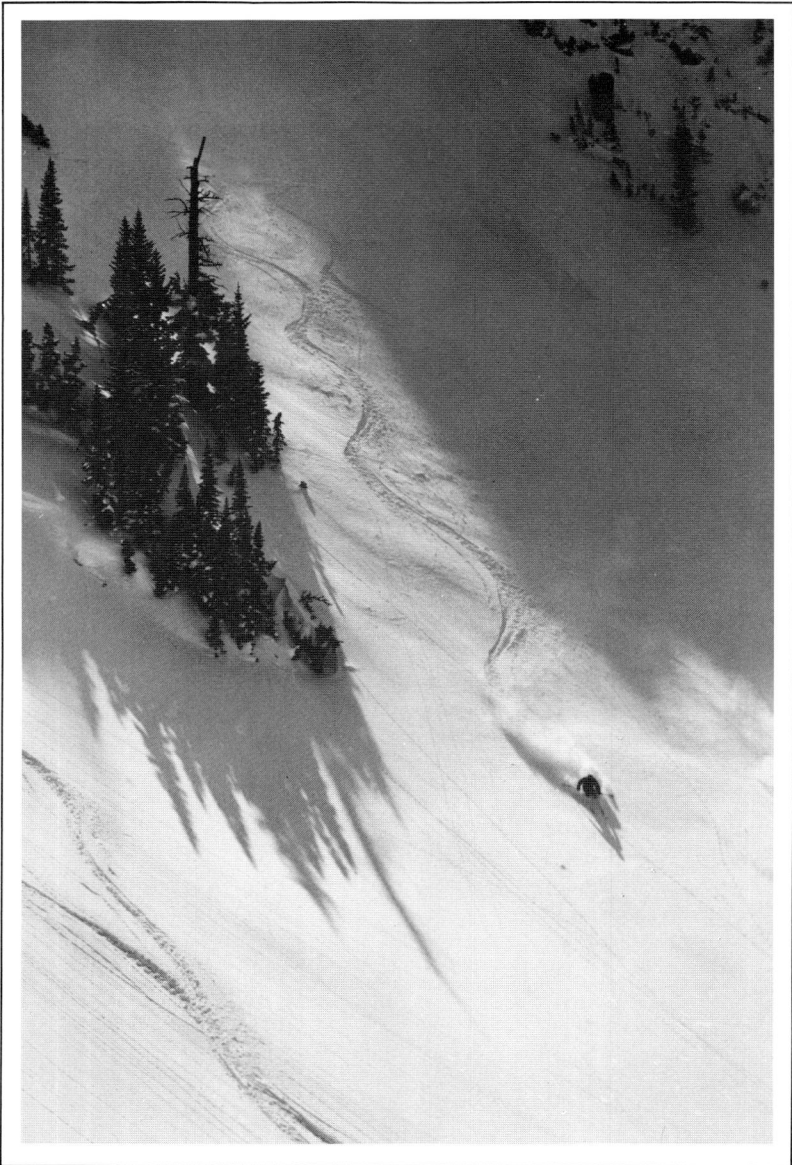

Bruce Christenson enjoys a late afternoon powder run in Millcreek Canyon. The generally benign terrain in upper Millcreek provides numerous opportunities for ski tourers of intermediate ability.

Chapter 4

MILLCREEK CANYON

Millcreek has become one of the most heavily used canyons in the Wasatch Mountains. It has long been a favorite for fishermen, hikers, picnickers, and bikers in the summer, but winter use has become popular only in recent years since Salt Lake County and Forest Service officials blocked off the upper road to motor traffic. Growing numbers of skiers, snowshoers, and even hikers are enjoying the tree-lined, snow-covered road above the gate. It is also the only canyon adjacent to Salt Lake City which is not currently in the water shed, so dogs are allowed. The road was described in Volume 1 as one of the better places for beginning cross country skiers.

The area that is not so well known and not so heavily used is the terrain far above the highway near the ridge that separates the Millcreek and Big Cottonwood drainages. Some of the high bowls provide excellent opportunities for intermediate and advanced ski tourers who enjoy a run in the powder. One difficulty with Millcreek tours is that they are most easily done from Big Cottonwood Canyon. A shuttle is involved unless one is prepared to hike several miles along the Millcreek road and then up a side canyon to the ridge. A considerable elevation and distance advantage is gained by using Mill D North Fork or Butler Fork as an approach.

Millcreek is one of the most heavily wooded of the Wasatch canyons. As its name implies, this fact was noted by the early pioneers who set up many sawmills there to help provide for the needs of their growing community. Most of the side canyons were named for the men who operated these mills. For skiers, the heavy vegetation has benefits as well as disadvantages. The upper bowls are generally less avalanche-prone than their counterparts in other canyons (with some very notable

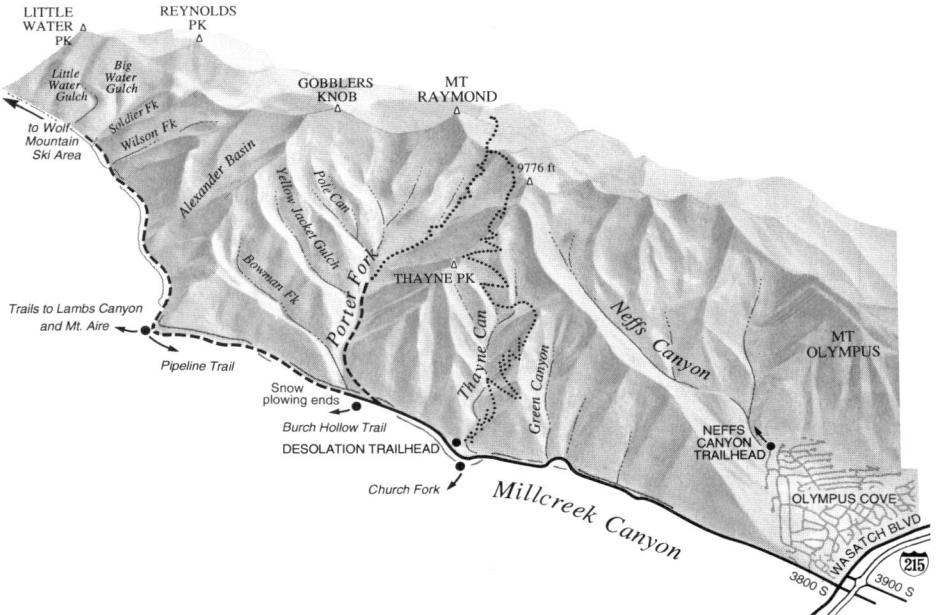

Figure 4.1   Millcreek Canyon is a convenient place for Salt Lake area tourers. The road is ideal for beginners, and side canyons have terrain to challenge expert skiers.

exceptions). Early in the season, however, when the snow cover is thin, the lower sections of most Millcreek forks are too brushy for enjoyable skiing.

Another potential problem in Millcreek Canyon is the relatively low elevation of much of the touring terrain. Prevailing snow conditions are very critical to the enjoyability of a ski tour. Late in the winter, when temperatures begin to rise, the snow is often heavier than that in the Brighton and Alta areas.

The tours described in this chapter are all in the intermediate class, with the exception of Alexander Basin, which is in a class by itself, and the north face of Gobblers Knob. They are listed in geographic order, starting at the upper end of the canyon, which is generally in order of increasing challenge of the descent. The lower forks have more trees and brush to dodge, lower quality and quantity of snow, and steeper sections near the highway. Figure 4.1 is a representation of the south side of the canyon showing all of the basins and drainages that are described in this chapter.

The tours are divided into two groups—those in the upper half of the canyon and those in the lower half. Upper Millcreek touring areas

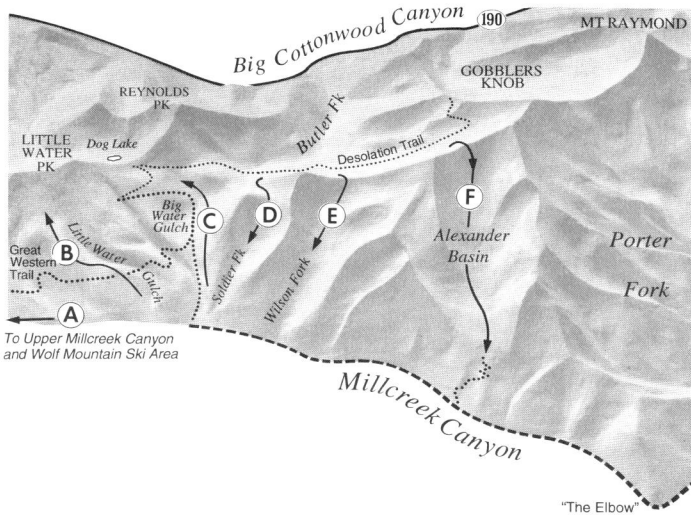

Figure 4.2   Ski tours in upper Millcreek Canyon. The numbered routes, which are described in the text, are (A) Upper Millcreek Basin, (B) Little Water Gulch, (C) Big Water Gulch, (D) Soldier Fork, (E) Wilson Fork, and (F) Alexander Basin.

are best accessed from the south (Big Cottonwood Canyon) or from the east (Wolf Mountain Ski Area). Lower Millcreek tours usually start and end in the canyon.

UPPER MILLCREEK TOURS

Tours in the upper half of Millcreek canyon usually involve a car shuttle but are otherwise most enjoyable. Tourers must always be aware that the steep bowls at the heads of Wasatch canyons must be treated with great respect, but the upper basin of Millcreek, as well as several side canyons, provide excellent opportunities for intermediate skiers. Notable exceptions are Wilson Fork and Alexander Basin, which should not be skied unless avalanche conditions are favorable. The six tours described in this section are illustrated in Figure 4.2.

Upper Millcreek Basin (H.P.A.)

The easiest of the Millcreek tours is a run down the bottom of the drainage from the upper basin. It is ranked intermediate rather than beginner only because of its length. Regardless of the starting point, the climb is more than 3.5 miles and at least 2300 vertical feet. Three

Figure 4.3   Upper Millcreek can be approached from the Wolf Mountain Ski Area, Big Cottonwood Canyon, or Lower Millcreek. The plowed highway ends about eight miles from the top of the canyon.

routes are described here for the hike to the top, each starting from a different canyon: Millcreek, Mill D North in Big Cottonwood, and one of the canyons near the Park West/Wolf Mountain/??? Ski Area.

Access From Lower Millcreek. The tour along the canyon bottom into the upper reaches of Millcreek was described in Volume 1. It is a beautiful area for the skier who enjoys a long, relatively flat outing. There is usually very little traffic beyond the first two miles, although an occasional skier makes it beyond the end of the highway. One can climb the 8.0 miles to the ridge overlooking Park City and the Uintas beyond. The major advantage of this alternative, of course, is that no car shuttle is needed.

Access From Big Cottonwood Canyon. The head of Millcreek Canyon can be reached most easily from Mill D North Fork in Big Cottonwood. A climb of only 2300 feet over 3.7 miles is required. The route is described in Chapter 5 and illustrated in Figure 5.10. Follow the Mill D trail and turn right toward Desolation Lake. After climbing through the aspens, bear left and go up the northerly branch by Powder Park and up to the Park City overlook at the head of the canyon. (Don't hesitate to take a break for lunch and a few turns along the way.) A short traverse along the Park City ridge leads to a good spot to start a run down through the aspens.

Access From Wolf Mountain. The east ridge at the top of Mill-creek Canyon borders the Wolf Mountain Ski Area between Murdock Peak and Red Pine Canyon to the south. The 2600 foot ascent from the parking lot can be done via chair lift or by hiking up a downhill ski trail. (Red Pine Canyon is currently being used by a snowmobile concession and is closed to skiers.) Regardless of which route is chosen, it is wise to check with the Ski Patrol before attempting this tour. They will be aware of avalanche conditions at the higher elevations.

Descent. The run down Millcreek is the same regardless of the starting point of the tour. Simply ski through the aspens at the top and follow the stream bed for about 2.5 miles to where the new Great Western Trail bears left (south) and traverses for about a mile, with little change in elevation, to Little Water Gulch. From there, a skier can follow the Little Water drainage down to the end of the Millcreek highway. Before the new trail was constructed, it was easy to follow the Millcreek stream for this whole section of the descent. Unfortunately, beavers have harvested quite a few aspen trees in the area, and nobody has cleaned up after them.

From the bottom of Little Water Gulch, skiers must follow the road for another 4.6 miles to where the snowplow stops. This provides a total of 3600 feet of elevation change. The terrain is quite gentle and should provide little difficulty even for the novice skier, but the tour requires good physical condition. This is particularly true right after a heavy snow storm when much of that 8 miles is not steep enough to allow the skis to glide without some effort. Note in Figure 4.3 that it is possible to drop into upper Millcreek from the south ridge of the canyon. Caution is urged on these slopes due to potential avalanche hazard.

Little Water Gulch (H.P.A.)

The first peak on the Millcreek/Big Cottonwood ridge is Little Water, which lies at the head of the gulch with the same name. The peak is 1.4 miles from the end of the canyon, and the gulch intersects the Millcreek stream just above the end of the highway.

The area got its name from the springs that originate there, contributing to an abundant year-round flow of water in Millcreek Canyon. The quantity of water was one reason for the number of sawmills that once existed there. The water is now used primarily for irrigation in the valley, although at one time there was a plan to divert much of it to Lamb's Canyon via a tunnel. The proposal was part of the Little Dell project which was recently completed in Parleys Canyon.

Figure 4.4   The Water Gulches are easily accessed from Mill D North in Big Cottonwood. They intersect the main canyon near the end of the highway.

Little Water Peak. The peak can be reached from Wolf Mountain Ski Area or from the Millcreek highway, but the most direct approach is from Mill D North Fork in Big Cottonwood Canyon. Simply climb to Dog Lake (2.8 miles and 1400 vertical feet of elevation gain) and follow the ridge east less than a mile to the peak. See Chapter 5 and Figure 4.4 for details. The top elevation is only 9422 feet, so the total climb involves only about 2100 vertical feet.

Descent. The two most common descent routes from Little Water Peak are shown in Figure 4.4. First is Little Water Gulch. The run down to the Millcreek stream is straightforward. There may be some brush early in the season, but it should present no problem for midwinter tours. The snow is often best on the west side of the gulch. Total descent to the end of the highway is 1.8 miles and 1600 vertical feet.

The second descent route is in the drainage just east of Little Water Gulch. The steep open bowl northeast of the summit should be avoided; it usually has a large cornice at the top, and avalanches are common. A less hazardous alternative is to go north along the ridge from the peak and then down through the trees as shown in the photo. The remainder of the tour is a relatively gentle descent to the Millcreek stream and then a 4.8 mile slide (or slog if the snow is deep) to the car.

Big Water Gulch (H.P.A.)

The most accessible of the Millcreek side canyons is Big Water Gulch. Dog Lake lies near its head, so the approach from the Big Cottonwood side is only a 1400 foot climb. The bottom of the gulch is at the end of the Millcreek highway. This area is very heavily used by hikers and bikers in the summer months, so winter is the best time to enjoy it.

Big Water almost became part of "Sugarbush West", a downhill ski area proposed for the end of the Millcreek Canyon road. In the early 70's, the individual who owned the Sugarbush ski area in Vermont acquired control of a square mile of private land at the end of the road. He applied for permits to develop a large part of upper Millcreek into a huge ski and condominium complex. This would have involved widening the road and destroying parts of the stream bed. Fortunately, the Forest Service and Salt Lake County agreed that the idea was not a good one, so fishermen, picnickers, and ski tourers continue to enjoy this beautiful canyon unencumbered by condominiums and destination skiers.

To get to the top of Big Water Gulch, follow Mill D North Fork to Dog Lake (Chapter 5, Figure 5.9). The west side of the gulch often has the driest snow, so it is best to traverse northwestward along the side of Reynolds Peak for a ways as shown in Figures 4.4 and 4.5. A trail through the fir trees makes this easy. A short hike along the ridge, over a small shoulder, leads to an open area that is a good place to start the descent. Distance from the Big Cottonwood highway is 3.2 miles.

Descent. The route down is very simple. It follows the drainage for 1.4 miles and 1200 vertical feet to the road, and then winds its way another 4.6 miles to the point where the plows stop.

Soldier Fork

Soldier Fork is the next canyon west of the Water Gulches. It is somewhat steeper than its easterly neighbors, with some avalanche hazard in the upper bowl, but the skiing can be delightful among the aspens and firs when there is enough snow to cover the undergrowth. The bottom of Soldier Fork is just below the end of the Millcreek highway.

An easy touring route to the top of Soldier Fork is simply a continuation of the one into Big Water Gulch. From Dog Lake (see Chapter 5) traverse along the north side of Reynolds Peak to the head of Butler Fork. Follow the ridge between Millcreek and Big Cottonwood canyons (Figure 4.5) beyond the head of Big Water to the point that is chosen as a starting place for the run down to the highway. The central part

Figure 4.5   The Millcreek/Big Cottonwood ridge between Dog Lake and Gobblers Knob provides access to Big Water Gulch, Soldier Fork, Wilson Fork,
and Alexander Basin.

of the upper bowl is the most protected from avalanche hazard, with
groups of trees going all the way to the top. The west side of the fork
is more open and steep (Figure 4.6).

An alternative approach to Soldier Fork is via Butler Fork, which
is also described in Chapter 5. This is slightly shorter, but it has more
elevation to gain. The hike from the bottom of Mill D North to the
top of Soldier via Dog Lake is 3.3 miles with 1600 feet of vertical. The
Butler Fork route is 2.1 miles and 1900 vertical feet.

Descent. The run down Soldier Fork to the Millcreek stream is 1300
vertical feet over 1.1 miles, with an additional 4.5 miles to the end of
the plowed highway.

Wilson Fork

The canyons that empty into Millcreek get longer, steeper, and narrower
as they get closer to Gobblers Knob. The northeast facing headwall at
the top of Wilson Fork should be avoided in all but the most stable

Figure 4.6   Soldier Fork and Wilson Fork are somewhat more challenging than the tours farther up Millcreek Canyon, but both have good intermediate terrain. Note that the west sides of both forks are steeper and more susceptible to avalanches.

snow conditions. The lower part of the fork has a gully that can be challenging to the intermediate skier, particularly if several people have already made tracks in the snow. As Figure 4.6 illustrates, the problem areas can be avoided if a good route is chosen.

The alternatives for climbing to the top of Wilson are the same as those just described for Soldier. The most common is to hike up Mill D North Fork to Dog Lake, as described in Chapter 5. From the lake, traverse around the north side of Reynolds Peak. A 1.8 mile westward climb along the Millcreek ridge takes a tourer to the highest point of Wilson Fork (Figure 4.5). The total climb is 2600 feet over 4.7 miles. Another possibility is to ski up Butler Fork to the end and then follow the ridge to the top of Wilson. This is 3.5 miles with an elevation gain of 2900 feet.

Descent. After enjoying the view and some lunch, the cautious skier will certainly want to retrace his climbing route down to the low point in the center of Wilson's upper bowl. The trees offer good protection for a descent at this point. Another safe way off the peak is to follow the ridge that goes in a northerly direction between Wilson Fork and

Alexander Basin. About 1000 vertical feet down the ridge, one can safely bear right into the Wilson drainage.

The narrow gully in the lower part of the fork is sheltered from wind and sun, so it can be a good place for powder snow. If it has been too heavily skied, however, it may be preferable to stay in the aspens on the west side of the canyon. The trees are far enough apart to be enjoyable for a reasonably competent skier. The total downhill run from the top of Wilson Fork to the highway is 1.8 miles with 2500 feet of vertical. Another 4.2 miles gets one to the car.

Alexander Basin (H.P.A.)

The only Millcreek fork that has been classified entirely as an advanced tour is Alexander Basin. It is steeper at both top and bottom than any other drainage; there is considerably more avalanche hazard, as Figure 4.7 indicates; and a longer climb is required to get to the top.

Alexander Basin was named after Alva Alexander, who cut and hauled timber in the area. He and his sons ran a sawmill there in the nineteenth century. Judging from the number and size of the stumps visible in summer, the basin must have been one of the most heavily logged side canyons in Millcreek.

A legend is associated with one of the mills at Alexander Flat. The owner reportedly had a problem with tools disappearing. He was not successful in discovering how they were being removed, and soon he didn't have enough tools to be able to continue operation. In desperation, he called in Brigham Young for advice. The Mormon leader suggested that the owner may have offended the spirits of the people who had lived there previously by building the mill on sacred ground. The mill was moved and the problem never again occurred.[1]

Three tours are described in Alexander Basin. In order of increasing difficulty, they are lower Alexander from Porter, the east branch of the basin, and upper Alexander. The last is so steep and dangerous that it should be attempted only by an expert skier. The first two tours are extremely challenging but relatively safe.

Lower Alexander Basin from Porter Fork. The easiest route into the basin is over the ridge from the west and into the lower part

---

[1]The sage advice of Brigham Young has in many cases proven to be relevant to modern day situations. For example, he was once asked about what constitutes health, wealth, joy, and peace. "In the first place," he stated, "good pure air is the greatest sustainer of animal life. Other elements of life we can dispense with for a time.... You can live without water or food longer than you can without air, and water is more important than meat and bread."

Figure 4.7   The most hazardous area in Millcreek Canyon is upper Alexander Basin (B). The east branch (A) is much safer, as is the route into the lower part of the basin from Porter Fork (C).

of the cirque, *(C)* in Figure 4.7. Most of the hazardous areas can be avoided by carefully selecting the point of descent from the ridge.

The climb starts with a hike up the Porter Fork road to the end of the cabin area. Continue southward on the jeep road for 0.2 mile beyond the houses to where the terrain levels off above the first switchbacks. Turn left (east) at that point and climb up the ridge south of Pole Canyon that is visible in Figure 4.8. Just below the open slopes that extend to the summit of Gobblers, traverse left through the trees to the ridge that separates Porter and Alexander. The ascent is 4.1 miles with 3300 vertical feet of elevation gain.

Descent. The run down to Millcreek includes a pleasant north-facing slope with widely spaced trees, a flat section, and then 1000 vertical feet of very steep, densely wooded terrain that will challenge even the most capable skier. There are a couple of narrow chutes down through the trees that often offer a relatively clear path if there is enough snow to cover the logs and undergrowth. Deep untracked snow is important for controlling speed since there is little room to make turns. It's sort of like a natural (and therefore very inexpensive) luge run!

The downhill part of this tour has a vertical drop of 2100 feet over 1.4 miles, followed by a 3.4 mile run along the Millcreek highway.

East Branch of Alexander Basin. By far the best alternative for this canyon is the east branch, which borders Wilson Fork. The ascent route is exactly the same as that previously described for Wilson Fork—start at Mill D North or Butler in Big Cottonwood and climb the ridge to the peak at the top of Wilson Fork. The hike from Mill D is 4.7 miles with 2600 vertical feet. The east branch of Alexander starts at this peak.

Descent. The safest descent is along the ridge that separates the east branch from the main basin, *(A)* in Figure 4.7. The route goes down through the trees to the basin, across a flat area, and then drops steeply to the Millcreek highway. Distance from the top of Wilson is 1.9 miles with 2400 feet of elevation difference.

Upper Alexander Basin. Figures 4.6 and 4.7 show two views of the approach to the upper end of the basin. It is simply an extension of the climb to the top of Wilson Fork. The ridge between these two points is quite flat but has a couple of narrow rocky spots that may require removal of skis.[2] Total climb from Mill D North is 2600 feet over 5.1 miles.

Descent. Figure 4.7, a photo of Alexander Basin, illustrates the hazards awaiting anyone who challenges the upper headwall. There are a few trees, but they offer little protection on such a steep slope. The greatest exposure is from the cliffs that rise more than 800 feet to the summit of Gobblers Knob. The skier who can't resist the challenge will have an exciting 2.1 mile run down to the highway.

LOWER MILLCREEK TOURS

Most touring in the lower half of the canyon involves Porter Fork, which is the largest of the Millcreek side drainages. Other possibilities are Thaynes Canyon, on the south side of Millcreek, and the pipeline trail on the north side.

---

[2]It is advisable to tie your skis to yourself when scrambling up or down the rocks. A dropped ski might not be found until summer.

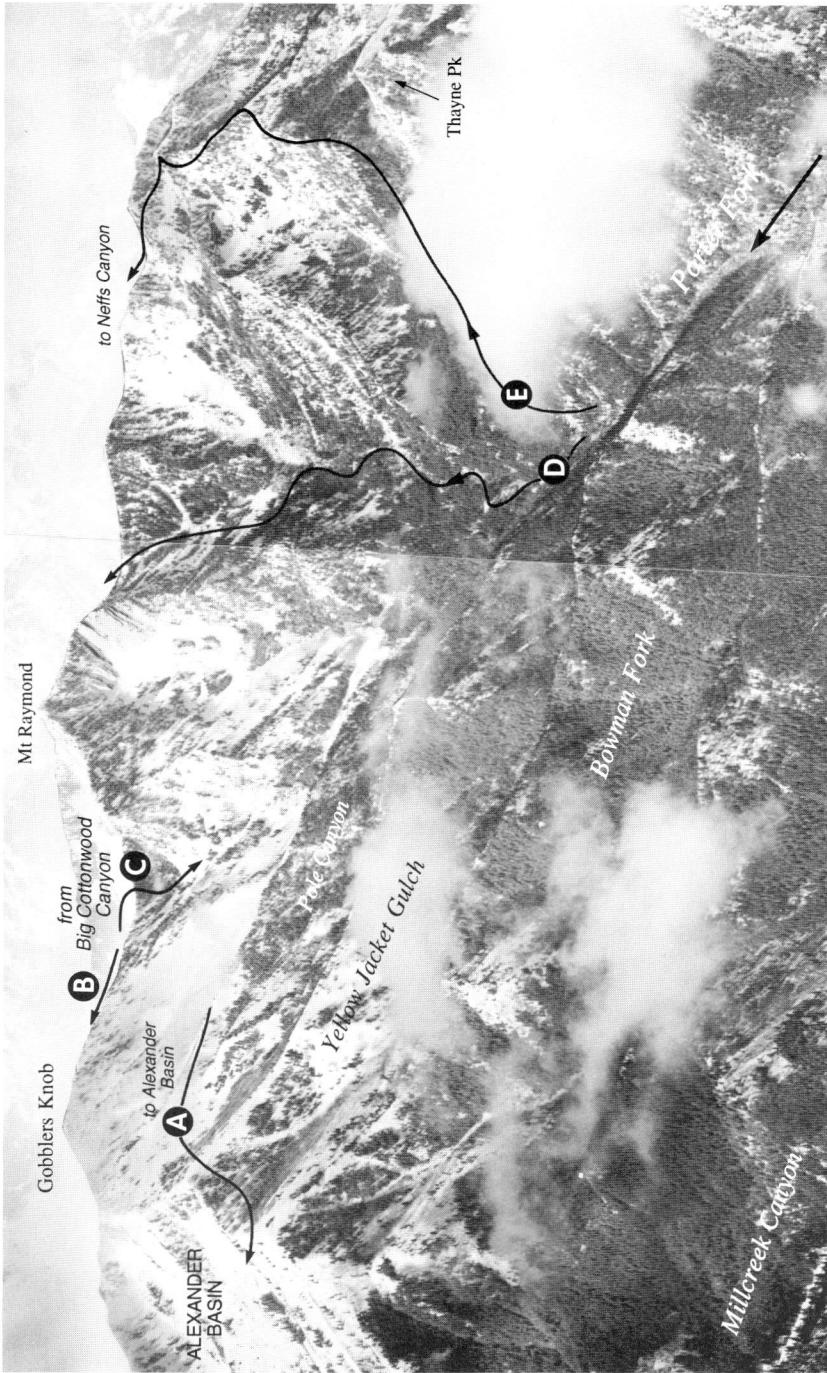

Figure 4.8   The largest Millcreek side canyon is Porter Fork. Some of the tours that are described involve Alexander Basin (A), Gobblers Knob (B), Big Cottonwood (C), upper Porter (D), and Neffs (E). Mount Raymond is also at the head of Porter, but its north face is too steep and rocky for good skiing.

Porter Fork (H.P.A.)

At least five of Porter Fork's many branches are suitable for skiing, with possibilities for tours involving Big Cottonwood and Neffs canyons. The fork was named after Chauncy Porter, who set up the first sawmill in Millcreek Canyon. It has also been the home of several mines that were worked for many years; in fact, at least one of them may still be active. Porter Fork's most famous miner was Indian Pete, a drifter who settled in the upper reaches of the canyon in the 1880's to try to make his fortune. He was unsuccessful and met an untimely end in an avalanche in 1889. The Indian Pete Mining and Milling Company was formed a few years later, and his name was carried on in Millcreek history.

Lower Porter Fork is presently a summer cottage area with a paved road that winds 1.3 miles up from the Millcreek highway.

The four tours described in this section go to the pass west of Mount Raymond (the "standard" tour), the saddle between Mount Raymond and Gobblers Knob (usually approached from Big Cottonwood), Neffs Canyon ridge, and Gobblers Knob. These are intended to be in order of increasing difficulty, but snow conditions and route selection make a tremendous difference in Millcreek's narrow and brushy terrain. Skiing at such a low elevation can be an uncertain proposition.

Standard Porter Fork Tour. The Porter Fork road intersects the Millcreek highway about 0.2 miles above the Log Haven restaurant. Ski tours from the bottom of the fork start along the road through the cabin area. Above the summer homes are some switchbacks followed by more gentle terrain. The road continues through an aspen forrest and into an open area below a steep bowl. Straight ahead is a picturesque rock formation with a large cave high above the trail. To get to the pass west of Mount Raymond, bear left at this point and continue climbing along the drainage to the east of the cave rock. This leads to the pass overlooking Big Cottonwood and other areas to the south. Total climb from the highway is 3400 vertical feet over 3.5 miles.

Descent. Options for the descent are somewhat limited. The most obvious is to retrace the climbing route back to Millcreek. An alternative is to ski the slopes on the west side of the fork down to the cave rock. Care must be taken, however, to avoid the avalanche paths that come down through the trees in this area. (See *(D)* in Figure 4.8.) Lower Porter Fork is much too heavily wooded to allow any deviation from the road.

Porter Fork from Big Cottonwood. The saddle between Mount Raymond and Gobblers Knob is most easily (and safely) reached from

Butler Fork in Big Cottonwood Canyon. The approach (described in detail in Chapter 5 and illustrated in Figure 5.13) involves a climb up the west branch of Butler and a traverse across the upper part of Mill A Basin to the pass. This is 3.0 miles with a 2200 foot elevation gain.

Descent. The safest route from the saddle follows the drainage until the gully narrows and steepens. At that point, traverse left to the jeep road, which can be followed down through the switchbacks and cabin area. The descent is 3.6 miles with 3400 feet of elevation change.

Neffs Canyon from Porter Fork. A short section of the west ridge of Porter is common to Neffs. The terrain below this ridge is much too steep to be a safe climb in winter. A better approach to Neffs, shown as *(E)* in Figure 4.8, is along the ridge. From the end of the cabin area in Porter, turn right and climb the ridge that goes west from the road. After about 300 feet of elevation have been gained, bear right and traverse into an open side canyon. The ridge on the north side of that canyon is a good climbing route all the way to the top of Neffs. Total climb from the Millcreek highway is 3.5 miles with a gain of 3800 feet.

The descent into Neffs is described in Chapter 7.

Gobblers Knob. The north slope of this peak is the wide expanse of white that is visible from Salt Lake in the winter. Formerly known as Porter Peak, this 10,246 foot summit is now called Gobblers Knob. It may have received its unusual name from miners in the area who tried to supplement their meager earnings by raising turkeys, an undertaking that was no more successful than their diggings. The peak is the highest point along the Big Cottonwood/Millcreek ridge. Surprisingly, the rocks at the summit were once on the floor of an ancient sea. Fossils are in abundance for the summer visitor to observe.

Gobblers looks inviting to the powder lover, but the area can be extremely hazardous unless avalanche conditions are absolutely stable. (See the photo in the accompanying sidebar.) Also, there is little protection from the wind, so the snow is often not as good as it appears from the valley. The other major disadvantage of making the long climb to the summit of Gobblers is the potential for disruption by helicopter skiers.

The peak should be approached along one of the ridges that lead to the top. The safest route is from the saddle between Gobblers and Raymond, which is about 900 feet below the summit. The pass is most easily reached from Butler Fork in Big Cottonwood Canyon, as described above. Alternatively, a car shuttle can be avoided by climbing up from the bottom of Porter Fork.

If the latter option is chosen, simply hike up the Porter Fork road

GOBBLERS KNOB IS NOT FOR TURKEYS

Late in February 1980, the north side of Gobblers Knob released one of
the largest avalanches to occur in the Wasatch. The slide started near
the summit, then became channeled into a ravine that winds through
dense timber toward a summer home area. A 30-foot high "tidal wave"
of snow descended the gully, splintering and uprooting large trees as it
passed. The mass of debris stopped just a few hundred feet short of the
uppermost cabin; it had run nearly two miles and had dropped about
3400 feet. Fortunately, no one was skiing in the gully at the time.

The Gobblers Knob avalanche emphasizes the need for tourers to
be aware of terrain *beyond and above* their immediate route and of the
area's avalanche history.

Gobblers' north flank was the site of an avalanche fatality a year
later. A group of experienced tourers was following a track made by
others earlier that day. One tourer strayed ahead of his companions
and was caught in a slide. All had beacons and shovels, so locating and
digging out was done quickly. But not quickly enough. This example
illustrates that even experienced tourers cannot always predict when
avalanches will occur and that *even a short burial can be fatal.*

to the end of the cabin area. Continue southward on the jeep road for about a quarter mile beyond the houses to where the terrain levels off above the first switchbacks. Bear left (southeast) away from the road at that point and hike up through the aspens until the pass is visible. This area can be confusing because the trees are too thick to allow a view of either Raymond or Gobblers until you have climbed quite a distance. Be careful to avoid the avalanche paths visible in Figure 4.8 and in the sidebar on the opposite page.

Total climb to the summit of Gobblers from Big Cottonwood via Butler Fork is 4.0 miles with 3100 feet of elevation gain, or 4.5 miles and 4300 feet via Porter Fork.

Descent. The descent route for the cautious tourer is back down the ridge to the saddle, then down through the trees into Porter Fork. Another possibility is the ridge to the north between Porter and Alexander Basin. It is best to ski about 1000 vertical feet down the ridge into safe terrain, then either traverse left to the Porter Fork drainage or turn right and find a good entry into Alexander Basin.

Thaynes Canyon

The next canyon west of Porter Fork is Thaynes Canyon. It starts near the Millcreek Inn, just above the Tracy Wigwam Boy Scout camp. An ascent of this canyon utilizes the Desolation Trail, which starts at the mouth of Thaynes and traverses very gradually across Thaynes Canyon and Porter Fork, eventually going over the ridge into Big Cottonwood just west of Mount Raymond. The Thaynes part of the trail is very low in elevation, but it can be a nice ski tour if there is enough snow.

Pipeline Trail

A number of trails have recently been constructed on the north side of Millcreek Canyon. One of these follows an old water pipeline from the mouth of the canyon to "the elbow" (a sharp bend in the road about five miles upcanyon). Designed to be used by mountain bikers, its slope is quite gradual in most places. The trail can be accessed from Church Fork, just across Millcreek from Thaynes Canyon, and from Burch Hollow, near the parking area at the end of the plowed section of the highway. The main disadvantage of this trail for ski touring is its location on the south-facing slope of the canyon□

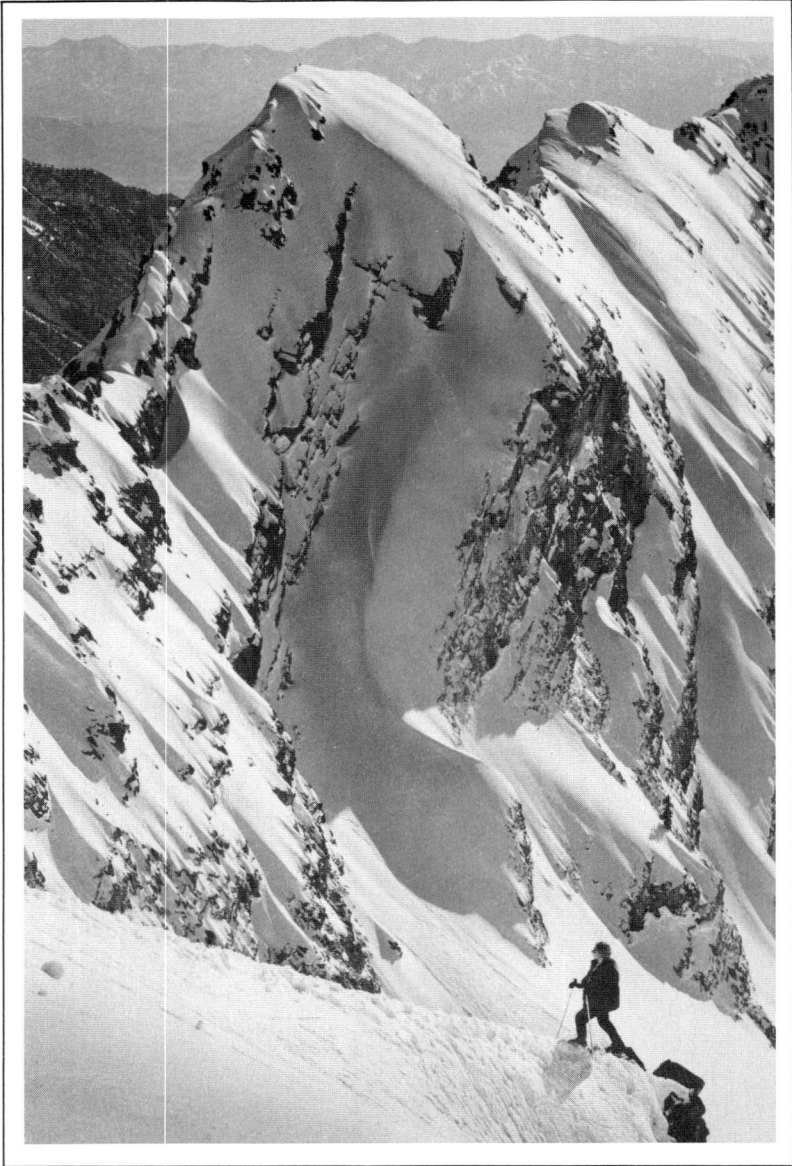

The Twin Peaks Wilderness Area in Big Cottonwood Canyon provides many opportunities for advanced touring and ski mountaineering. Karin Caldwell enjoys the view from a ridge near the summit of Mount Monte Cristo.

Chapter 5

BIG COTTONWOOD CANYON

"Would you like to escape from the bonds of winter, away from the murky atmosphere of cities; breathe air untainted by the smokes of civilization; see your favorite summer-time canyon retreat in a new and strangely beautiful setting, and enjoy a fuller portion of the fellowship of man? Then try SKIING, the king of winter sports, headline event of the modern renaissance of outdoor winter-time recreation."

Thus begins a February 1935 *Salt Lake Tribune* article titled "Skiing Becomes Winter Sport King in Utah." In the full-page article, S. Dean Green describes Brighton as "the Center" of pleasure and adventure to be found "in canyons and over mountain trails at the city's very doors."

Skiing in canyons and over mountain trails was not new to the area around Brighton. In 1910, the power company's line patrolman, E. R. Wright, had the responsibility of skiing along power lines strung between area mining camps in search of breakages and malfunctions. Five years later, a group of nine "healthy young students" from Latter Day Saints University and Salt Lake High School (later renamed West High School) began making barely noticeable "sporting news" headlines related to skiing in Brighton Basin.

"Ski Party Leaves for Mountain Top," the first of the headlines stated on Thursday, January 22, 1915. The excursion described commenced from a point "some distance from the mouth of Cottonwood Canyon." For two days, the *Tribune* later reported, the group had occupied themselves "sliding down the steep slopes about Twin Lakes." During their return to the valley four days later, one or two "luckless" participants had to trudge many weary miles without skis due to "nu-

Figure 5.1   The Wasatch Mountain Club's lodge at Brighton, under construction during the summer of 1930. Photo by S. Dean Green.

merous mishaps and broken implements."

Calling themselves the Rough Neck Ski Club, the group continued making Brighton excursions—and headlines—throughout the remainder of the season. The following season's March 6 headline was their last: "Boys Have Narrow Escape In Canyon—Make Trip on Skis and Get Lost in the Blinding Blizzard." The exertions of their outings must have proven immense, for by now the group had diminished to only two participants.

Ascending to Brighton by way of Big Cottonwood Canyon was not very practical; the canyon road was narrow, steep, and long. During the early 1920's, members of the Wasatch Mountain Club rediscovered what miners of the previous generation had already known—it was easier to access Brighton from Park City. By mid-decade, the Mountain Club's Park City to Brighton outings had became routine, and by 1928 the recreation group began construction of their clubhouse deep in the Brighton Basin. "Unquestionably, Brighton is and will continue to be the perfect local retreat of its kind," wrote a club officer, urging members to speed construction.

The Wasatch Mountain Club's lodge was sufficiently complete by the early 1930's to accommodate an expected increase in the ranks of area skiers. But the country was on the brink of the Depression, the canyon roadway remained unusable during winter, and the would-be throngs of skiers would not materialize until later in the decade.

In December 1938 Club President Charles Pfeiffer (after whom the Pfeifferhorn is named) threw open the doors of the Mountain Club's lodge to the new generation of skiers. "Anyone who skis is welcome to make our lodge his headquarters at Brighton," Pfeiffer announced as he outlined an impressive program of races and cross-country tours to be sponsored by the mountain club for the Alta-Brighton-Park City area.

For the remainder of the 1930's and into the 1940's, the Mountain Club's lodge at Brighton served as a center of Utah skiing. For a time after 1944, the Club operated a public surface ski lift known then as the Great Western Ski Lift. In a bylined article published in 1945, Wasatch National Forest Supervisor F. C. Koziol praised the "great missionary and motivating force" of the Wasatch Mountain Club in the development of Utah skiing.[1]

In 1980, thanks to extensive research by Claire Davis, the Wasatch Mountain Club's lodge was placed on the National Register of Historic Places. The dedicatory plaque states:

WASATCH MOUNTAIN CLUB LODGE

Constructed 1929-1930, this lodge was built by the Wasatch Mountain Club. Organized in 1920, the Wasatch Mountain Club is one of the earliest private organizations in the Intermountain West dedicated to the appreciation and conservation of nature. The cabin is one of the few surviving structures from the period when the canyons of the Wasatch Range were first developed for recreation.

Throughout the 1960's, '70's and '80's *public* (non-member) use of the historic building extended far beyond use by skiers. "Over the years," the *Tribune's* Robert Woody wrote, "it has been a retreat for church groups, a meeting place for clubs, a gathering hall for family

---

[1] Wasatch Mountain Club members who were responsible for the Lodge's success between the late 1930's and the 50's eventually moved on to other skiing-related endeavors. Fred Speyer, the Austrian mechanical engineer who dazzled club members with his *gelandesprungs* during the mid-30's, moved on to Alta, where he made functional Alta's first ski lift. Speyer managed the Alta ski area between 1943 and 1960. C. B. "Chick" Morton, one of the movers behind the Club's Great Western Ski Lift, took over management of the Alta area in 1960 and continued in that capacity until his retirement late in the 1980's. Wasatch Mountain Club "Commissary" directors James and Elfrieda Shane built—and continue to operate—the Goldminer's Daughter lodge at Alta. Ray Watrous moved on to operate the Little Mountain Ski Area above Emigration Canyon. Former Club President Harold Goodro organized the University of Utah's Department of Recreation and Leisure, which today is responsible for teaching outdoor recreation skills to hundreds of students annually.

Figure 5.2   Three generations of Wasatch Mountain Club members gather at the club's annual "Old Timers' Party" during the summer of 1994. Now on the National Register of Historic Places, the two-story log structure has been utilized by thousands of outdoor enthusiasts not affiliated with the mountain club.

reunions, a surrogate wedding chapel, a stage for amateur musicals and a forum for intellectual and spiritual inquiry." Leaders of many groups have indicated that the lodge was *the only canyon facility* available that their group could afford to utilize.

During the Forest Service's Environmental Assessment phase of the Club's Special Use Permit renewal process in 1993, over a hundred letters extolling the Club's lodge at Brighton were received by forest officials. A segment from a letter by former Salt Lake City Mayor Ted Wilson reflects some of the sentiments expressed:

> "The lodge has provided a retreat for many who enjoy the beauty of the mountains in a simple and non-commercial manner. It would be a shame to lose such a source of non-commercial access in this age of expanding ski resorts and commercial activities."

The Salt Lake Tribune ———————————————————— January 22, 1939

WIMPY RACERS NEED NOT APPLY

Throughout the early history of ski competitions in Utah, one fact remains constant—cross country racing never achieved the status of "main event." In 1920, after three seasons of jumping tournaments near Salt Lake, a "cross country run" was planned "should a forthcoming jumping tournament fall through."

Exhibition ski jumping by a troupe of traveling professionals dominated the early to mid-1930's. Their grace, competence—and jump distances nearing 300 feet—dazzled audiences numbering in the thousands. Success of these Ecker Hill events elevated organizer Marthinius Strand into the National Ski Association's leadership; as First Vice President, he promised more and better tournaments for Utah.

He was a man of his word. In 1938 Strand announced four major tournaments for Utah. Pending the International Skiing Federation's (FIS) sanction, the largest would have been the 1942 World Championships in combined jumping, cross country, and relay events that would have commenced and terminated at Brighton.

Fortunately for the racers, Germany received the championships. Had they come to Utah, competitors would have been challenged by a course (illustrated above) with uphill portions totaling more than 8000 vertical feet, a maximum elevation of 10,000 feet, and exposure to some 50 avalanche paths.

Big Cottonwood Touring Today

The ski touring terrain in Big Cottonwood Canyon is the most varied and also the most accessible in the Wasatch Mountains. Several beginner outings have been described in Volume 1—the Guardsmans Pass road, Spruces Campground, and the Solitude Nordic Ski Center, which includes Redman Campground and Silver Lake. Big Cottonwood tours described in this volume are suitable for advanced beginners, intermediates, and expert skiers.

Sooner or later, most beginning tourers tire of flat terrain and wide roads populated by snowmobiles and decide to venture into more challenging areas. The tours labeled "advanced beginner" are suitable for this type of person. The slopes in these areas are generally not steep enough to avalanche, or even to intimidate, but all have places that can be quite challenging to someone who is not yet able to maneuver between the trees. This can be less of a problem in deep powder, which slows a skier down, so individuals who can't turn should save these tours for the right snow conditions. Included in this category are the Brighton Lakes area, Mill F East Fork, Mill D North Fork, lower Silver Fork, and lower Mill D South Fork. Unfortunately, the Brighton and Solitude ski areas have recently expanded, eliminating the popular advanced beginner tours to Lake Solitude and Snake Creek Pass.

Intermediate tours involve steeper descents and often are exposed to considerable avalanche hazard. Several such outings are described in this chapter, starting with Catherine Pass, Twin Lakes Pass, and Mount Wolverine in the Brighton Basin. On the north side of the canyon Willow Fork, Beartrap Fork, Butler Fork, and Mill A Gulch provide excellent intermediate terrain. Silver Fork, Greens Basin, lower Days Fork, Mill D South Fork, and lower Mineral Fork offer similar opportunities on the south side. Solitude and Brighton have consumed Clayton Peak, Mill F South Fork, and Honeycomb, three of the most accessible drainages that used to be available to intermediate tourers.

The remaining touring areas in Big Cottonwood are suitable only for expert skiers who have considerable experience with route selection in hazardous terrain. The canyon has an enormous variety of advanced touring terrain. Most of it is located along the south side of the canyon in the many glacial cirques and forks that originate at the Little Cottonwood divide. Because many of the touring routes into these canyons cross steep and open north-facing slopes whose avalanche conditions are automatically suspect, skiers must be especially wary. Days Fork, Lake Blanche, Mineral Fork, and Broads Fork all have runs that will challenge even the expert downhill skier. Mount Raymond and Gobblers Knob are also very steep and hazardous at the higher elevations.

Many tours in this chapter utilize routes for the ascent that are not the same as those recommended for the descent. A significant vertical advantage can often be gained by starting and ending in different places. For example, Days Fork could be done from the bottom with a climb of more than 3000 feet of elevation, but the total climb from Alta or Brighton is less than 2000 feet (or only 1000 feet if the Evergreen Lift is used). The tour is longer from Brighton, but the ascent is easier and the view is superb along the ridge. The second reason for different routes is safety. The steep slopes and open bowls that provide the best downhill skiing are also the most hazardous. A tourer should minimize exposure to avalanche danger, so traversing back and forth to get up such an area should be avoided whenever possible. In the backcountry, discretion is the better part of skiing!

Few areas are plowed for parking along the Big Cottonwood highway, so tourers should learn about parking regulations in the canyon each year. During some winters, parking has been allowed only on the north side of the road during one weekend day, and the other side during the other day. Neither should skiers take for granted UTA bus service in the canyon. Sometimes bus drivers have disembarked and picked up tourers anywhere they requested, but in other years they have been allowed to stop only at one or two specified locations.

Tours in this chapter are not listed in order of increasing or decreasing difficulty. The descriptions appear in a geographic progression to allow for easier reading. Tours in the Brighton area at the head of the canyon are discussed first. Next described are tours on the north side of the highway. Routes on the south slopes of the canyon conclude the chapter.

BRIGHTON BASIN TOURS

The upper end of Big Cottonwood Canyon contains a delightful combination of gentle wooded terrain and dramatic alpine cirques. People with minimal downhill skiing ability can tour among the large fir trees in the basin, while enjoying the scenic high peaks from a distance. For those with more advanced skills, nearly every slope in the Brighton area is accessible when snow conditions are right.

All of the tours in the Brighton area are labeled "endangered" because of continuing ski area expansions. Each year a little more terrain is lost to backcountry skiers. The backcountry skier's worst nightmare, however, is a concept called "Interconnect," which would link Park City's ski areas with those in Big and Little Cottonwood canyons. Very few additional ski lifts would be required to allow downhill skiers to freely move among almost all of the ski resorts in the central Wasatch. Already Brighton and Solitude are essentially connected. Alta and Snowbird could easily become connected, and Deer Valley creeps closer to Park City each year. Alta skiers can ski to Brighton with no significant amount of climbing, and it is possible to go from Solitude to Alta with a minimal uphill traverse. A trip from the top of Park City to Solitude is completely downhill. Fortunately, Forest Service and Salt Lake County planners have resisted approving the concept, but, like the quest for the Winter Olympics, the plan to interconnect the ski areas continues to raise its ugly head.

Clayton Peak (R.I.P.)

The excellent touring terrain along the slopes of this peak is now part of the Brighton Ski Area.

Snake Creek Pass (R.I.P.)

This magnificent and extremely popular ski tour was also eliminated by expansion of the Brighton Ski Area.

Brighton Lakes (End.)

Dog Lake is about a mile from the Brighton Ski Area parking lot, and lakes Mary, Martha and Catherine are strung beyond it like emeralds on a necklace. All are accessible by advanced beginners. The best route for hiking up the mountain is to follow the Brighton Lakes Trail, which starts near the Wasatch Mountain Club lodge and climbs through the woods west of the Crest ski lift. Steep slopes on the right eventually force a tourer onto the groomed ski trail, but the traffic is usually not too heavy along the edge. It is sometimes disconcerting to watch the flailing masses of skiers and snowboarders hurtling in one's direction, but exposure to the collision hazard is relatively brief.

The Lakes Trail departs from the ski area about three quarters of a mile from the parking lot where the groomed ski run makes a sharp left turn toward the top of the Majestic ski lift. Turn right at this point and traverse up through the firs to a flat area that overlooks the village of

Figure 5.3   The Brighton Basin has some spectacular scenery for the tourer whose skills allow for a bit of downhill skiing. The lakes area (A) is a delightful alternative for advanced beginners, and Catherine Pass (B) is a good destination for intermediates. Both areas, however, have some avalanche hazards.

Brighton. Dog Lake is just a short distance to the south, and the other lakes are farther up the drainage to the west.

Dog Lake. (R.I.P.) Since the construction of Brighton's Crest ski lift, downhill skiers can easily access the steep, tree-covered slopes on the east side of Dog Lake. These delightful powder runs are now so heavily used that the area has lost its appeal to ski tourers.

Cross country skiers who wish to explore the west and south sides of Dog Lake can bear left from the Brighton Lakes Trail mentioned previously and ski south across the flat area. An old jeep road, originally built to service the Cottonwood Mine at the south end of the lake, can be followed along the west shore. Some very steep avalanche slopes hang just above the mine, so when conditions are at all unstable, tourers should not venture far from the lake.

Lake Mary. Lake Mary is about 0.2 miles and 200 vertical feet above Dog Lake, and is most easily reached via the Brighton Lakes Trail just mentioned. The trail follows the drainage westward from the Dog Lake turnoff up to the Lake Mary dam, as shown in Figure 5.3. Mount Tuscarora, Wolverine, and Millicent provide a spectacular backdrop for the lake.

Lake Martha and Lake Catherine. A quarter mile past Lake Mary is Lake Martha, and Lake Catherine lies just above. The terrain steepens during the ascent, so less skilled skiers might want to terminate their tour at Lake Mary. The upper part of this drainage is detailed in the next paragraph.

Descent. Returning to the parking lot is the hard part of this tour. The Brighton Lakes Trail is the only reasonable alternative for inexperienced skiers. After returning to the packed ski run, one can ski down through the trees on the left, or brave the packed slopes and dodge the shredders. In either case, some turning ability is required. The traverse and kick turn technique also works quite well in this situation.

Catherine Pass (End.)

The most popular skiing and hiking route between Brighton and Alta goes over Catherine Pass. The pass is easily reached from either community with about 1400 feet of climbing in moderately safe and gentle terrain. Catherine Pass and the lake just to the east were named after Catherine Brighton, the wife of William Brighton. The Brightons homesteaded in the basin and later ran a hotel that catered to the mining traffic between Alta and Park City. Brighton was a popular local resort spot even then.

The route to Catherine Pass is an extension of the tour to the lakes area described in the previous section. Above Lake Mary, stay to the left and climb along the ridge overlooking Dog Lake until it gets steep and rocky. Bear right at this point and take a gentle upward traverse to Lake Catherine. The exposed slopes on the left in this area can be avoided by taking a lower line through some large fir trees as shown in Figure 5.3.

The climb from Lake Catherine to the pass is the most hazardous part of this ski tour. The steep slopes on Sunset Peak to the left and Mount Tuscarora to the right are all prone to avalanche. Just below the pass, however, a small secondary ridge goes straight down toward the lake. (See Figure 5.4.) This provides the tourer with a somewhat safer approach if the snow is stable. It is best to stop at the lake when avalanche conditions are particularly bad. The total distance from Brighton to the pass is about 2.2 miles.

Descent. The safest route down from Catherine Pass is the one just described, but there are other variations for those desiring a steeper and longer run in the powder. One alternative is to follow the ridge to the south and east toward Sunset Peak. If conditions permit, the slopes on

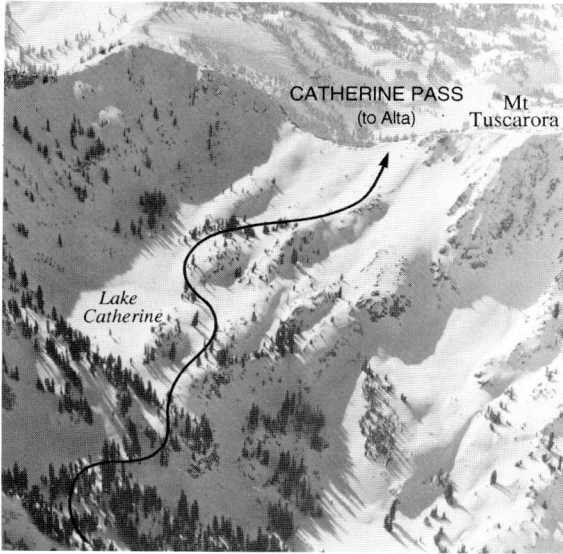

Figure 5.4   Lake Catherine is surrounded by very steep slopes, so the route to the pass must be chosen carefully. Notice the small ridge that can provide protection from avalanche paths coming off the nearby peaks.

either side of the summit can be skied all the way to the lake. The bowl can be extremely dangerous in midwinter, however, and usually must be saved until spring.[2]

Another possible return route from Catherine Pass is to ascend the ridge north of the pass and traverse over the top of Tuscarora to Mount Wolverine. The lower part of the ridge is often quite rocky and brushy, but the run down to Brighton can be worth the effort. Details of the descent possibilities from Mount Wolverine are found in a later section.

The third return alternative is to ski down the west side of the pass to Alta and return to Brighton via Grizzly Gulch and Twin Lakes Pass. Chapter 6 contains information on the Alta side of both passes.

Twin Lakes Pass (End.)

A second touring alternative between Brighton and Alta for intermediate skiers is Twin Lakes Pass, where the power line crosses the ridge between Big and Little Cottonwood Canyons. During the mining days, the road over Twin Lakes Pass was a heavily traveled route in both

---

[2]This was the scene of a double fatality in November 1985, when two members of a group of tourers skiing the bowl under Sunset Peak were caught in an avalanche.

Figure 5.5   Twin Lakes Pass can be approached from the dam by a relatively safe route along the power line (A). The traverse around Wolverine Cirque from the Millicent lift (B) is very exposed to avalanche hazard and is not recommended.

winter and summer. Summertime sightseers made a round trip from Salt Lake to Brighton, then over the pass and down Little Cottonwood to the valley. The pass is only about 1200 vertical feet from Brighton or Alta, with a climb of about 1.7 miles from either town.

Skiers headed for Twin Lakes Pass from Brighton will find it difficult to avoid the downhill traffic at the ski area unless they condescend to ride a chairlift. If this alternative is chosen, the Evergreen Lift, which ends at the Twin Lakes dam, is the best choice. It has 500 feet less vertical rise than the nearby Millicent Lift, but the route to the pass from the top of Evergreen is much safer. (See Figure 5.5.)

The tourer who elects to begin at the parking lot can start out to the left of the Millicent Lift and climb up the groomed ski run that eventually crosses under Millicent and ends at the top of Evergreen. It is usually safer to stay in the unpacked snow beside the downhill runs when hiking up a ski area.

From the Twin Lakes dam, the best touring route to the pass goes around the lake and intersects the power line. Some good terrain features are available to provide protection most of the way from this point.

The power line is a good guide, since it stays generally in the trees or along the top of a minor ridge. Note the hazardous avalanche zones that have to be crossed if one strays too far in any direction.[3]

Descent. Many alternatives exist for the return from Twin Lakes Pass. The simplest is to follow the ascent route. Several other possibilities are described in later sections on Mount Wolverine, Grizzly Gulch (Chapter 6), Silver Fork, and Days Fork. A pleasant round trip tour is to ski down Grizzly Gulch to Alta, then ski back to Brighton via Albion Basin and Catherine Pass. One other variation (when conditions are very stable) is to traverse south from Twin Lakes Pass and ski the lower part of Wolverine Cirque.

Mount Wolverine (End.) (H.P.A.)

The highest of the peaks between Brighton and Alta, Mount Wolverine is formed by the intersection of three ridges—one from Twin Lakes Pass and one from each of its sister peaks, Mount Millicent and Mount Tuscarora. At 10,800 feet, Wolverine stands above all others at the head of Big Cottonwood Canyon. It is a very rugged peak that is often exposed to severe wind and weather. Snow conditions at the peak's higher elevations are usually difficult, making this one of the most challenging of the tours that we have rated as intermediate. The large cirque on the north side of the mountain is extremely hazardous and should only be attempted when conditions are totally safe.[4]

Three routes are practical to the summit of Mount Wolverine. All follow ridges with steep sections and rocky areas with wind-eroded snow. In some places it may be necessary to remove skis and walk. The edges of cornices should be avoided, since it is difficult to tell how far they overhang. The windward sides of ridges, generally less susceptible to avalanche danger, should be used whenever possible.

From Twin Lakes Pass. The easiest approach to Mount Wolverine is from Twin Lakes Pass, which is accessible from Brighton, as described previously, and from Grizzly Gulch, as discussed in Chapter 6. From the pass, simply follow the ridge south to the summit. Total distance from either Alta or Brighton is about 3 miles with a climb of 2100 feet.

---

[3] A ski tourer died in this area in a 1987 avalanche. One particularly sad detail of this fatality was that the victim had an avalanche beacon in his pack, but it was not turned on. Rescuers arrived from nearby ski areas within 15 minutes of the burial, but another hour was required to locate him.

[4] In April 1993, a cross country skier jumped off a cornice into one of Wolverine Cirque's steep chutes, setting off an avalanche that swept him to his death.

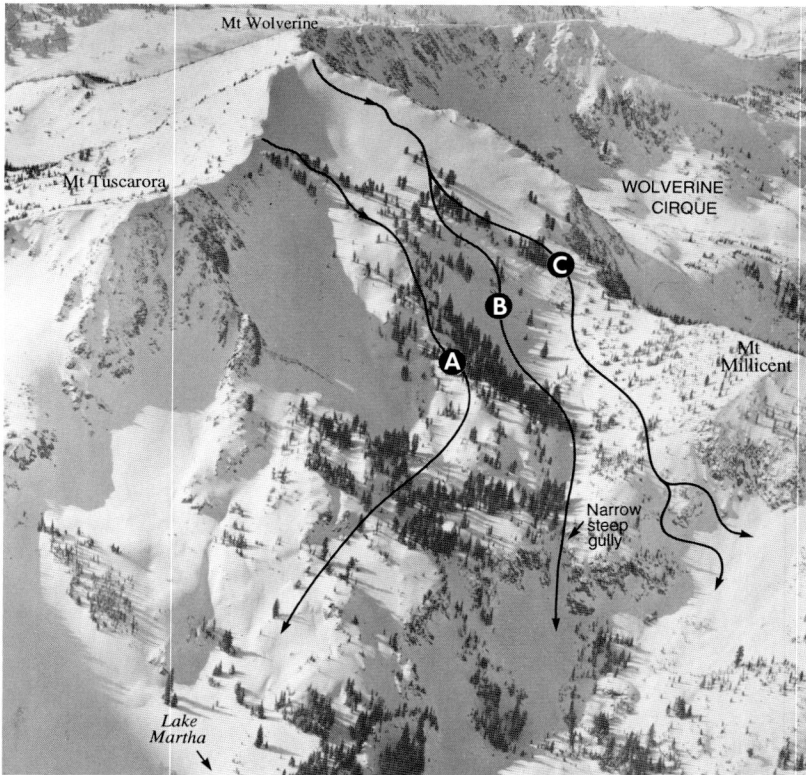

Figure 5.6   Mount Wolverine is the highest peak in the Brighton basin. When the snow has accumulated enough to cover the rocks, there are challenging intermediate powder runs down to the lakes. Labeled routes are described in the text. Wolverine Cirque is extremely dangerous and not recommended.

From Catherine Pass. The second route to Mount Wolverine ascends the ridge north of Catherine Pass over the top of Mount Tuscarora. One route to the pass has been described in an earlier section, and another is found in the next chapter. The total distance to Mount Wolverine is about the same as the Twin Lakes route, but the ridge above Catherine Pass is often more difficult to negotiate.

From the Millicent Lift. The third variation is to climb the ridge from the top of the Millicent ski lift to the saddle southwest of Mount Millicent's summit, then continue along the ridge to Wolverine. This is the most direct route, about a mile shorter than the others, but is also the steepest and rockiest of the three. One advantage is that half of the work can be eliminated by riding the chair lift.

Descent. Three variations are described for the descent of Mount

Wolverine. All of these routes can be quite rocky early in the winter, so the tour is best saved for later in the year. The avalanche hazard also dictates that this area be avoided until the deep, early-season snows have stabilized. Figure 5.6 shows the possibilities.

Route (A). The safest descent route is from the saddle between Mount Wolverine and Mount Tuscarora. A line of trees that goes down toward Millicent provides some protection in the upper section. Below these trees the terrain flattens out. It is best to bear right at this point, as illustrated in the photograph, following the ridges near the avalanche gully under Mount Tuscarora. At the point that overlooks the Brighton lakes, bear right again for the final descent to Lake Martha. This part of the route is exposed to much avalanche danger, so it is important to avoid the steep slopes on the side of Tuscarora. From the lake, the tourer has the option of skiing over Catherine Pass to Alta or continuing down to Brighton.

Route (B). This route is more hazardous, but it has some very steep areas for the powder lover's enjoyment. The bowl at the top of Wolverine is often quite wind-packed, but on a good day it can be a superb run from the summit. Stay to the left at the bottom of the bowl and drop into the gully that starts at the saddle between Wolverine and Millicent. When the snow cover is sufficiently deep, this gully is skiable all the way to Lake Mary, but its lower section is steep and cliffy, and can be quite dangerous.

Route (C). The tourer who likes some "steep and deep" terrain for descent can consider traversing along the south slope of Mount Millicent and rounding the ridge eastward to ski the east slope of the mountain. (See Figure 5.6.) This is an excellent run in late spring when the snow has solidified and stabilized. Traversing left (north) after partial descent puts one onto the ski trail joining Brighton ski resort's Millicent and Majestic ski areas.

UPPER BIG COTTONWOOD–NORTH SIDE

This section describes ski tours in the area bordered by the Guardsmans Pass road, the Park City ridge with its popular mountain biking trail, the Millcreek Canyon ridge, and the North Fork of Mill D. The north side of Big Cottonwood is somewhat more benign than the south side. Steepness and difficulty of access to side canyons increases as one descends Big Cottonwood, but all of the tours in the upper part of the canyon are rated as advanced beginner or intermediate. Despite the

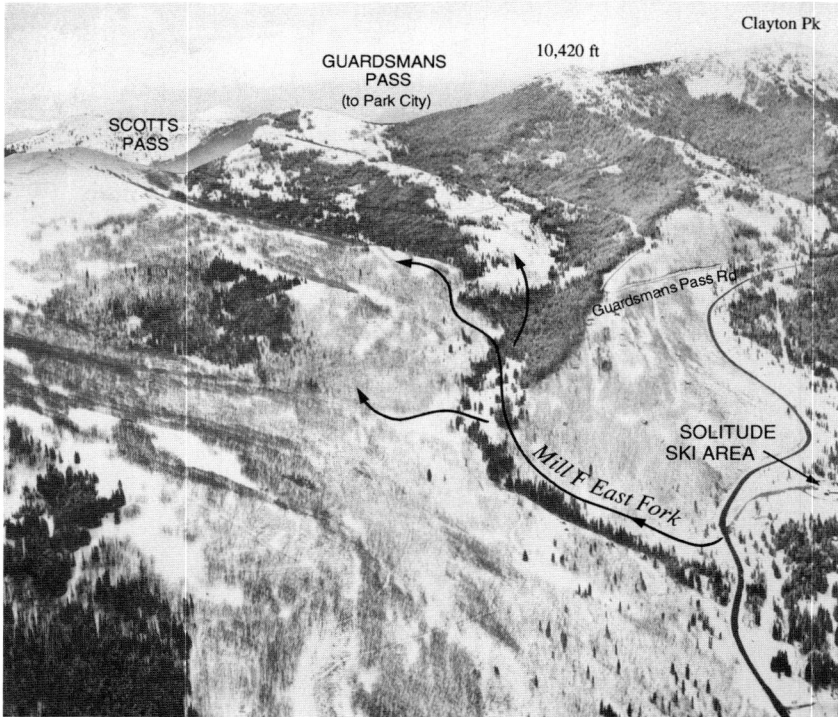

Figure 5.7   Mill F East Fork starts across from the Solitude ski area and ends at the Park City ridge. Two of its branches lead to Scotts and Guardsmans Passes.

south and west exposures of the side canyons, there are plenty of slopes sheltered from the sun for skiers to enjoy.

Mill F East Fork (End.)

Mill F is the uppermost of the "mill" forks in Big Cottonwood Canyon. These drainages were named for the series of seven saw mills set up by the settlers in the 1850's and 1860's to provide lumber for their extensive building program. Output of just three mills in the vicinity of Mill F and Brighton produced more that one million board feet annually for many years. The trees have since grown back in Mill F, but the fork is once again in danger of being "defoliated." This time the assailants are proponents of Interconnect, rather than loggers. Unless the developers have their way, this fork will remain a delightful option for advanced beginners.

The east fork of Mill F, visible in Figure 5.7 begins across the highway from the Solitude Ski Area, and its two branches lead up to Scotts Pass and Guardsmans Pass. The best access route starts just across from the upper Solitude entrance. The Mill F tour goes north from the highway through some aspens past a few summer homes and then into an open area. The canyon goes up to the right (east) at this point. A road provides a good touring route along the left side of the drainage almost to Scotts Pass, which is about 2.5 miles and 1500 vertical feet from the highway. One of the more noteworthy landmarks of the tour is a handsomely decorated outhouse beside the trail with aspens painted on all sides. It looks inviting but is kept locked.

A half mile beyond the outhouse, a power line comes in from the right and follows the road to where the terrain steepens just below the pass. The open tunnel on the left is an entrance to the old Iowa-Copper mine.

The only difficult part of this tour is the last quarter mile from the end of the power line to the pass. It requires some traversing and kick-turning, but the view of Park City and the Uinta Mountains beyond is outstanding. Scotts Pass is at the head of Thaynes Canyon, which is part of the Park City ski area.

The second branch of Mill F East Fork leads to Guardsmans Pass. An easy way to get into this drainage is to turn right through an open area just beyond the decorated outhouse. The main road to the pass is soon encountered. The terrain is just as good and the view at the top is equally spectacular, but unfortunately the snowmobiles have better access to this branch. It might be better to save it for a midweek outing.

Willow Fork

Willow Creek flows southwest from a couple of small lakes that lie in a flat area about a mile from the Big Cottonwood highway. Most of the lower part of the drainage is privately owned, with several summer cabins scattered among the aspens. Two upper bowls, which extend northward and eastward from the lakes to the Park City ridge, are part of the Wasatch-Cache National Forest and are popular destinations for intermediate ski tourers.

Willow Fork can be accessed from where it intercepts the highway, just above the Silver Fork summer home area, or skiers can save a bit of climbing by starting about a half mile farther upcanyon and traversing around the ridge that forms the eastern boundary of the fork. In either case, parking may be a problem. Skiers should be sure to put their cars as far off the pavement as possible to leave room for canyon traffic. Note

Figure 5.8   Willow and Beartrap forks are easily accessed from the bottom. Adjacent canyons can also provide excellent ascent and descent routes.

that parking is not allowed at the Silver Fork Lodge without permission of the owner.

Starting elevation for a Willow Fork tour is about 8000 feet. The hike to the lake area, which is called Willow Heights, is less than a mile, with about 500 vertical feet of elevation gain. At this point, two good options exist for skiers. They can ascend the east bowl, which is relatively open with a few patches of evergreens, or they can bear left and explore the aspen-covered north bowl. The snow usually stays good in both bowls, but some south-facing areas are often softened and crusted by the sun, particularly in late winter.

The east branch of Willow Fork is usually the place to find the best skiing. The ridge is gained in about 1.3 miles and 1500 vertical feet. The high point at the head of the fork provides a superb view of Park City and the Uintas to the east, the high peaks in Big and Little Cottonwood Canyon to the south, Gobblers Knob, Mount Raymond, and Salt Lake City smog to the west, and more Wasatch Mountains to the north. After a few runs in the powder, skiers may prefer to return to their cars via Mill F East Fork, the next Big Cottonwood side canyon above Willow. The upper part of the north branch of Mill F, called "USA Bowl" because of the pattern of the trees that outline it, is a favorite when relatively low angle terrain is mandated by avalanche conditions.

The north bowl of Willow involves only a 1000 foot climb to the ridge and provides access to Beartrap Fork. (See Figure 5.8.) This is a delightful option for the descent with lots of evergreens to protect the snow from afternoon sun. Beartrap intercepts the highway only a mile or so below Silver Fork and is described in the next section.

Another possibility for a Willow Fork tour is to ascend Mill F East Fork and follow the Park City ridge from Scotts Pass. This is a much longer route and would require a car shuttle, but it is more scenic. The high peaks on the south side of Big Cottonwood, as well as the Uintas to the east, are visible along the way.

Beartrap Fork

Beartrap Fork joins Big Cottonwood just below the settlement at Silver Fork. In the 1860's, the Littleford family, who lived at the mouth of this fork, reportedly trapped bear in the area. Several summer homes have been built there in recent years, apparently with the belief that the Littlefords got all the bears. Relatively few ski tourers venture into Beartrap, probably because parts of it are narrow and steep, but it is a delightful area for an intermediate tourer.

A pleasant way to tour Beartrap is to approach it from Desolation Lake as described in the next section. To access the head of Beartrap from Desolation, simply follow the ridge on the west side of the lake to the first low spot, which overlooks an open area that is a good entry point for Beartrap. This is route *(C)* in Figure 5.10. Tourers must beware of the avalanche slopes around Desolation Lake. Total climb from the mouth of Mill D is 4.3 miles and 2300 vertical feet.

If one chooses to ascend Beartrap instead of Mill D, a good place to begin is just below Silver Fork where a road traverses up through the aspens to a summer home area. The only place that might be confusing is just beyond the flat section that starts about 0.5 mile from the highway. The canyon branches here, and the right branch is the one to follow to the ridge overlooking Desolation Lake. (See Figure 5.8.) Near the top, the steep slopes on the east side should be avoided, but otherwise there appears to be little avalanche danger in Beartrap. The ascent is 2000 feet over 1.8 miles.

Descent. The run down into Beartrap requires no guide. It's quite narrow and wooded in places, so the easiest way down is to ski where the snow is best. The bottom of the canyon is skiable if the snow is deep enough, but some places are too brushy. About half way down to the highway, the fork widens and becomes relatively flat. If the car is parked at Mill D, just keep to the right at this point and ski parallel to the highway for a mile or so.

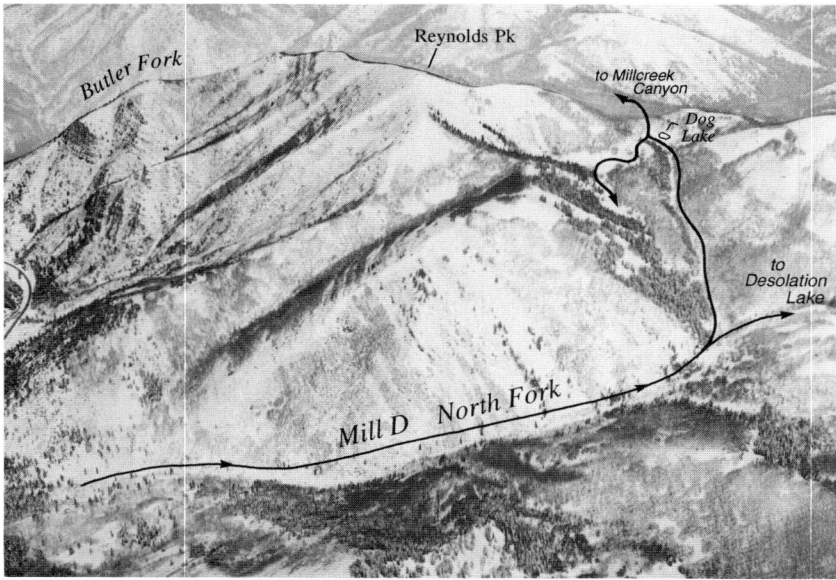

Figure 5.9   Dog Lake is at the top of the west branch of Mill D North Fork. The preferred descent route is shown in the photo, along with an access point for Millcreek Canyon tours. The steep bowl on the east side of Reynolds Peak should be avoided.

Mill D North Fork

All the lakes in Mill D North Fork are small muddy puddles in the summer. They are popular destinations for mountain bikers who can reach them from Big Cottonwood, Millcreek, and Park City. This canyon is equally popular in winter, since it is one of the few places where relative novices can enjoy Utah's incomparable powder snow.

The trail up Mill D starts just below and across the highway from the off-road parking area at the Spruces Campground. The easiest winter access to the fork is the summer home road that traverses up the east side from the highway. Just beyond the last cabin on the left, a trail goes through the aspens toward the bottom of the drainage and stays near the stream all the way to the lakes. About 2.0 miles from the highway, the canyon branches left to Dog Lake (yes, there really are two Dog Lakes in Big Cottonwood) and right to Desolation Lake and the Park City overlook. The elevation gain to this point is only 850 feet, so most tourers with advanced beginner skills can comfortably go that far. The terrain beyond that becomes more challenging.

Dog Lake. It is just a short climb from the branch point in the Mill

D North trail (about 0.8 mile and 550 vertical feet) to Dog Lake. Part of the trail is quite narrow and steep, but that section can be avoided on the way down. Simply cross the lake and continue in a westerly direction over a small rise into the drainage that parallels the ascent route, as shown in Figure 5.9. That drainage intercepts the trail just above the turnoff to Desolation Lake. If avalanche conditions permit, the open areas in the firs on a descending skier's right can provide good practice terrain for powder skiing.

Reynolds Peak. This 9427 foot peak is most accessible from Mill D North Fork, but is also commonly approached from Big Water Gulch in Millcreek Canyon or from Butler Fork. The open east face drops steeply into Mill D near Dog Lake and should be avoided in most situations. The north side of the mountain, however, is less steep and lightly forested, and it often contains some of the nicest powder to be found. By adding only 600 vertical feet and less than a mile to the tour, one could climb the ridge from Dog Lake to the summit. The peak can be seen in Figures 5.9, 5.12, and 4.4.

Desolation Lake. Desolation Lake is about two miles and 1100 vertical feet from the branch point in the Mill D trail. Most of the trail is in flat open meadows, but some parts are a bit steeper. Shown as route *(A)* in Figure 5.10, it starts out with a climb through an aspen forest, then bears to the right into the bottom of the drainage. From there one follows the open meadows, keeping to the left (north) in the wooded areas. The route passes north of a small pond before reaching Desolation, which is in the uppermost bowl of the fork. A new hiking/mountain biking trail was constructed to Desolation Lake in 1993 and 1994. It traverses through the aspens along the north side of the drainage and is another possible ascent route.

The south side of Mill D has many extremely hazardous slopes which should be avoided. This was the site of a 1979 avalanche fatality described later in this chapter.

Park City Overlook. A smaller drainage parallels the part of Mill D that goes to Desolation Lake. This drainage is entered by bearing left after climbing through the aspens above the Mill D North trail branch point. (See route *(B)* in Figure 5.10.) Fondly known as "Powder Park," this is a popular area for tourers who are learning to ski in deep snow, since the slopes along its right side are quite open but sheltered from wind and sun. The top of this drainage is a point common to three canyons—Big Cottonwood to the west, Millcreek to the north, and Red Pine on the Park City side. The spot is marked by an old dead tree that stands defiantly as the king of the mountain. The 360 degree view

Figure 5.10   Desolation Lake is tucked in a bowl high in the east branch of Mill D North Fork at the end of the Desolation Trail (A). This canyon provides access to upper Millcreek Canyon (B), Beartrap Fork (C), and terrain south of the Wolf Mountain (Park West) ski area (D).

from this point is superb. Total climb from the branch point in the Mill D trail is 1.2 miles and 1500 vertical feet.

LOWER BIG COTTONWOOD–NORTH SIDE

The side canyons in Big Cottonwood become steeper and narrower as one descends westward. The terrain described in this section is suitable only for intermediate and advanced tourers. All of the side canyons terminate at the Millcreek or Neffs canyon divide and provide good opportunities for cross canyon tours. These are usually done by ascending the south-facing Big Cottonwood slopes and enjoying the dryer snow on north-facing slopes in the other canyon.

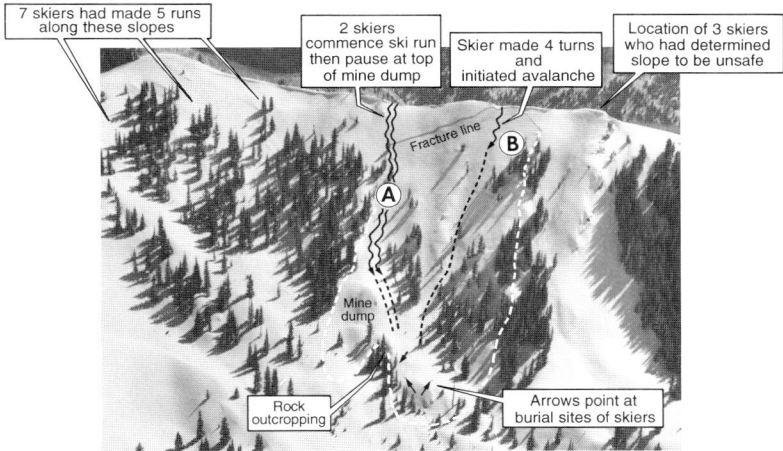

7 skiers had made 5 runs along these slopes

2 skiers commence ski run then pause at top of mine dump

Skier made 4 turns and initiated avalanche

Location of 3 skiers who had determined slope to be unsafe

Fracture line

B

A

Mine dump

Rock outcropping

Arrows point at burial sites of skiers

OVERCONFIDENCE KILLS*

April 2, 1979, was a bluebird day. Two feet of snow had dumped on the Wasatch earlier in the week. Aware of avalanche activity nearby, seven experienced tourers left Silver Fork at 10:00 and climbed into upper Mill D North Fork. They observed no signs of instability during the ascent or during five runs off the ridge above Desolation Lake.

At about 5:00 pm, they decided to go for "just one more run" on an untracked, slightly steeper slope a little farther west. The first three skiers, who were ahead of the others, decided that the planned run looked too dangerous and continued along the ridge. Unaware of those concerns, the following skiers decided to ski it. Two of them went part way down *(A)* and stopped mid-slope to wait for the others. A third started down *(B)* and triggered an avalanche.

The mid-slope skiers tried to outrun the slide, but were engulfed in moving snow. One managed to swim and was only partially covered. The other was knocked over a rock outcropping and buried, as was the skier who started the avalanche. A beacon search began immediately, and the victims were dug out in about 20 minutes. One didn't survive.

This tragedy illustrates the importance of not letting down one's guard, even after several uneventful runs. The Forest Service evaluation included three recommendations. *Concerns voiced by members of a group should be communicated to all others. No more than one tourer should be exposed to possible hazard at the same time. A skier should not stop in a potentially dangerous location while others are above.*

* Condensed from *The Snowy Torrents, Avalanche Accidents in the United States 1972-79*, Knox Williams and Betsy Armstrong, U. S. Forest Service.

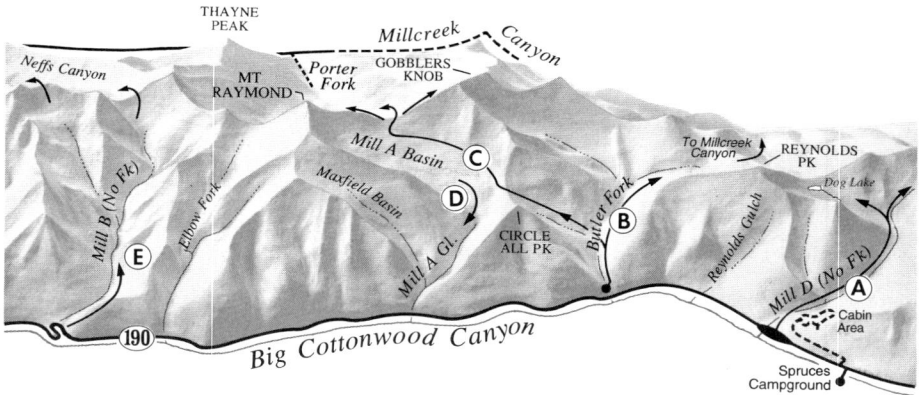

Figure 5.11   Some of the popular ski touring routes on the north side of Big Cottonwood Canyon are (A) Mill D North Fork, (B) Butler Fork, (C) Mill A Basin, and (D) Mill A Gulch. The rocky and brushy terrain in Mill B North Fork (E) makes it less suitable for enjoyable touring.

Butler Fork (H.P.A.)

Butler Fork is on the north side of Big Cottonwood where the canyon makes a sharp bend. It is one of many Wasatch forks named after the operator of a mill or mine that played an important part in the canyon's early history. In this case it was Neri Butler, who ran a steam sawmill there in the 1800's. This was one of the areas that provided timber for the Mormon pioneers to build their "oasis in the desert." It is difficult to imagine what these mountains must have been like before tens of millions of board feet of lumber were hauled into the valley.

Near the bottom, Butler Fork is a fairly narrow, steep-sided canyon, but it soon widens. The fork rises 1700 feet in about 2.3 miles, where it ends at the ridge overlooking Millcreek Canyon just north of Reynolds Peak. (See Figure 5.12.) About 0.5 miles from the highway, a branch of Butler bears to the left (west) and eventually terminates at the ridge separating it from Mill A Basin. Both parts have good skiing, but the east branch of the canyon is easier, with gentler terrain and more room to maneuver between the aspens.

Descent. Several alternatives exist for a Butler Fork ski tour. The most obvious option is to climb up the east branch and return the same way. Another possibility is to go up the west branch and ski down Mill A Gulch (see next section) or continue up to the saddle between Mount Raymond and Gobblers Knob, which is at the head of Porter Fork in Millcreek Canyon (described in Chapter 4). The main branch of Butler is commonly used as a route to Alexander Basin or one of the other

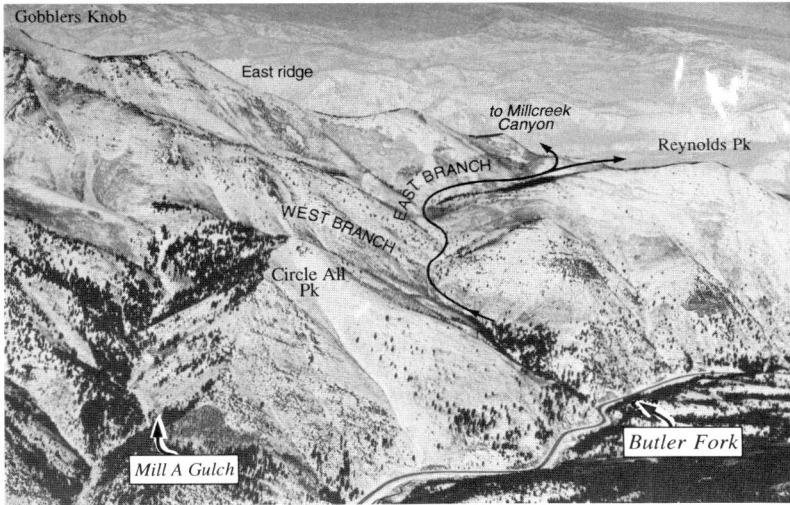

Figure 5.12   The main (east) branch of Butler Fork can be skied to its head at the Big Cottonwood/Millcreek ridge near Reynolds Peak. A popular tour involves a descent of the north slope of Reynolds into Butler from Dog Lake in the Mill D North Fork drainage. It's also possible to ascend the east ridge of Gobblers Knob from Butler Fork.

Millcreek tours described in the previous chapter. Another relatively simple alternative is to climb up the east branch to the top, traverse 0.4 mile through the firs behind Dog Lake, and go down Mill D North Fork. (This tour could just as easily be done in the opposite direction.) Finally, one could climb Reynolds peak and ski back down into Butler from there.

Gobblers Knob. For the ski mountaineer, Butler Fork provides three routes to the 10,246 foot summit of Gobblers Knob. None are appropriate for intermediates due to the steep terrain and high potential for avalanches. The peak is at the intersection of several ridges, most of which have some steep and rocky sections. The easiest route, labeled *(A)* in Figure 5.13, goes to the saddle below Mount Raymond and follows the west ridge to the top. Two other routes follow ridges that are steeper and rockier. The south ridge, visible in Figures 5.13 and 5.14, separates the two parts of Butler Fork and is the most direct alternative. The longest route, shown in Figure 5.12, is the east ridge, which starts at the head of Butler's east branch.

Descent. All possibilities for descending from the summit of Gobblers are exposed to hazardous avalanche areas. Skiers should study the photographs in this and the previous chapter and select a suitable route

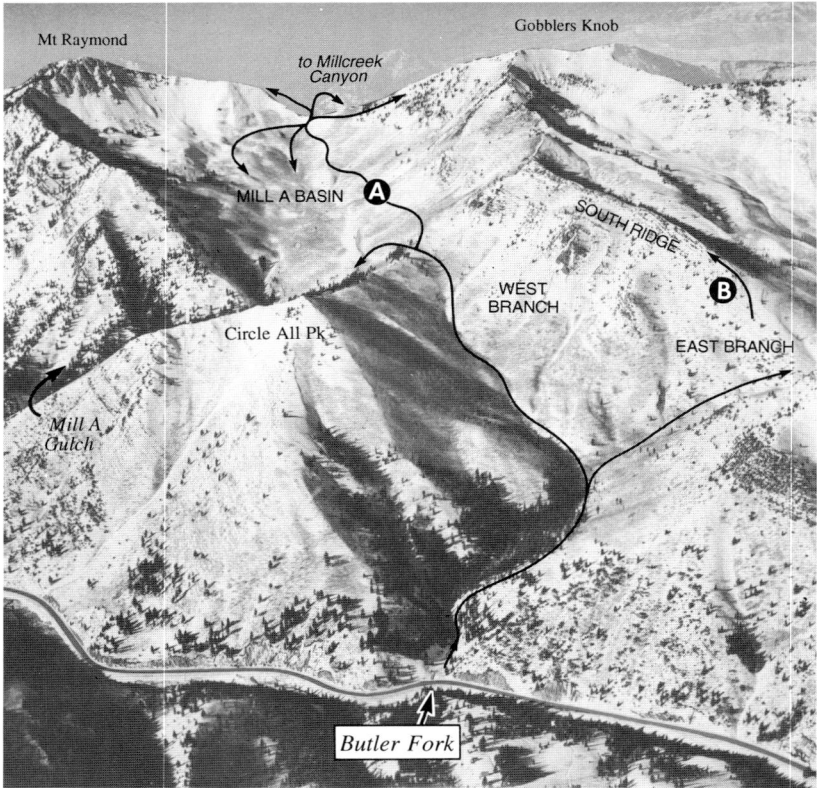

Figure 5.13   The west branch of Butler Fork is used primarily for access to other areas.   Route (A) leads to the saddle between Gobblers and Mount Raymond, where skiers can choose between an ascent of one of the adjacent peaks and a descent of Mill A or Porter Fork in Millcreek. Route (B) is the challenging south ridge route to Gobblers Knob. Descent possibilities in upper Mill A Basin can also be seen in the photo.

based on current snow conditions and the ability levels of the members of the touring party.

Mill A Gulch

John Maxfield operated the first of the sawmills built by the Big Cottonwood Lumber Company, a venture organized by Brigham Young and other prominent pioneers to provide building materials for their growing community. Today the Maxfield name is more closely associated with the mine developed by his sons in Mill A Gulch in 1872. The mine produced a fortune in gold, but not for the Maxfields. Before the mine

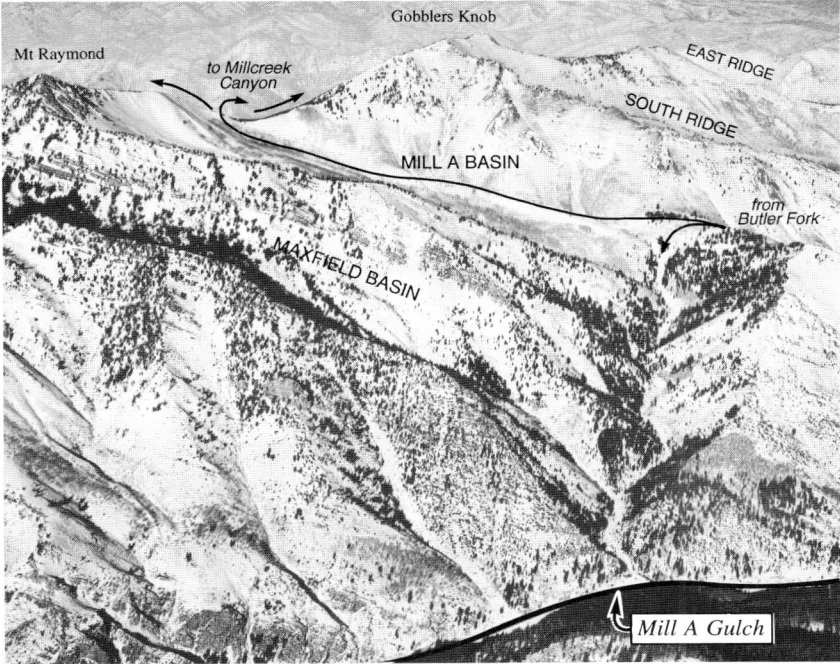

Figure 5.14　Mill A Gulch leads to the Big Cottonwood highway from the basin between Gobblers Knob and Mount Raymond. The gulch is usually approached from Butler Fork.

became operational, they sold the claim for the mere sum of two mules, a wagon, and $80.

Mill A is a fairly narrow canyon with lots of aspens, but its slope is gradual enough to make the run down quite pleasant. The ascent to the top of the gulch is best accomplished via the west branch of Butler Fork, since there is more room to traverse back and forth in Butler. Also, the bottom of Mill A is in a No Parking zone of the Big Cottonwood highway; vehicles may not be left in that area due to avalanche danger below the gullies visible in Figures 5.13 and 5.14. The major hazard in the gulch proper is from snow sliding from the steep sides into the bottom of the drainage.

To reach the ridge separating Mill A Gulch from the Butler Fork trailhead requires a climb of only 1.6 miles and 1500 vertical feet. An alternative that often has better snow requires continued ascent to the saddle between Gobblers Knob and Mount Raymond (Figure 5.13). This adds an extra 1.4 miles of distance and 700 feet of elevation to the climb.

Descent. There are several options for the descent from the Butler

Fork ridge. The route shown in Figure 5.14 drops into the bottom of the gulch and follows it back to the highway.

Mount Raymond. A more advanced ski mountaineering tour ascends the ridge to the summit of Mount Raymond (10,241 feet). This is not a particularly difficult climb, but the descent from the summit can prove more challenging than an intermediate skier might enjoy. The steep cirque on the east side of Mount Raymond can be a powder hound's delight, but the avalanche hazard there is usually quite high. Most skiers follow the ridge back to the saddle and drop into Mill A from there.

Mill B North Fork

The Neffs Canyon section of Chapter 7 describes two alternatives for tours from Big Cottonwood. Figure 5.11 illustrates the branches of Mill B North Fork. Neither side of this canyon has a route that is either obvious or easy to ascend.

UPPER BIG COTTONWOOD–SOUTH SIDE

Not many ski touring opportunities remain in this part of Big Cottonwood Canyon since Solitude expanded its commercial operations into Mill F South Fork and to the head of Honeycomb Fork. The only drainages that remain for backcountry skiing are Silver Fork and Greens Basin. Silver Fork, in fact, remains endangered. It was removed from Solitude's master plan only after immense opposition from noncommercial recreation advocates. Tourers should be alert to requests for a change in that policy.

Mill F South Fork (R.I.P.)

Mill F South Fork was a very popular and accessible area for cross country skiers, but it has been consumed by expansion of the Solitude Ski Area.

Honeycomb Fork (R.I.P.)

Honeycomb is another drainage that has been taken over by downhill skiers. The new lifts at Solitude make this terrain accessible to anyone who is willing to put up with a short hike back to the bottom of the ski area. It is no longer enjoyable for ski touring.

Silver Fork (H.P.A.)

The history of Silver Fork is full of the trauma and tragedy that went hand in hand with the mining boom around the turn of the century. The canyon is dotted with abandoned mines and mine dumps left by men who made their fortunes extracting silver ore. Some weren't so fortunate, however. Avalanches took many lives in those years. The hope for overnight wealth overpowered the discretion that should have been foremost in their minds when the heavy snows began to accumulate. A reminder of the old mining days that is still visible in winter is a tiny cabin perched high on a cliff between the two upper bowls of Silver Fork. Its precarious location and durability stand as a tribute to someone who was determined to beat the odds.

The lower part of Silver Fork was described in Volume 1 as a good beginner ski tour. An intermediate skier could continue beyond the flat section at the bottom, climb another mile or two, and have an enjoyable run back down without encountering much hazardous terrain. The best ascent route starts on a road along the west side. The stream should be crossed about 0.3 mile above the large mine on the left, shown in Figure 5.15, since the terrain is somewhat safer on the east side above that.

Silver Fork can be enjoyed from top to bottom with much less climbing if the tour is started from Brighton or Alta. The pass at the top of the east bowl is almost the same elevation as Twin Lakes Pass, and only a short traverse away. The total distance down to the highway is about 3.5 miles and between 2000 and 2400 vertical feet, depending on the route chosen. This is a difficult intermediate tour due to the steepness at the top and the avalanche potential.

The routes to Twin Lakes Pass are detailed elsewhere. (From Alta, simply ascend Grizzly Gulch to its end. From Brighton, take the lift or hike to the Twin Lakes dam and follow the power line to the pass. From Solitude, a lift can be taken to the top, followed by a traverse to the pass.) The traverse from Twin Lakes Pass to the top of Silver Fork's east branch is only about 0.7 mile, but it crosses several avalanche paths, as shown in Figure 6.4. Great care should be taken in this area when avalanche conditions are at all threatening. To reach the west branch of Silver Fork, continue along the ridge about 0.7 mile (over Davenport Hill) to the southwest crest of the canyon. Both branches of Silver Fork offer excellent skiing.

Descent. The east branch is the easier and safer one, although a tourer should use considerable caution in either of the upper bowls.

Figure 5.15   Silver Fork is one of the most challenging and dangerous intermediate tours in the Wasatch. Both of the upper bowls are steep and prone
to avalanche.

There are two possible descent routes in the east branch. One can ski
down through the trees below the saddle, or traverse to the right across
the steeper areas to access gentler terrain. Both alternatives expose the
tourer to dangerous slopes.

The west bowl of Silver Fork is usually better skiing, but the terrain
is more challenging and considerably more hazardous. A group of eleven
experienced tourers were caught in an avalanche there in January 1967.
They were skiing down the steep north-facing slope from the low point

Figure 5.16 The west bowl of Silver Fork is more hazardous than the east, but there are several lines of trees that offer a degree of protection. This area has become a favorite haunt of the helicopter skiers.

in the ridge when a slide released and buried three of them. One was injured seriously, but fortunately no fatalities occurred. Figure 5.16 is a closeup that shows the avalanche areas and how exposure to hazard can be minimized. Simply stay on the ridge near the southwest corner of Silver Fork and ski down among the large trees that may help hold the snow in place.

The two branches of Silver Fork converge at the bottom of the upper bowls. The best route down from that point is the the same as that described for ascending from the bottom. The east side is good for the first half mile or so, then the west side is better below that. The stream bed itself can be good skiing late in the year when the snow cover is very heavy, but there are some narrow sections to watch for.

Greens Basin (H.P.A.)

Greens Basin is a small drainage that is nestled between Silver Fork and Days Fork. It was named after a turn-of-the-century sawmill owner who cut down trees and sliced them into lumber needed by local miners and the Salt Lake Valley building trade. Greens Basin is one of the really nice touring areas that was omitted from the first edition of *Wasatch Tours* in 1976.

The climb to the top of Greens Basin is relatively short, less than three miles and 2300 vertical feet from the highway. An ascent can easily be accomplished in half a day, with time left for some great powder runs before lunch. The wooded terrain offers some security from the dreaded avalanche and excellent protection from wind and sun. The basin's northeast exposure helps keep the snow light and dry. Greens Basin is probably the Wasatch tour with the most reward for the least investment of time and energy.

Greens Basin is conveniently accessed from the Spruces Campground parking area, about 9.5 miles up Big Cottonwood at an elevation of 7400 feet. The trail into Days starts at the northwest end of the parking area, crosses the campground, then climbs along the east side of the drainage. The initial 300 vertical feet are relatively steep, and the trail is quite narrow for a short distance. After that first steep pitch, the trail into Days Fork is intercepted by a Forest Service trail coming in from the left (southeast), shown as route *(D)* in Figure 5.18. This trail traverses for about a mile to a large flat meadow in the bottom of Greens Basin. The steep wooded terrain on three sides of this meadow can be delightful for an intermediate powder skier.

The safest ascent route from the meadow follows the southeast ridge through aspens and firs to the top of the basin, which is a 9700 foot prominence on the Silver Fork/Days Fork ridge. This is a popular starting point for skiers who are willing to risk the avalanche hazards of the chutes that drop steeply from the ridge into Silver Fork. A less risky alternative is to descend back through the trees of Greens Basin to the meadow and then retrace one's tracks to the Spruces parking area.

LOWER BIG COTTONWOOD–SOUTH SIDE

Most of the advanced tours in Big Cottonwood are located in this area. The simplest and most popular commence at Alta and go directly over the ridge into Days and Cardiff forks. The most spectacular series of tours includes Mineral Fork, Mill B South Fork (Lake Blanche), and Broads Fork. All are shown schematically in Figure 5.17. Each successive fork is steeper, longer, and more dangerous than its easterly neighbor. Fortunately, the lower parts of many of these canyons are suitable for intermediates, so one need not be an expert skier to enjoy the spectacular alpine scenery in these drainages.

Days Fork (H.P.A.)

Days Fork, which empties into Spruces Campground, was another of the very active mining areas during the last part of the nineteenth century.

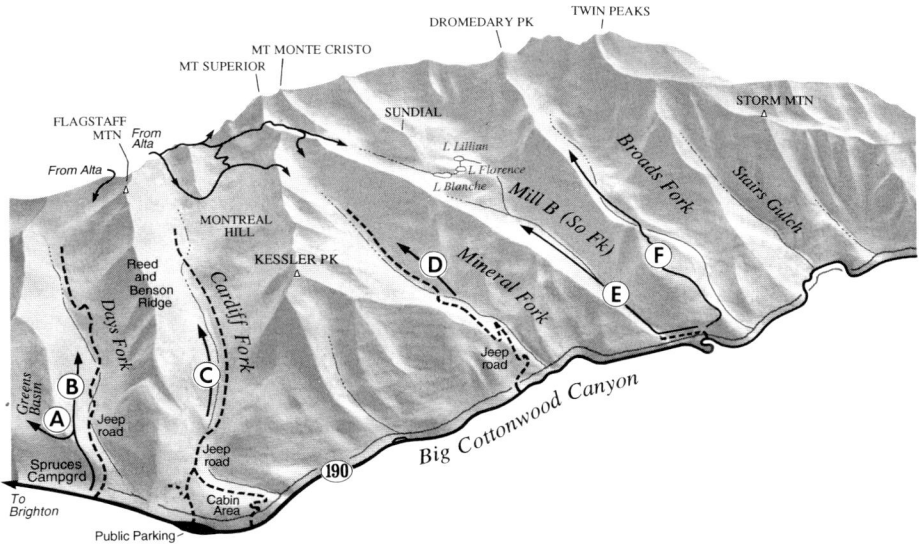

Figure 5.17   Some of the touring areas on the south slopes of Big Cottonwood Canyon below Brighton are (A) Greens Basin, (B) Days Fork, (C) Mill D South Fork, (D) Mineral Fork, (E) Mill B South Fork, and (F) Broads Fork.

Numerous remnants of its eventful past remain for the summer visitor to enjoy, but in winter, only bumps in the snow can be seen. Days Fork is similar to Silver Fork in many ways. The terrain is extremely steep at the top (so much so that we classify upper Days Fork as an advanced tour), but the lower section is more moderate. Part of this canyon would be an excellent beginner tour, except that the lower 300 vertical feet is quite steep and tricky to negotiate.

Lower Days Fork.   Days Fork can be done as an intermediate tour by ascending from the highway *to the base* of the upper cirque, a climb of about 4 miles and 2500 vertical feet. The route to follow is generally along the bottom of the drainage, but the beginning can be a bit confusing. Several small streams coming into Big Cottonwood Creek in this area are often open and difficult to cross. The simplest approach from the Spruces Campground is to go toward the pavilion which is beyond a clump of large fir trees near the east end of the parking area. If there is plenty of snow to cover the streams, simply bear right at the pavilion and cross the open area. Go through an aspen grove and work your way up the center of the fork. If the streams are open, they can be avoided by crossing the open area near the pavilion and traversing back and forth up the left side of the canyon for the first quarter mile.

Figure 5.18   The lower part of Days Fork has delightfully gentle terrain. The upper bowl is very hazardous and prone to avalanche. Routes shown in the photo are (A) ascent from the bottom, (B) access from Alta, (C) alternate descent along the west slopes, and (D) access to Greens Basin.

Descent. The easiest route back to the highway is along the same path as the climb. Another alternative, *(C)* in Figure 5.18, is to ski the west side of the canyon on the way down. A tourer could traverse up to the Reed and Benson Ridge overlooking Mill D South Fork and find an open spot in the trees for a descent back into the Days Fork drainage. A particularly good one (if the wind hasn't been too active) is the last

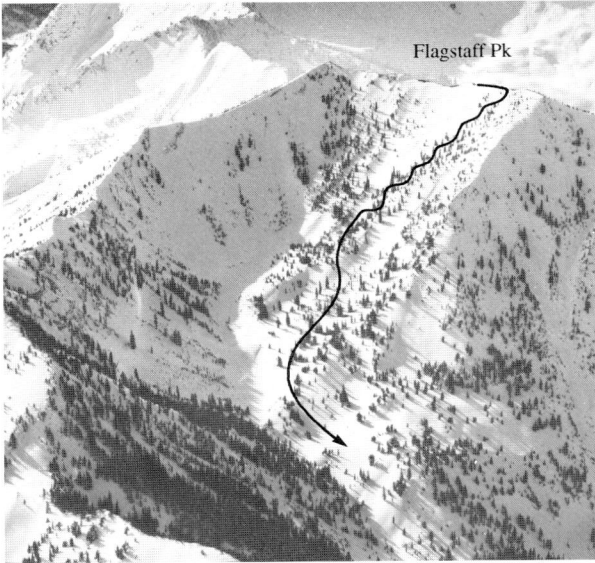

Figure 5.19   The safest descent into the cirque at the head of Days Fork is through the trees on the west side. However, great care should be exercised regardless of the route chosen.

1000 vertical feet along the ridge ending at the campground.

Upper Days Fork. Figure 5.19 illustrates that the upper bowl has a much different character than the lower part of this canyon. The entire south side is a series of avalanche chutes that a sensible skier would avoid in all but the most stable conditions. The trees on the west side of the Days Fork cirque provide some protection for the tourer, but care must always be exercised in the top part of this canyon. The section below the upper cirque is generally safer, as mentioned earlier in the chapter. Total run from the top to the highway is 3150 feet over 4.1 miles.

Flagstaff Peak. Three possibilities are described for an ascent of the 10,530 foot peak at the head of Days Fork.

(1) The safest approach is along the ridge from Twin Lakes Pass. The route is the same as that into Silver Fork, except it is a few hundred yards longer. The tour can be done from Alta or Brighton with a total ascent of 1900 feet in about 4.5 miles. This is quite a long route, but it avoids the steep slopes that otherwise must be climbed, and the view is unparalleled. It is described in detail in Chapter 6 and illustrated in Figure 6.4.

(2) The most popular route to Flagstaff is shown in Figure 6.6. A

steep ridge goes straight up to the summit from the town of Alta. The gullies on each side should always be avoided; they are the avalanche paths that have repeatedly put Alta in the news. This is a south-facing slope that often stabilizes within a few days of the last storm. In the cold, windy, snowy part of the winter, however, great care should be exercised in any area as exposed as this. This route is at its best when the sun gets higher in late winter and early spring.

(3) The third way to Flagstaff is up Days Fork from the Big Cottonwood highway. The only advantage of this alternative is that it eliminates the hitch-hiking or car-spotting required of a two canyon tour. The disadvantages are the distance and elevation of the climb and the length of time that the skier is exposed to the avalanche hazard of the upper cirque. Skiing down is dangerous enough, but climbing up is definitely not recommended.

Mill D South (Cardiff) Fork (H.P.A.)

As mentioned in Volume 1, the lower part of Mill D South Fork has good beginner touring terrain. Advanced beginner skiers can follow a road for two or three miles from the Big Cottonwood highway without encountering any uncomfortably steep slopes. This canyon also has the advantage of a large parking area plowed at the bottom by the State of Utah. Anyone skiing the lower part of this fork will have to share the trail with snowmobiles, so we recommend that the canyon be done as an intermediate tour from Alta to assure at least a couple of miles of challenging but peaceful skiing in the upper section.

Anyone who decides to do this tour from the bottom should be alert for the fork in the road about 0.7 miles from the highway. The right fork crosses the Cardiff stream and leads up the canyon, while the left one goes only a short distance and stops near Donut Falls.[5] Evidence of an active past is visible all the way up Mill D South. The area just below Donut Falls used to be known as Taggart Flat, named after a family that was killed in an avalanche during the late nineteenth century. A glance at the steep slopes on the side of Kessler Peak just west of the trail will tell the tourer why that wasn't a good spot to build a house. The number and the size of the nearby tailings piles attest to the extent of past mining operations.

From Alta. The route to Cardiff Pass (sometimes called Pole Line

---

[5]This part of the canyon is very narrow with steep sides. A fatality occurred here in February 1981 when an avalanche dumped about 10 feet of snow on three skiers who were touring up the gully.

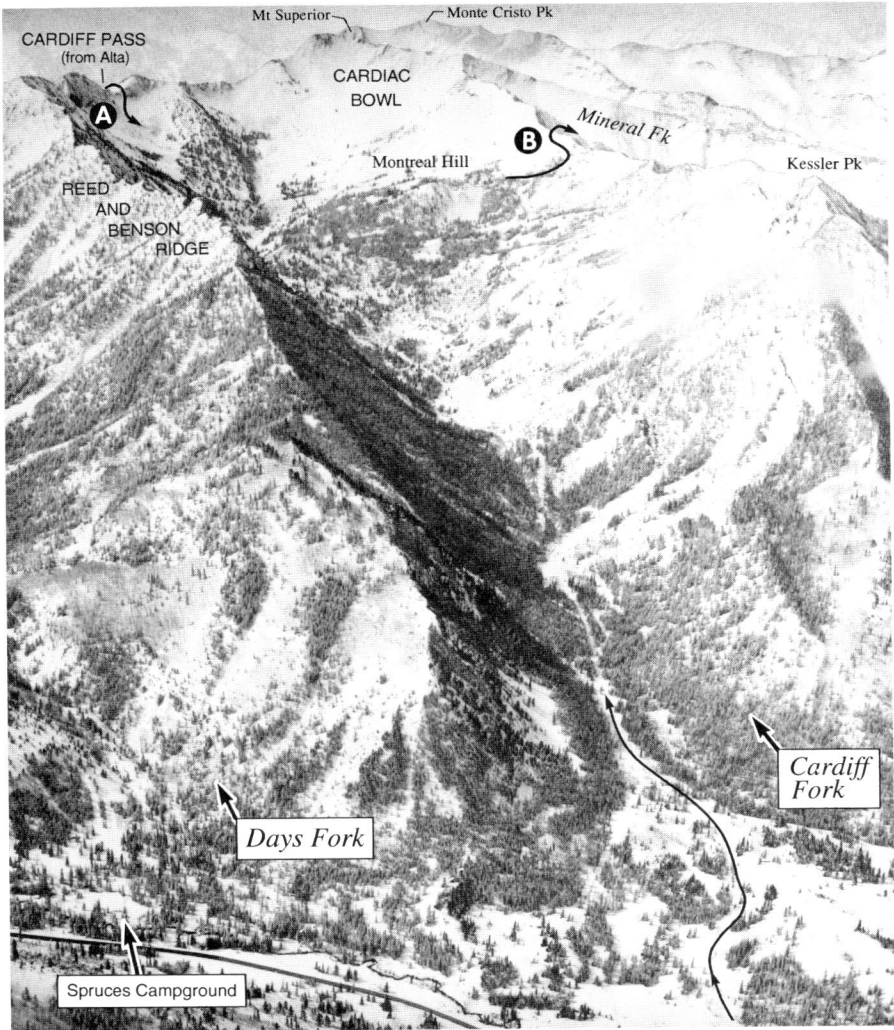

Figure 5.20   Several possibilities exist for the run down Cardiff Fork. The safest and easiest is the east branch (A) in the upper left corner of the photo. The hazards of the west branch, known as Cardiac Bowl, are shown in a later photo. The route from Montreal Hill into Mineral Fork (B) is also marked in this picture.

Pass) from Alta is described in Chapter 6 and shown in Figure 6.6. Note the avalanche paths on either side of the recommended route that the careful tourer should always avoid. The climb along the power line is generally quite moderate, although there are a couple of steep sections. The total ascent is about 1400 vertical feet and a bit over a mile.

Descent. The run down into Cardiff has many variations, as Figure 5.20 shows. Most of the canyon is quite gentle, but the upper bowls have some extremely steep areas that should be avoided unless conditions are particularly stable. The fork is divided into two parts by a ridge that runs about a mile down to the Cardiff Mine. The pass is at the top of the east side of the canyon. The easiest descent route into Mill D South is directly below the pass, through the trees and across an open slope to the bottom of the drainage. Even this area is prone to avalanche, so care should be exercised.

Another possibility for the east bowl is to follow the ridge west from Cardiff Pass over the first high point and down to the next saddle. The slope below often has better snow.

The west bowl of Cardiff Fork, also known as "Cardiac Bowl," is one of the most hazardous areas in the Wasatch and should be treated with great respect. The northeast side of Mount Superior drops more than 1000 feet with an average slope of more than 40 degrees and is suitable only for expert skiers with advanced avalanche training. The Lake Blanche tour described later in the chapter has more information on this area.

The lower part of Cardiff is simply a run down very gentle terrain, along a jeep road, to the highway. If more challenge is desired, one can climb to the left from the Cardiff Mine to the top of Montreal Hill for a few extra turns before the terrain flattens.

Mineral Fork (H.P.A.)

Mineral Fork is very similar to Days, which was described earlier in the chapter. As its name implies, this canyon was also a center of mining activity around the turn of the century when visions of gold and silver dominated the minds of many would-be millionaires. Mineral Fork is the home of the Regulator Johnson Mine, perched high in the upper cirque at an elevation of 10,200 feet in the middle of an active avalanche area.[6] It is truly amazing that such a venture could succeed with the technology that was available at the time.

Lower Mineral Fork. The top of Mineral is extremely hazardous, as Figure 5.21 illustrates, but most of the fork is quite heavily wooded. An old mining road climbs gradually along the stream from the highway to the upper bowl. Only the lower part of the canyon is of sufficient difficulty to preclude a beginner rating for lower Mineral Fork. The

---

[6]In March 1943, a cook shack at a mine in Mineral Fork was destroyed by an avalanche. One of its three occupants was killed.

Figure 5.21 Lower Mineral Fork is quite heavily wooded and narrow, so the tourer is restricted to an old mining road that intercepts the Big Cottonwood highway about 1.5 miles above the S-curve. Upper Mineral is extremely steep and prone to avalanche.

bottom section of the road switches back and forth for about 700 vertical feet before it levels off.

Above the switchbacks the Mineral Fork road wanders through a fairly dense oak and aspen forest that allows the tourer few opportunities to deviate. About 2.3 miles from the Big Cottonwood highway, the canyon opens up and becomes much steeper. A competent skier could climb another 1400 vertical feet into the upper cirque, but avalanche conditions become an important consideration. The chutes on the west side of the canyon frequently slide all the way to the stream. Total climb from the highway to the base of the cirque is about 4.0 miles and 2900 vertical feet.

Descent. There are few alternatives for the descent other than the route just described. One could climb up either side of the canyon and ski back down to the road. The west side is less steep than the east side, but both have many areas with high avalanche potential, so great care should be exercised.

Upper Mineral Fork. For a ski tour that has only four miles of downhill, Mineral Fork has an unusually large number of possible approaches. The top of the canyon can be reached from Alta, from lower Cardiff Fork, from the S-curve in Big Cottonwood, or by hiking up from the bottom. All are advanced tours that include exposure to hazardous terrain during both the climb and the descent. Two of the most straightforward routes into upper Mineral are described here. Both are shown in Figure 5.22, which is a photograph of the cirque.

The safest approach marked in the figure avoids the big open bowl at the top and allows the tourer to ski on somewhat protected terrain. The approach is from Cardiff Fork, so it can be reached from Alta or Big Cottonwood Canyon. Figure 5.20 shows a moderately thick line of fir trees leading to the ridge from the top of Montreal Hill, which is just above the Cardiff Mine. The best ascent route is to climb through the trees to the ridge, and then up the ridge another 100 yards to a favorable descent area. The run down to the jeep road in the bottom of Mineral Fork is the most challenging part of the tour. The canyon is quite flat below that except for the portion just above the Big Cottonwood highway. Total descent is 3500 feet over a distance of 3.9 miles.

The second possibility for upper Mineral should be attempted only by the most competent and knowledgeable ski tourers. It can be a superb powder run, but the potential for an avalanche is extremely high. The route comes over the ridge from Mill B South at the southwest corner of the upper Mineral Fork cirque. Route *(C)* in Figure 5.25 shows the approach. From Alta, one can go over Cardiac Pass, then traverse down and to the right for about 0.3 mile, staying as high as possible. (More details on Mill B South are found in the next section.) The pass into Mineral is a small notch at 10,500 feet elevation. Skis may need to be removed for a short rock scramble in order to get there. Once over the ridge, however, there is almost always enough snow to ski right from the top. The true glutton for punishment could get to this pass by climbing about five miles and 4300 vertical feet along the Lake Blanche

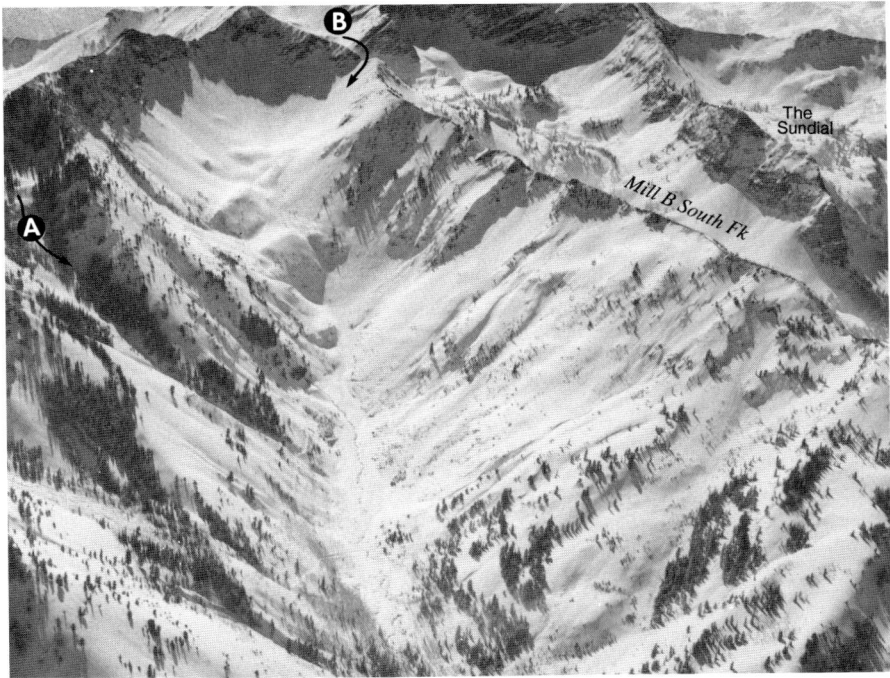

Figure 5.22   The two routes into upper Mineral Fork originate in Cardiff Fork (A) and Mill B South Fork (B). The latter is very steep and hazardous in winter and spring.

hiking trail. Total descent into Mineral Fork is about 3800 feet over 4.1 miles.

Mill B South Fork (Lake Blanche)

Lake Blanche[7] is considered by many to be among the finest advanced ski tours in the Wasatch Range. Throughout its nearly five mile length, this canyon possesses a unique blend of alpine characteristics—jagged summits, treeless cirques, mountain lakes, meadows, and dense forests. The upper part of Mill B South is wide open, with lots of room for skiers to carve their most graceful turns. The lower section, on the other hand, is a steep and narrow hiking trail that can provide even the most experienced ski mountaineer with moments of excitement (or even

---

[7]Lake Blanche, along with nearby Lakes Lilian and Florence, are rumored to have been named by the early pioneers after three zealous ladies of the late nineteenth century who served law and order by moonlighting as police decoys in the nearby mining camps.

Figure 5.23   Ski tourer Bob Irvine on the summit of Superior, with Monte Cristo in the background. Short skis, such as those he is packing, are excellent for late spring skiing.

despair) when the snow is hard and daylight is rapidly disappearing.

There are three common variations to the Lake Blanche tour. One is the "standard" route starting from Alta, and the others are "anti-establishment" alternatives commencing from upper or lower Big Cottonwood Canyon. The latter two will appeal to those who detest the traffic jams, high-rise condominiums, and commercial atmosphere of the Alta-Snowbird complex. They also have the advantage of eliminating a car shuttle. (We should mention that the car shuttle involves only the 4.3 miles in Big Cottonwood Canyon thanks to the excellent UTA bus service available to skiers in recent years.)

Mill B South Fork from Alta. The "standard" Lake Blanche ski tour consists of an ascent from Alta to Cardiff Pass, a traverse and climb to "Cardiac Ridge"[8] between Cardiff Fork (Mill D South) and Mill B South, and then a descent to the S-curve in the Big Cottonwood highway. From Alta, one follows the power line to Cardiff Pass (see Figure 6.6). Care should be taken to avoid the avalanche prone slopes on either side of the pole line; it was laid out to avoid avalanches, and the tourer should take advantage of this well planned route.

---

[8]The name of Cardiac Ridge was first coined by Charles Chauncey Hall, a prominent Salt Lake orthopedic corporation (now retired from practice) and active ski tourer, who observed that a person could have a heart attack just *looking* at this dangerous area.

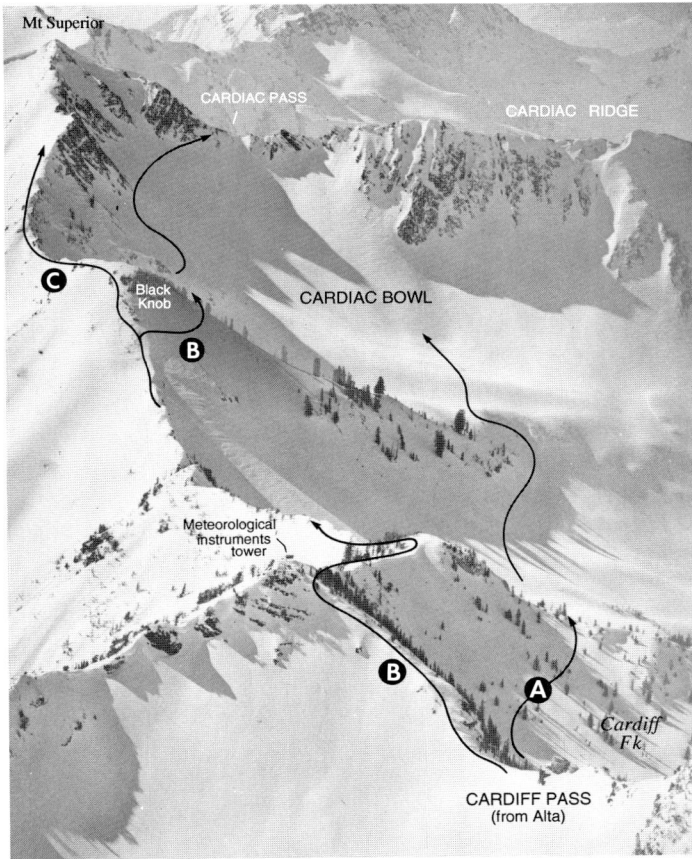

Figure 5.24   Three routes are available from Cardiff Pass to Cardiac Pass, none of which is completely safe. Cardiac Bowl, northeast of Mount Superior, is one of the most hazardous avalanche areas in the Wasatch.

From Cardiff Pass there are two recommended ways to reach Cardiac Pass, gateway to the east branch of Mill B South Fork and Lake Blanche. The merits of these and other routes have been examined and extensively debated by avalanche connoisseurs and Forest Service professionals. The general conclusion seems to be that none are particularly safe. Route *(C)* in Figure 5.24 follows the ridge directly to the summit of Mount Superior. Although it is relatively free from avalanche hazard, it is not frequently used because of its steepness and general difficulty.

The two alternatives to be described, *(A)* and *(B)* in the photograph, involve some loss of elevation in order to stay on safer terrain, but the extra climb is well worth the effort. One route drops down into Mill D South Fork and stays below the extremely steep areas, and the other follows the ridge as far as possible to stay above many of the dangerous slopes. Regardless of which of these routes is chosen, the cirque below Cardiac cannot be avoided.

(A) The safest of the two approaches is the lower one.[9] Unfortunately, it requires the most climbing. From the pass, the tourer descends into the fork by angling down and to the left toward the secondary ridge that separates the east and west sides of upper Cardiff. After a short climb to this ridge, one again loses elevation and traverses in a westerly direction, being careful to stay well away from the steep slopes that could send a "white death" down on fellow tourers. The climb into the cirque below Cardiac Pass is then done on relatively safe terrain.

(B) The higher route follows the Mount Superior ridge from Cardiff Pass for about 0.7 mile to the "Black Knob," a rocky shoulder at the head of an avalanche slope visible in Figure 5.24. The ridge is quite steep in spots, so some traversing back and forth is often necessary; the south side is often safer for this purpose, since the cornices tend to form on the Big Cottonwood side.[10] From the shoulder, the route traverses north below the Black Knob and crosses the top of the avalanche slope just mentioned. After that, a fairly steep gully has to be crossed to reach the cirque below Mount Superior and Cardiac Pass.

Cardiac Pass can be reached by approaching the cirque high from the left side, then traversing under the cliffs below the summit of Superior. (A touring party was involved in an avalanche there in February 1972.) One can also zig zag directly up the middle of the cirque to the pass. (Another party was swept down in a slide there in December 1969.) The third alternative is to traverse to the pass from the right to avoid the north-facing slopes. (A group was involved with an avalanche in that area in the mid-1970's.) The climb from Alta to Cardiac Pass is 3.0 miles and, depending upon the route, involves between 2300 and 2900 feet of vertical climb.

Descent. The run down into Big Cottonwood Canyon has many possibilities, two of which are described here. They are labeled *(A)* "upper" and *(B)* "lower" in Figure 5.25, a photo of the higher regions of Mill B South Fork. The two routes converge at Lake Blanche, which lies just below the Sundial massif, and separate again in the lower part of the canyon. Above the lake, the upper descent route involves considerable

---

[9] This route was first suggested by Dr. Ronald Perla, one of the leading avalanche authorities in North America, who spent several years at the now-defunct Alta Avalanche Study Center.

[10] A hiker was killed there when he lost his footing, slid down the snowslope, and tumbled over a cliff.

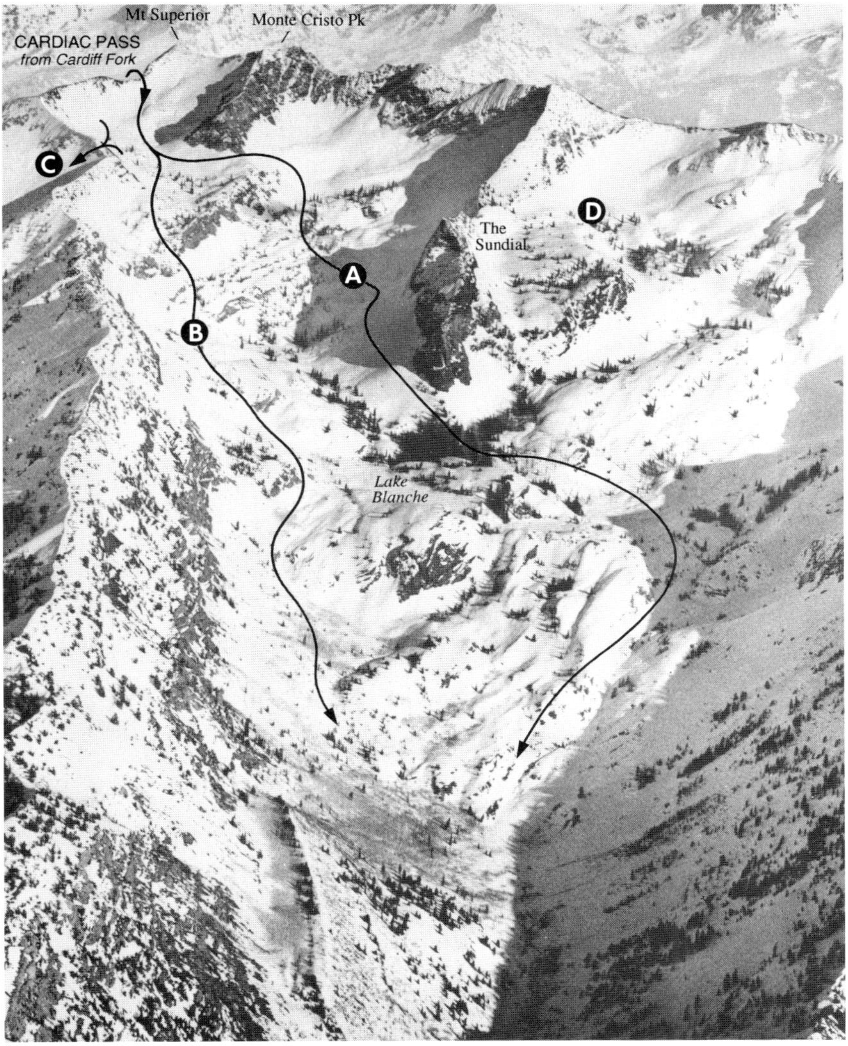

Figure 5.25   Mill B South Fork has many touring possibilities. The two main descent alternatives are (A) the "upper" and (B) the "lower" routes shown in the picture. An access into Mineral Fork (C) is shown in the photo, along with the infrequently skied area in the west branch of the canyon (D). The prominent ridge known as "The Sundial" is represented in the emblem of the Wasatch Mountain Club.

avalanche hazard. It also requires much traversing and climbing, but the snow is often better. The lower route to Lake Blanche also has some avalanche danger, but the descent is smoother.

Below the lake, the choice of routes depends largely upon snow conditions and enthusiasm remaining among members of the party. The lower route generally follows the hiking trail, which is quite narrow and steep in spots. It has the advantage of offering good walking terrain if the snow ends before the tour (not an uncommon occurrence). The upper route crosses several hazardous areas, but the snow on the east-facing slopes is protected from the sun and often allows one to ski all the way to the bottom. The total length of Mill B South from Cardiac Pass is 4.9 miles with 4600 feet of elevation change.

Mill B South Fork from Lower Cardiff. In order to avoid the congestion in Little Cottonwood Canyon, the Lake Blanche ski tour is often done from Big Cottonwood via Cardiff Fork. This alternative, unfortunately, involves a climb of almost twice the distance and one and a half times the elevation gain as the standard approach from Alta. The tour basically follows the old mining road up Mill D South to the Cardiff Mine complex, as described in an earlier section. From this point, a gradual traverse is taken to the right and up into the cirque below Cardiac Pass (Figure 5.20). Routes and avalanche hazards in the upper reaches of Cardiff Fork have already been described. Total distance from the highway to the pass is 5.3 miles with an elevation gain of 3600 feet.

Lake Blanche from the S-curve. The third alternative for Mill B South avoids the avalanche hazards in upper Cardiff. This tour starts at the bottom of the S-curve in Big Cottonwood and follows the Forest Service road along the stream for about 0.3 miles and then goes up the hiking trail to Lake Blanche. Several possibilities are available from the lake. One can stay to the left and take the previously described "lower" descent route to Cardiac Pass. Another option is to climb over the east ridge and ski into Mineral Fork, as described in the previous section. It is also possible to climb to the right of The Sundial into the high valley bordered by the Dromedary and Sundial ridges; Figure 5.25 shows that there is some delightful skiing terrain in this branch of Mill B South, but the only reasonable approach is from the bottom.

Broads Fork

Unlike most of the lower Big Cottonwood tours, the ascent into Broads Fork is almost always done from the bottom. Although a route exists between Mill B South (Lake Blanche) and Broads, it is an unusually risky venture that is rarely attempted. The only safe, sane, and practical alternative for a tour into Broads Fork is the hiking trail that goes directly up the canyon and stops short of the upper cirque beneath the

Figure 5.26   The upper cirque in Broads Fork has one of the largest collections of avalanche slopes in the Wasatch. Bob Athay is said to have made 287 nonstop, consecutive turns on the slope that is affectionately known as "Bonkers."

summits of Dromedary, Sunrise, and Twin Peaks.

The hiking trail into Broads Fork starts at the lower end of the S-curve, just across the bridge from the Big Cottonwood highway. It traverses westerly and upward for about 0.4 mile to the top of a secondary ridge overlooking the highway. From this point, the trail bends to the south and, after another 0.5 mile, crosses the stream. For the next 1.2 miles, any of several minor, tree-covered ridges (often glacial moraines) can be followed to a prominent knoll that serves as an excellent viewpoint for the Broads Fork bowl. Because of severe avalanche hazard in the cirque, the tour generally ends at this point. Total climb is 2100 feet over 2.1 miles.

Figure 5.26 shows the spectacular avalanche terrain in upper Broads Fork. The outstanding alpine scenery is the high point of the tour. The descent, like that of the hiking trail below Lake Blanche, will challenge all but the expert skier. It is not advisable to abandon the trail in favor of following the streambed into the lower portion of the drainage. Broads Fork is an excellent example of a hanging valley; just above the Big Cottonwood stream, the canyon becomes very steep. In addition, its lower slopes are covered with thickets of nearly impenetrable brush.

Stairs Gulch

Stairs Gulch is *almost* never entered in winter. The Forest Service and other knowledgeable agencies wish that it be *absolutely* never entered in either winter or spring. Stairs Gulch is a very narrow, winding canyon that goes about two miles from the Big Cottonwood highway to its crest at the ridge below Twin Peaks. In that distance, the canyon rises 4600 vertical feet, which means that it has an average slope of almost 30 degrees. (It is actually much steeper at the top.) The upper part of Stairs Gulch is an immense rock slab that frequently sends powerful avalanches into the main gully below. The Big Cottonwood highway has been buried to depths of 40 feet or more on several occasions. The photograph of the canyon and a highway-crossing avalanche in Figure 5.27 illustrates why the area is not recommended for ski touring, snowshoeing, hiking, or any other activity in winter or spring□

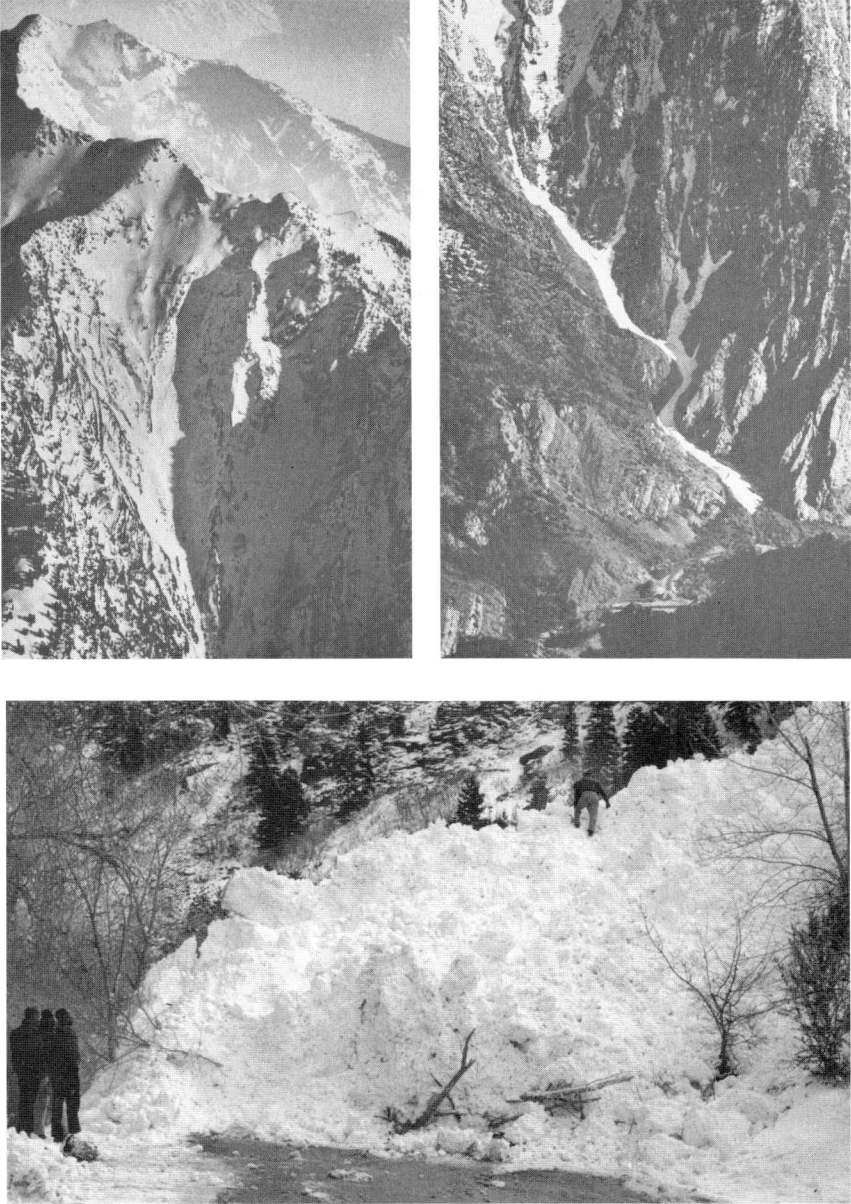

Figure 5.27   Nearly all of the snow that falls on the steep upper slopes of Stairs Gulch avalanches into the narrow gully at its base. On April 17, 1994, a giant, slow-moving avalanche, not unlike that pictured in the bottom photograph, nearly overran a group of *nineteen* members of an outing club who had assembled in the bottom of the canyon to practice snow climbing.

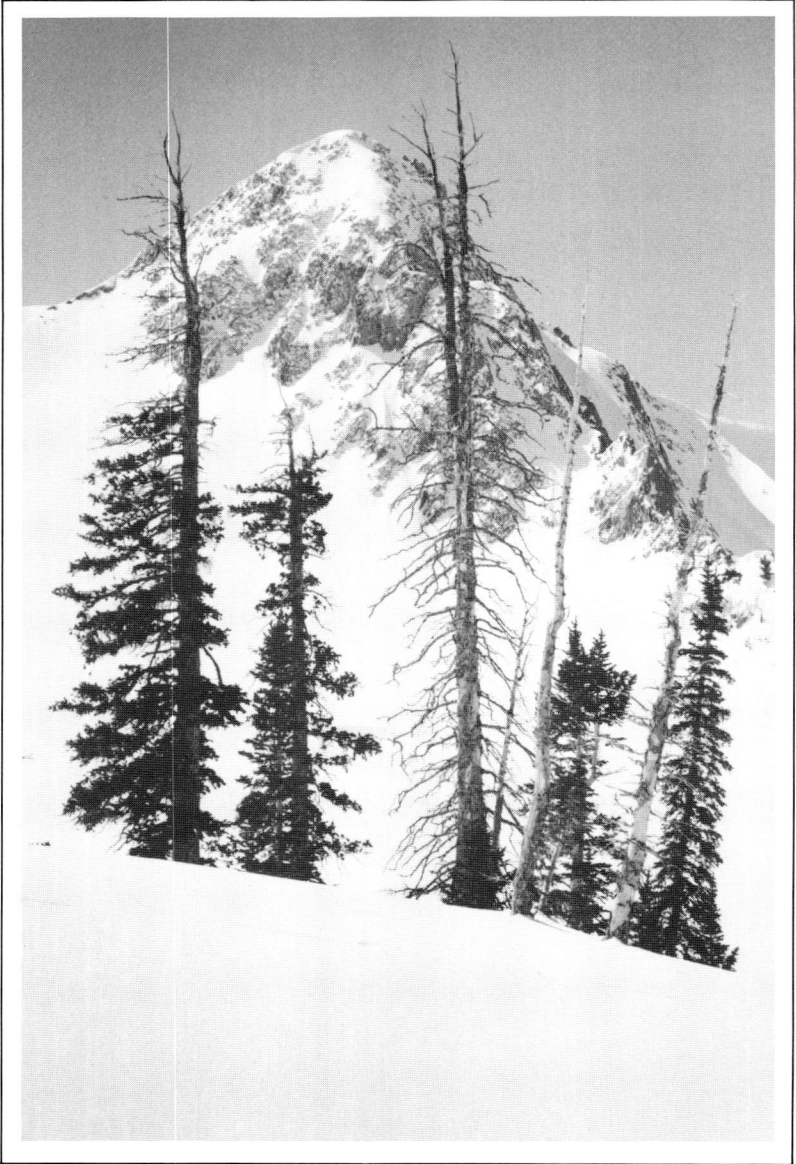

Once proposed for an aerial tramway and a surrounding destination ski area that few locals could afford to patronize, the Pfeifferhorn is now protected from commercial exploitation by its inclusion in the Lone Peak Wilderness.

Chapter 6

LITTLE COTTONWOOD CANYON

Little Cottonwood Canyon has had a colorful and controversial history for over a century. Until the miners came looking for gold and silver, the canyon was used primarily as a source of granite for the Salt Lake Temple and lumber for buildings in the valley. In 1868, Alta had only a steam sawmill and a boarding house, but five years later its population is reported to have grown to several thousand.

By 1880, most of the timber had been cut off the slopes around Alta, leaving the area particularly susceptible to avalanches from the surrounding mountainsides. "Six Poor Souls Hurled Into Eternity" reads the headline of the January 15, 1881, issue of *The Daily Tribune*. The article describes a "fearful" avalanche that swept from the Davenport Divide crushing the Grizzly Boarding House. In the five day period of January 12 to 17, 1881, fifteen lives were lost to snow slides in Little Cottonwood and American Fork Canyons. On March 11, 1884, under a headline of "Death In A Snowslide", the *Tribune* again describes Alta's visitation by a "Horribly Destructive Avalanche" which left "Ten Men and Two Women Killed and Terribly Mangled".

> "It is as though the hand of God had swept quickly over the earth, and with no noise, confusion, or notice, had quietly blotted out of existence so many lives and so much property, as a man would snuff out a candle...
>
> The slide was the most fearful and destructive that has ever visited Alta. It started from the summit of Equitable Gulch and with the rapidity of a flash made its way to the Rattler Ravine above Grizzly Flat. Continuing downwards it

Figure 6.1   *"Effects of the snow-slide. Alta. Cottonwood. Utah."* On February 14, 1885, sixteen individuals perished in an avalanche described as "the worst disaster yet to befall that snowy region." The photo, taken by C. R. Savage on July 3, 1885, shows remnants of some of the buildings. Photo courtesy of the Utah State Historical Society.

> struck and carried away the New Emma boiler house, black-smith shop, boarding house, and concentrating works, in-stantly killing twelve persons who had sought the place for safety."

Just a year later, on February 14, 1885, "The Worst Disaster Yet To Befall That Snowy Region" occurred, killing sixteen persons and destroying a good portion of Emmaville, a small cluster of businesses and residences just a short distance below the city of Alta.

Early in 1871, Alta became embroiled in conflicts with speculators. It was discovered that whole streams and power sites had been claimed by individuals described in the *Tribune* as men who "only want to bleed those who would turn them into sources of wealth for the workers." The speculator, the writer concluded, is a "nuisance and a pest. We do not know that they can be entirely got rid of." The problem of speculators resurfaced exactly a century later, but the "nuisances and pests" of the current generation are the resort and condominium developers who rely on public subsidies—in the form of unconscionably low Forest Service lease fees and state tax dollars for advertising—for their real estate

Figure 6.2 *"Three days on skis, Alta to Brighton then up over Scott's Peak and down Mill Creek."* The first cross-country ski tourers arrive at Alta in 1923. Photograph by J. R. Griffiths/W. H. Hopkins, courtesy of the Wasatch Mountain Club.

projects and resort expansions.

Just as Little Cottonwood Canyon is rich in lore and history, it is also rich in ski touring opportunities. Of all the canyons in the Wasatch, Little Cottonwood provides access to the largest variety of terrain for the backcountry skier. But the threat of avalanches hangs as heavily above the skier of today as it once hung above the miner of yesteryear.

Since the Alta Ski Lifts company expanded into Albion Basin, little ski touring terrain remains for the neophyte. Several areas, however, are still available for those whose skiing abilities are more intermediate. In the Alta area are Catherine Pass, Grizzly Gulch, Silver Fork Pass, and Cardiff Pass. Farther down the canyon, below the concrete reminders of man's "progress", are White Pine and Red Pine gulches. (If Snowbird officials get their way, however, White Pine will go the way of the many other canyon recreation areas that have been sacrificed to "destination skiers.") Advanced skiers will enjoy touring Maybird and Hogum forks, with the Pfeifferhorn and other nearby summits serving as winter mountaineering diversions.

Little Cottonwood Canyon is also the starting point for a number of trans-canyon tours into Big Cottonwood, American Fork, and Bells canyons, as well as the Dry Creek drainage above the community of Alpine. Trips into Big Cottonwood are described in Chapter 5. Tours into American Fork Canyon and those into Alpine are in Volume 3 of *Wasatch Tours*.

The Little Cottonwood Canyon tours are discussed in what the authors believe to be an approximate order of increasing difficulty. Since the side gulches of Little Cottonwood are steeper, longer, and more rugged as one descends the canyon, each route described becomes more challenging. Figure 6.3 illustrates the concept.

Due to the constricted nature of the canyon highway during winter and difficulties associated with snowplowing, only three trailhead areas are practical for tours originating in Little Cottonwood.[1] A number of tours start at Alta's uppermost parking area. Several Little Cottonwood Canyon tours (and trans-canyon tours to Big Cottonwood) commence from central Alta (from the Forest Service garage across the pavement from the Alta Lodge). A formal Lone Peak Wilderness trailhead at the base of White Pine Gulch provides access to White Pine and the upper basins of the canyon's remaining gulches.

A "supertours" section, describing a series of exceptionally long and arduous ski tours, is included at the end of this chapter.

TOURS FROM UPPER ALTA

A number of excellent–but not as good as they used to be–intermediate and advanced ski tours are possible from Alta's upper parking area. Two trunk routes (pictured in Figure 6.4) depart from the parking area: one ascends Albion Basin to Catherine Pass, the other ascends Grizzly Gulch to Twin Lakes Pass. Several interesting side excursions can be made from either route.

Catherine Pass (End.)

One of the easiest intermediate outings in the Wasatch is the tour up the Alta ski area to Catherine Pass, which overlooks Brighton to the east. This tour was more appealing before ski lifts were thrust into Albion Basin, but the spectacular scenery compensates (somewhat) for

---

[1]Tourers who anticipate touring in Little Cottonwood Canyon are warned that Sheriff's deputies are likely to issue citations (or impound notices) for vehicles parked along the highway. As roadside snow melts during springtime and as traffic decreases at the end of the ski season, the enforcement policy often becomes less rigid.

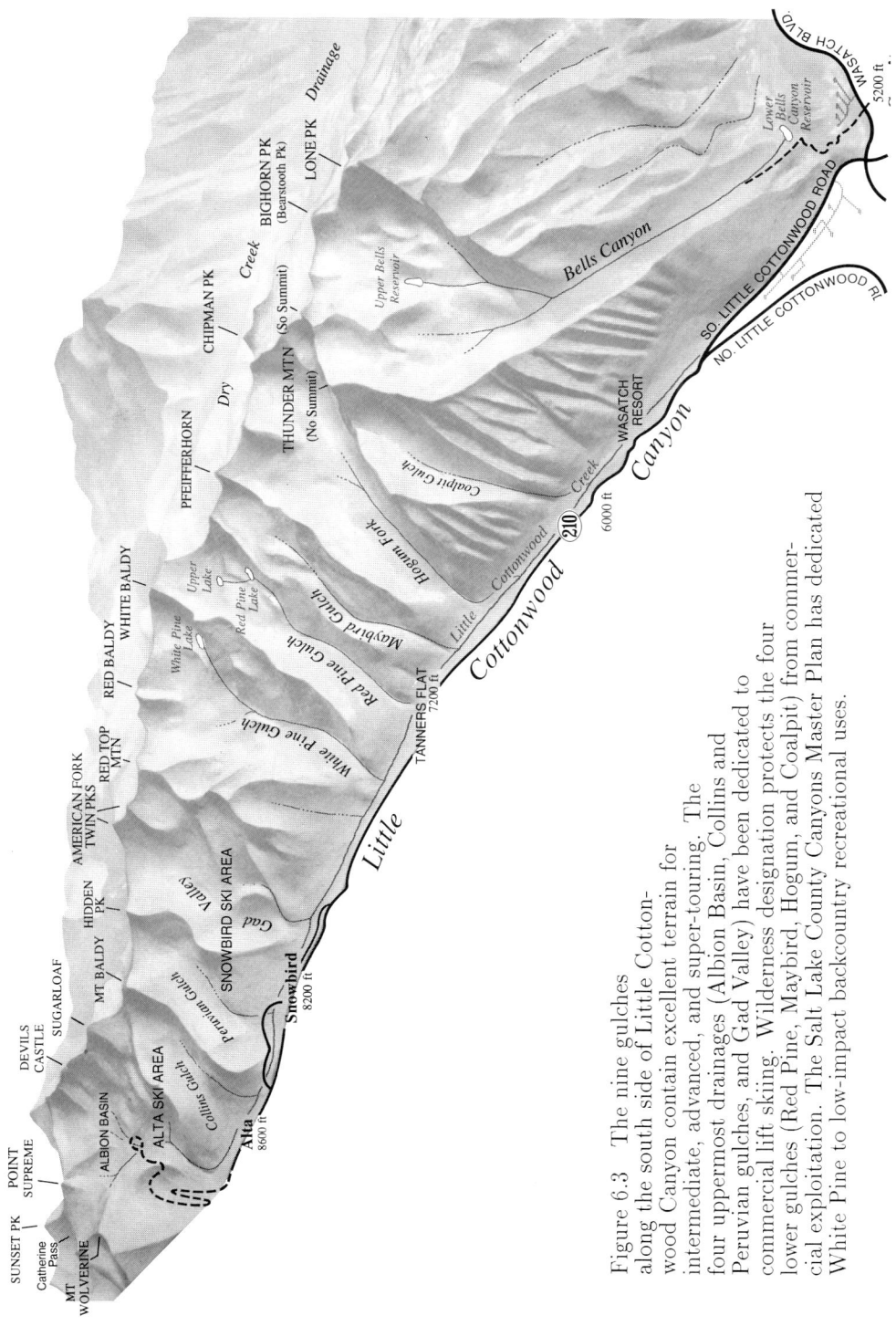

Figure 6.3 The nine gulches along the south side of Little Cotton- wood Canyon contain excellent terrain for intermediate, advanced, and super-touring. The four uppermost drainages (Albion Basin, Collins and Peruvian gulches, and Gad Valley) have been dedicated to commercial lift skiing. Wilderness designation protects the four lower gulches (Red Pine, Maybird, Hogum, and Coalpit) from commer- cial exploitation. The Salt Lake County Canyons Master Plan has dedicated White Pine to low-impact backcountry recreational uses.

Avalanche search and rescue operation in "Snake Pit Gulch," Alta, January 1, 1941. Photograph by F. C. Koziol, courtesy of U.S. Forest Service.

UTAH'S FIRST TOURING FATALITY*

New Years Day 1941. With 14 inches of fresh (though heavy) snow in the upper canyons some 1500 area skiers converged on Alta, at that time and still Utah's premier ski area. A group of five skiers left Alta to ski in Albion Basin, following a route that ascended above the south side of Snakepit Gulch. During the traverse of the steep hillside known today as Greely Hill, the only skier without climbers began to lag. He was "in no hurry," he told his companions, urging them to go ahead. After feeling "the snow slip once," the four frontmost skiers hurried on to their destination. They skied the upper basin for 45 minutes and on return found that Greely Hill had avalanched, covering Snakepit with deep mounds of debris.

The massive avalanche had been observed by another tourer (in a group of three) from the valley below. "I saw three men in one group and a fourth man apart from the group," the witness was later quoted. "All were in the path of the slide and about two thirds of the way up the mountain.... The man who was apart from the rest started to schuss down the slope to beat the slide. He attained a terrific momentum but struck some trees and was engulfed by the snow." The witness couldn't tell what had happened to the others.

In organizing the search, rescuers assumed that four individuals had been buried. Within an hour of notification, searchers came across a pair of broken skis identified as belonging to one of the victims. A day later, after no "missing" skiers were reported to authorities, the number of suspected victims was reduced to one.

The search took two days and ultimately involved over 200 volunteers drawn from Alta's two lodges, from personnel of the Salt Lake Air Base at Fort Douglas, and from C.C.C. camps stationed at Bountiful and Big Cottonwood Canyon. The search was painfully meticulous. Parallel trenches 8-9 feet in depth were dug in the 50-75 foot deep depositions of snow. Shovelfuls of snow had to be relayed to reach the surface. Long probing rods, thrust down from the floor of the trenches, failed to reach the ground. A Caterpillar tractor churned through the snow; portable generators powered searchlights through the night.

The victim's body, buried seven feet under the surface and located 75 feet downslope of the broken left ski, was found on the second day of the search. The victim's neck appeared to have been broken.

The aftermath of the tragedy left Forest Service and County officials pledging to "study" the possibility of posting dangerous areas, enlarging patrols to police winter sports grounds, and initiating educational programs "to help skiers detect dangerous snow conditions and slopes."

---

* Distilled and condensed from contemporaneous newspaper accounts.

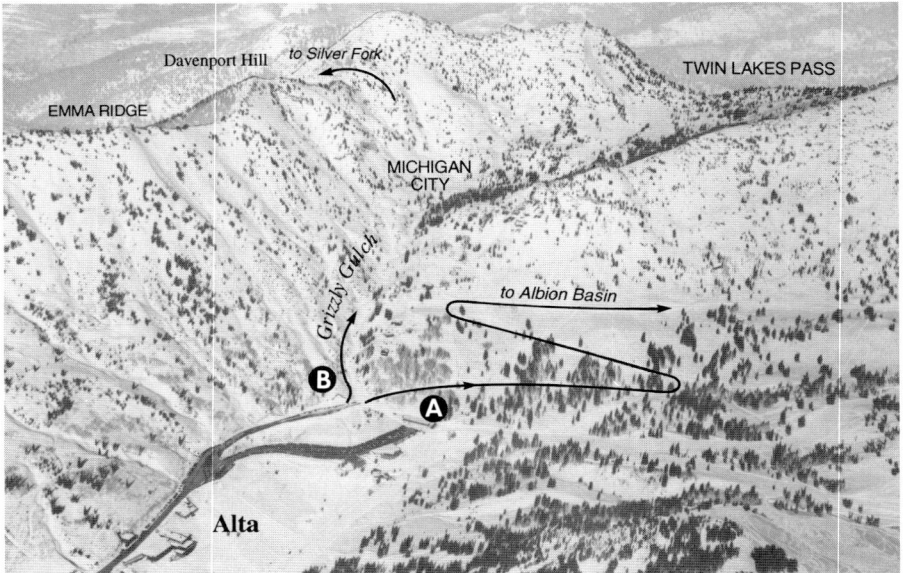

Figure 6.4   Alta's upper parking lot provides access to two excellent inter-mediate to advanced touring areas. Route (A) leads to Albion Basin and Catherine Pass. Route (B) leads up Grizzly Gulch to Twin Lakes Pass and adjacent areas. *Note:* Grizzly Gulch can also be approached from the Forest Service garage along an old mining road above the north side of the highway.

the commercial intrusion. The Catherine Pass trail is the most popular route between Alta and Brighton in both summer and winter. The tour from the Brighton side is described in Chapter 5.

Access to Albion Basin is gained along the Forest Service road that is a continuation of the Little Cottonwood highway. The road is plowed only to the base of the ski lifts, so the tour begins at the end of the parking lot. To reach Catherine Pass, it is best to follow the road only until it passes under the Albion ski lift, then bear left along the ski trail to the top of the chair lift. From there, a gradual traverse up and to the left leads into the drainage below Catherine Pass, as shown in Figures 6.4 and 6.5.

For about half a mile the climb is quite gentle. It then flattens in a large meadow and becomes steeper just below the pass. The south slope of Mount Tuscarora, which rises sharply on the left side of the touring route, should be avoided if the avalanche situation is at all dangerous. Total elevation gain from the parking lot to the pass is about 1400 vertical feet over three miles.

Advanced Tours from Catherine Pass. From Catherine Pass

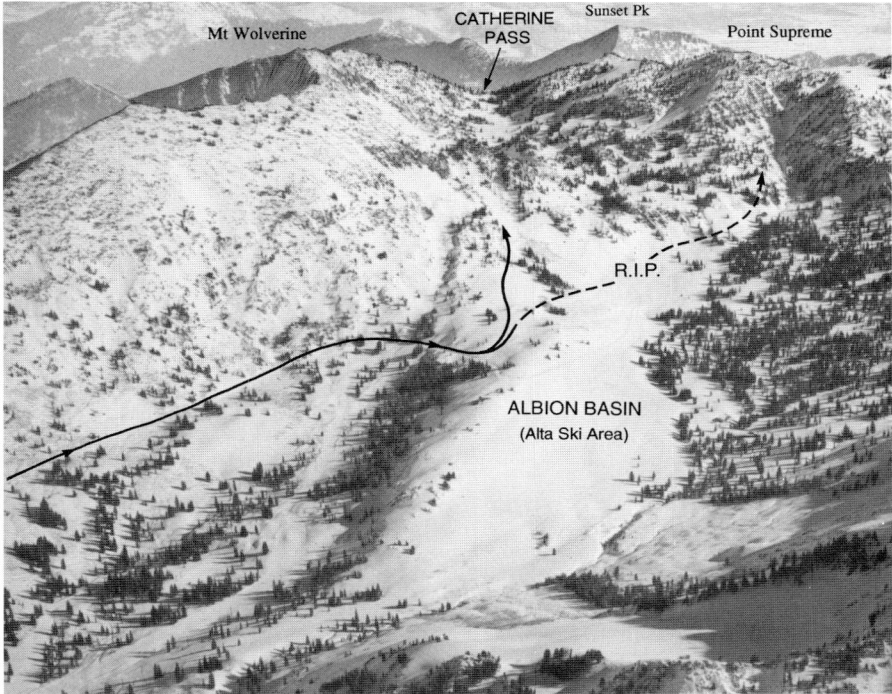

Figure 6.5   The Catherine Pass tour is one of the easiest intermediate ski tours in the Wasatch; it is also one of the most scenic.

the more adventurous and advanced tourer can follow the ridge north-ward or southward to some delightful summits. Descents can also be made into Big Cottonwood or American Fork Canyons, as well as to the town of Midway to the east.

Mount Tuscarora/Wolverine. Ascending the ridge *northward* 0.3 mile leads to the summit of Mount Tuscarora. Continuing along the ridge westward another 0.3 mile leads to the summit of 10,795 foot Mount Wolverine. The ridges are often corniced and have pockets of windblown snow depositions that can lead to avalanches. Skiers who choose these tour variants should be especially careful. See Chapter 5 for descent possibilities into Big Cottonwood Canyon.

Sunset Peak. A 0.2 mile climb *southward* along the ridge from Catherine Pass leads to a high prominence overlooking Albion Basin. Another 0.2 mile ridgeline traverse eastward leads to the 10,648 foot Sunset Peak.

Point Supreme (R.I.P.) From the high prominence south of Cather-ine Pass, it is possible to continue southwestward to the 10,595 foot

Point Supreme. Today, a saddle near the summit is occupied by the top terminal of Alta's Point Supreme ski lift.

Grizzly Gulch (End.) (H.P.A.)

During the late nineteenth and early twentieth centuries, Michigan City (located midway in Grizzly Gulch) was the scene of intense mining activity. Long after most Alta mines had been deserted by their disillusioned owners, Michigan City's mines continued to send ore down Cottonwood Canyon. In 1904 directors of Michigan City Mines undertook one of the more challenging transportation feats in local mining history. They constructed an aerial tramway to carry ore from Michigan City down to Tanner's Flat, a distance of about 4.5 miles. The tram carried thousands of tons of valuable cargo before it creaked to a halt in 1923. Many of the old wooden towers were dismantled and reused for the first Collins ski lift at Alta in 1938.

Two touring routes lead into Grizzly Gulch from Alta. The direct approach starts on the north side of the upper parking lot near the end of the plowed highway. The tour follows a narrow gully for about 0.8 mile until it widens into a broad flat area. This used to be the site of Michigan City. From there, a power line, which goes directly east, can be followed to Twin Lakes Pass, overlooking the Brighton ski area. (See Figure 6.4.) Total climb is 1.3 miles and 1200 vertical feet.

The second route is longer (1.9 miles and 1350 vertical feet), but its grade is more gradual and avoids the gully at the bottom. The ascent starts at the Forest Service garage at the west end of town and follows an old mining road that parallels the highway. This alternative intersects the first route near Michigan City Flat. Grizzly Gulch to Twin Lakes Pass is a scenic tour on gentle terrain, but there can be great avalanche danger from above during and after a storm, particularly the second route.

There are several popular descent alternatives. The most obvious return route is to retrace the ascent. Another is to ascend the ridge toward Mount Wolverine for 0.2 or 0.3 mile and ski down through the trees toward Alta. A third possibility is to cross Twin Lakes Pass into Brighton and to return via Catherine Pass. (See Chapter 5.)

Advanced Tours From Grizzly Gulch. Several excellent advanced ski tours are possible from Twin Lakes Pass or from the flats at Michigan City. Based on the number of complaints to the Forest Service, ski tours in this area may have a great potential for disruption by activities associated with helicopter skiing.

Mount Wolverine. It's relatively easy to ascend the ridge southward to the summit of Mount Wolverine. A small prominence, about half-way to the summit, can be used as a convenient stopping point for a descent back into Grizzly Gulch. It's also possible to continue ridge hopping to the summit of Wolverine and beyond.

Honeycomb Cliffs. Climbing the ridge northward from Twin Lakes Pass leads one to the crest of the Honeycomb Cliffs area that overlooks Brighton and Honeycomb Fork. The ascent is quite steep and avalanche-prone, but the views from the summit are breathtaking.

Silver Fork Divide. From Twin Lakes Pass one can traverse to the pass between Grizzly Gulch and the east branch of Silver Fork. The route is generally straightforward, since Twin Lakes Pass and the divide are at about the same elevation. The traverse crosses some serious avalanche slopes, so care should be exercised at all times. See Chapter 5 for descent possibilities into Silver Fork.

Davenport Hill. Davenport Hill is a high prominence located a short distance west along the ridge from the Silver Fork Divide. The hill can be climbed or bypassed (along the Alta side) to place the tourer at the crest of the west branch of Silver Fork. Descent options into Big Cottonwood are described in Chapter 5.

Emma Ridge. The 1.3-mile long ridge between Davenport Hill and Flagstaff Mountain is known as Emma Ridge. It was named after the notorious Emma Mine that was located on the hillside above Alta. As is evident from Figures 6.4 and 6.6 the ridge contains numerous rock outcroppings, steep and narrow chutes, and plenty of opportunities for mountain mishaps. Extreme care should be exercised in attempting this traverse or in descending any of the avalanche-prone snowslopes and gullies back to Alta.

TOURS FROM CENTRAL ALTA

The Central Alta trailhead, located between the Forest Service garage and the Shallow Shaft Restaurant (across the road from Alta Lodge) is one of the most significant touring trailheads in the Wasatch. It serves as access to Cardiff Pass, Flagstaff Mountain, Emma Ridge, Mount Superior, and to several superb ski tours in Big Cottonwood Canyon.

Cardiff Pass

One cannot overstate the importance of Cardiff Pass to Alta-oriented ski tours. This pass is the starting point for several superb Big Cottonwood

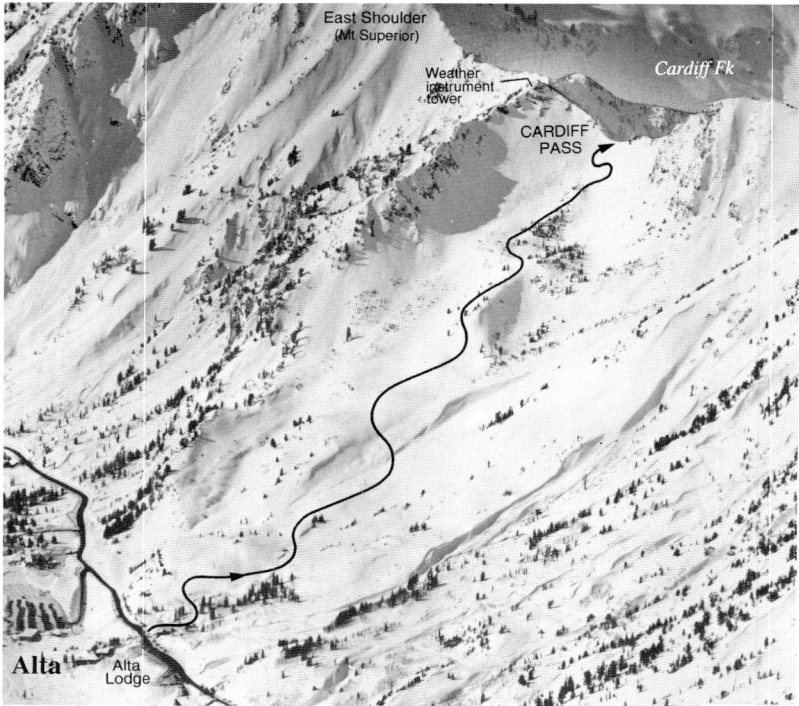

East Shoulder
(Mt Superior)

Weather
instrument
tower

Cardiff Fk

CARDIFF
PASS

Alta

Alta
Lodge

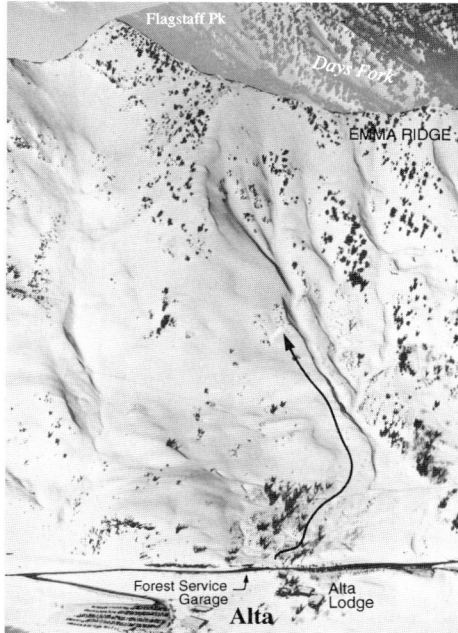

Flagstaff Pk

Days Fork

EMMA RIDGE

Forest Service
Garage

Alta
Lodge

Alta

trips, such as Cardiff Fork, Mineral Fork, and Lake Blanche. Many people like to climb to the pass just to enjoy the view and then ski back to Alta. Although the south-facing snow is not always appreciated by the average tourer, a number of Cardiff Pass connoisseurs delight in skiing it under any and all conditions. The pass is also a favorite among a growing number of snowboarders.

Some of the early miners reportedly used a different method of transportation down from their workings near Cardiff Pass. The *Alta Independent* described one such descent in 1873:

> "This morning, the snow being very hard, a man mounted his steed, a large shovel, and started to come down to the city. He came at a rate of 50 miles an hour for about 2000 feet when he found it impossible to keep his seat, and each was trying to beat the other to town. The shovel came on as gracefully as the soaring of an eagle; while the movements of the man resembled the gracefulness of a baby elephant; the acts he went through would make the most perfect acrobat feel the blush of shame in a professional line. He landed at the foot of the mountain unhurt, but considerably paled from exertion of the race."

The ascent to Cardiff Pass (illustrated in the top portion of Figure 6.6) commences at the Forest Service garage, follows a jeep road past the two Forest Service guard cabins to the gun tower used for avalanche control. From there, an upward and northwesterly traverse (along another jeep road) leads to a power line. This power line should be followed all the way to the pass, since it stays on a relatively avalanche-free secondary ridge. Many tourers erroneously steer for the open slopes west of the wires, thus exposing themselves to the serious avalanche threat illustrated in the avalanche chapter of Volume 1. Total distance to Cardiff Pass is about a mile with a 1400 foot elevation gain.

Figure 6.6 (Opposite page.) The *Central Alta* trailhead. *Top photo:* The ascent from Alta to Cardiff Pass is best accomplished by following the power line that was laid out to avoid avalanche slopes that threaten it from either side. *Bottom photo:* The ridge above the Alta Lodge is the most direct route to the summit of Flagstaff Mountain and to Days Fork in Big Cottonwood Canyon. The gullies and slopes on either side of the ridge are known for their ferocious avalanches (see page 120 in Volume 1). Even the ridge has been known to slide.

Flagstaff Mountain

Flagstaff Mountain is a popular destination among snowboarders, as well as lodge and lift employees who live in Alta. During springtime it's an excellent morning tour for taking advantage of crystalline corn snow. The route, depicted in the bottom portion of Figure 6.6, is very straightforward: simply follow the ridge up from the Forest Service garage trailhead.

While the route is straightforward, it is not free of hazards. The gullies on the east side of the ridge avalanche frequently, and are responsible for repeatedly thrusting Alta in the news. The steep, sparsely timbered slopes west of the ridge also have a history of avalanches. On February 24, 1979, a large avalanche released from this area, swept down the gully just west of the ranger stations, crossed the highway, and terminated in the open area between the Gold Miners Daughter parking lot and the Alta/Peruvian Lodge to its west. While most of the snow mass passed harmlessly along the side of the building, part of it stacked against the lodge two stories deep.

The ridge to Flagstaff Mountain is a south-facing slope, so it may stabilize within a few days of a snowstorm. In the cold, snowy, and windy parts of winter, however, great care should be exercised on slopes as open and exposed as this ridge. Distance from Alta to the southern summit of Flagstaff Mountain is 1.4 miles; elevation gain is 2000 feet.

Mount Superior

From the day the first photographs were taken of Alta during the late 1800's, the peak known as Mount Superior has always served as a spectacular backdrop to the small community. As the Rock of Gibraltar guards the entrance of the Mediterranean Sea, Mount Superior has stood sentinel for more than a century over the mines and morals of upper Little Cottonwood Canyon.

"When miners sin," a saying goes, "the snow slides." Rarely a week passed during the mining era when the area's bordels, bars, and breweries had not been overrun by Superior's devastating snowslides. As sins related to mining have given way to those associated with skiing, Mount Superior has continued to maintain a vigilant eye over the newly developing wintersports Mecca. Almost legend is "Valerie's Climax," an early 1970's avalanche that released from Superior's south shoulder to overturn a lodge employee's trailer.

Mount Superior played a superprominent role during the years of

Figure 6.7   *Top:* Scott Phillips contemplates the steep slopes of Mount Superior. *Bottom:* Although the south face of Superior can be skied directly from the summit, it is more commonly descended along the open slopes beneath its east shoulder.

Alta's emergence as the "mother nest" of North American powder skiing. Nearly every advertisement extolling Alta's snow included a photo of its arctic-like summit. Superior's photographic renown reached its zenith when it appeared on the cover of *Colorado* magazine as a backdrop to figure skater Peggy Fleming and *Denver's* bid to host a winter Olympics.

Burdened by heavy and cumbersome equipment, ski tourers of the 1920's gave little thought to ascending Superior's summit. Just getting to its base was a three-day undertaking! Some seventy years later, hot-doggers and shredders in colorful day-glow outfits descend its south face with such regularity that inclusion of possible routes in this book is warranted.

Ascent Routes. Two ascent routes (with several variations) provide *advanced* touring access to Mount Superior from Alta.

Cardiff Pass Route. The most common Mount Superior ascent route starts at the Forest Service garage, proceeds to Cardiff Pass, then continues either along the ridge or beneath it to the summit. The various routes from Cardiff Pass to the summit are clearly illustrated in the Lake Blanche tour description in Chapter 5.

East Shoulder Route. This ascent route is utilized only in late spring, *when all danger of avalanche has disappeared.* Pictured in the bottom photo of Figure 6.7, the route goes almost straight up the east shoulder of Superior to the base of the Black Knob, then follows the east ridge to the summit. Ascent is short and steep, 2700 vertical feet over a distance of only 1.8 miles.

Descent. *Only the most expert of skiers should attempt these descents; they should be done only after all avalanche and rockfall activity has ceased.*

East Shoulder. The most straightforward of the Mount Superior descent routes follows the east shoulder ascent route. In skiing the steep slopes below the Black Knob, it's important to avoid drifting too far to the east. A hiker, a few years back, was killed when he slipped on the steep snowslope and plunged over the cliffband beneath.

Direct South Face. Although the south face of Superior contains several lethal cliffbands, a knowledgeable expert skier can plan a descent that avoids them. Slope conditions, obviously, vary considerably throughout the skiing season. More cliffbands are present early in the season when the snowpack is shallow. The bottom portion of Figure 6.7, taken during spring, may suggest some descent possibilities available when considerable snow has accumulated.

Figure 6.8 The north wall of Little Cottonwood Canyon, showing Tanners Gulch and the dramatic peaks along the ridge.

North Wall of Little Cottonwood

The north wall of Little Cottonwood west of Mount Superior is one of the most avalanche-prone areas in the country. Snow accumulation pockets along its crest are steep and plentiful. Avalanches that release from these slopes funnel into narrow ravines or gullies before reaching the canyon's highway. Figure 6.8 illustrates the lethal nature of the north wall located beneath Twin and Dromedary peaks.

Tanners Gulch. Tanners is the largest of the gulches that descend from the crest. During late spring and summer, *after all snowslide (and freeze-thaw rockfall) activity has ceased,* it offers some excellent hard-snow climbing and skiing.

WHITE PINE TRAILHEAD

Little Cottonwood Canyon has a great deal of very difficult skiing terrain, all the way from Alta to Bells Canyon. The high cirques in all of the side canyons are extremely steep with little vegetation to hold the snow in place. Touring in these areas should only be done with great caution. It is usually best to save these tours until late in the winter, after the cold snowy season has passed. The lower parts of White Pine and Red Pine gulches contain the only remaining touring terrain suitable for intermediates in the part of Little Cottonwood below the commercial ski areas.

The White Pine trailhead in Little Cottonwood Canyon is probably the most used wilderness trailhead in the Wasatch. In the mid-1960's it consisted of a slightly wide shoulder along the highway and four rickety logs for crossing Little Cottonwood Creek. Today, a large paved parking lot greets hikers and tourers wishing to enter the Lone Peak Wilderness, and the stream is crossed on a sturdy footbridge. From the lot's overfull condition every weekend, it's apparent that nearly every backcountry recreationist in Salt Lake Valley uses it at one time or another.

The White Pine trailhead is located along the south side of Little Cottonwood Canyon, about five miles upcanyon from the large electronic informational sign at its mouth. The trailhead accesses several excellent touring areas near and within the Lone Peak Wilderness. Ski tours to be described in this section are: White Pine, Red Pine, Maybird, and Hogum gulches. Side routes to several popular summits will also be described.

White Pine Gulch (End.) (H.P.A.)

White Pine has been a canyon of many uses. At one time it was a major source of Engleman spruce, from which it gained its name. The lumber was used by miners in Little Cottonwood Canyon and by builders in Salt Lake Valley. Later, a road and a dam were built there as a part of Salt Lake's water storage program. In 1959 this canyon was the scene of one of the largest and most destructive avalanches to occur in the Wasatch Mountains for many years. Tree stumps ten feet high and three feet in diameter still stand as grim reminders of the incredible power that can be generated by a wave of moving snow.

Since Snowbird Resort arrived on the scene in the early 1970's, White Pine has become one of the more controversial canyons in the Wasatch. The public debate is centered over whether or not it should be added to the Snowbird Ski Area. The original Lone Peak Wilderness proposal to include White Pine Gulch within Lone Peak Wilderness was scuttled by Snowbird officials and a Utah congressional delegation that was exceptionally sympathetic to the corporation's wishes.

The Salt Lake County canyon master plan allocates White Pine to low impact backcountry recreational uses. But ski area owner Dick Bass still covets the canyon. If the developers are successful in annexing White Pine, another superb intermediate touring and hiking area will be spoiled for local backcountry users. Salt Lake Valley residents have already lost about half of the beginner and intermediate terrain that was available in Big and Little Cottonwood canyons in the early 1970's. Will the Californians—and Texans!—win again?

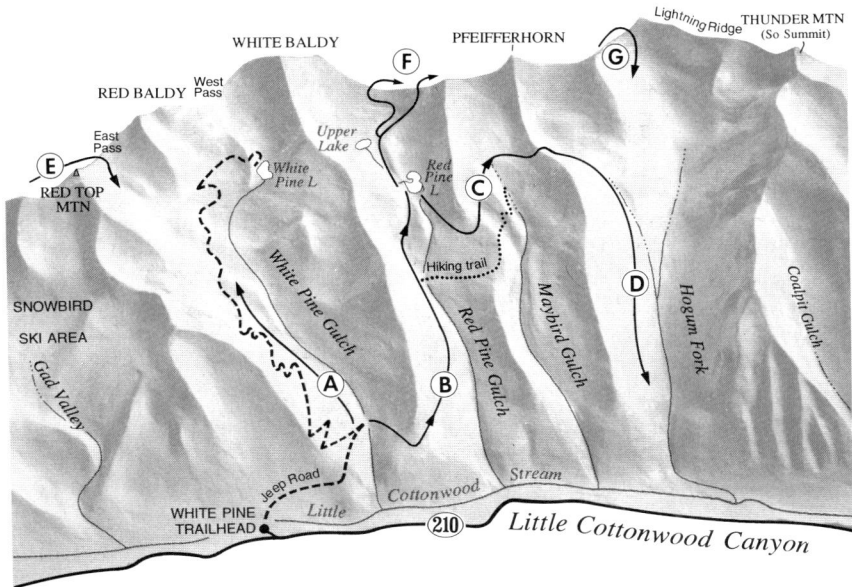

Figure 6.9   The White Pine Trailhead accesses seven major drainages. Routes discussed in this section include: (A) White Pine, (B) Red Pine, (C) Maybird, and (D) Hogum gulches. Route (E) enters upper White Pine Gulch from Alta. Routes (F) ascend the Pfeifferhorn, and (G) enters upper Hogum Gulch after traversing behind the Pfeifferhorn.

Most of White Pine's terrain is delightful for intermediate touring. Except for the lower 800 feet and the upper cirques, the canyon is not very steep. The easiest route to White Pine Lake follows a jeep road all the way from the bottom. (See in Figures 6.9 and 6.10.) The tour starts at the trailhead, crosses the footbridge, and follows the jeep road as it climbs gently westward from there. About 0.9 mile from the trailhead, the road bends sharply to the left, and a trail branches to the right. (The hiking and touring route to Red Pine Gulch follows the right trail across White Pine's stream.) After the sharp bend to the left, the jeep road switches back and forth and then levels off for the next 1.2 miles. It then continues along the left side of the canyon and passes several large avalanche runout zones clearly visible in Figure 6.10. Close examination of Figure 6.11 reveals that the final approach to White Pine Lake is also exposed to several major slide paths that should be avoided under uncertain snow conditions. The total climb along the road is 2400 feet over about five miles.

Upper White Pine from Alta. An interesting alternative for touring White Pine Canyon is to access it from the top by way of

Figure 6.10   Lower White Pine is one of the most popular intermediate touring areas in Little Cottonwood. Its upper bowls, which can be reached from American Fork Canyon (East Pass and West Pass), have some extremely challenging *and hazardous* terrain.

American Fork Canyon. This option, because it involves a very long car shuttle, is rarely exercised. A more practical—and elevation advantageous and scenic—option involves entering the top of American Fork Canyon *from Alta*, then traversing three upper basins of American Fork Canyon to intercept the "east pass" of White Pine Gulch shown in Figure 6.11. While at first blush this tour appears to be prohibitively long and arduous, many *advanced tourers* find the route quite delightful and rewarding. A variety of sub-options are described for tourers of different moral suasions.

The Fundamentalist Route. This option is de rigueur for chaste tourers who reject all forms of ski lifts and traffic jams. It commences early in the morning (before resort traffic) at the base of Alta's Collins Gulch or Albion Basin. In either case the route follows ski runs to the top of the Albion Basin/American Fork Canyon divide. From there,

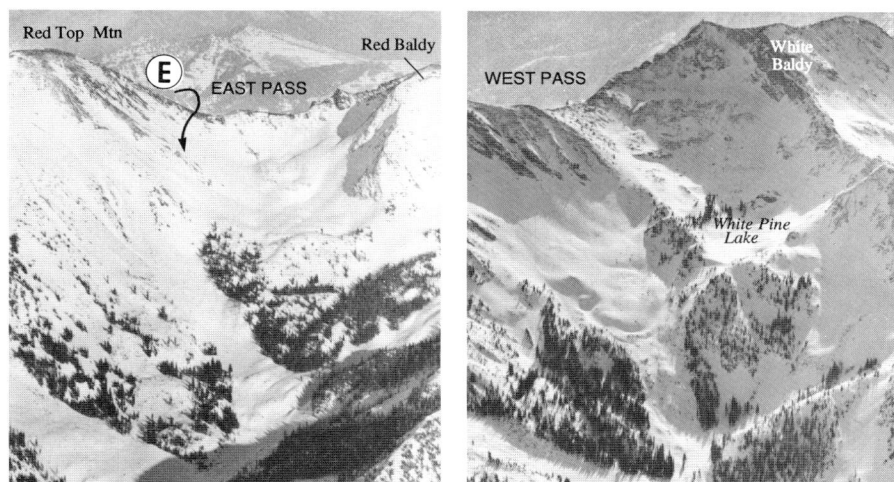

Figure 6.11   The upper basins of White Pine Gulch contain numerous major avalanche paths that should be avoided during periods of uncertain snow conditions. Route (E) from Alta enters White Pine Gulch at the "east pass." The "west pass" is used to access Silver Glance Lake and Silver Fork in the American Fork drainage.

Mineral Basin (the top of American Fork Canyon) is traversed to a high pass leading into Mary Ellen Gulch, which is ascended to a high ridge separating it from the Silver Fork drainage. A gently-descending traverse of upper Silver Fork leads to the east pass of White Pine.[2]

The Revisionist Option. This route is for tourers who have modified their touring morals to accommodate access by ski lift. Alta's lifts are most commonly used to transport those tourers to the Albion/American Fork ridge. Late in spring, some skiers ascend the northeast ridge of American Fork Twins directly from Snowbird.

The La Dolce Vita Alternative. This option is common to a very exclusive group of self-indulgent, extravagant, and hedonistic recreationists known as helicopter skiers.

Descent. A tourer who ventures into White Pine Gulch from the top is advised not to linger on the headwall in the upper cirque. Only expert fall-line skiers should attempt a descent as steep as this.[3] It is not an area for long traverses. The run to Little Cottonwood Creek from East Pass is 3100 vertical feet over about five miles.

---

[2] Ski tours in the drainages and upper basins of American Fork Canyon will be described in detail in Volume 3 of *Wasatch Tours*.

[3] A skier was killed here on April 29, 1993, when he lost control of his skis on the frozen morning snow. He slid and tumbled 1500 vertical feet to the basin below.

Figure 6.12   Red Pine Gulch provides access for many advanced and super tours, including Maybird, Hogum, Coalpit, Bells, Dry Creek, and American Fork. It is also a popular intermediate skiing area in its own right.

Red Pine Gulch

Like its easterly neighbor, Red Pine Gulch has excellent intermediate terrain below the upper cirque, but the top 800 feet should be saved for the experts. Red Pine Lake, with its exquisite alpine setting, is a popular destination for hikers in the summertime and backcountry skiers in the winter.

The Red Pine Lake tour, shown in Figures 6.10 and 6.12, commences at the White Pine trailhead and proceeds across the bridge over Little Cottonwood Creek and along the White Pine jeep road for 0.9 mile. The easiest way into Red Pine is to bear right where the White Pine road bends sharply to the left. After crossing the White Pine stream, the trail traverses northwestwardly around the White Pine/Red Pine ridge. From a small plateau on the ridge, the trail angles upward along the steep west-facing (and avalanche-prone) slopes of Red Pine Gulch. For the next 1.3 miles the trail stays on the west side, high above the stream bed. After climbing through a grove of aspens, the touring route intersects the stream near a small mine dump.

Two excellent routes lead from the mine dump to Red Pine Lake. The first one continues directly south along the open slopes on the east side of the canyon. The other route drifts to the right and climbs through Douglas fir trees (after which this canyon was named) to a knoll overlooking the lake. The possibilities are obvious in Figure 6.13, a closeup of the upper bowls. White Pine trailhead to Red Pine Lake is 3.3 miles with 2000 feet of elevation gain.

A number of touring options are available at Red Pine Lake. Anyone wanting more vertical can climb through the trees above the lake that are visible in the photo. (The avalanche path west of the trees should be avoided.) An ascent of only 400 feet gets one to upper Red Pine Lake. The descent back to the lower lake should also be in the protection of the trees.

Several advanced and ski mountaineering options become possible from the upper lake, as shown in Figure 6.13. The most popular alternative is to follow a spur ridge to the dividing ridge between Little Cottonwood and Alpine's Dry Creek. It is also possible to climb to a pass into Dry Creek or to the summit ridge of White Baldy. Route *(C)* continues into Maybird Gulch, to be described in the next section.

Descent. At least three alternatives exist for returning to the highway from Red Pine Lake. The simplest is to retrace the upward route all the way to the car. If more powder skiing is desired, the west side of the canyon is often better. A simple traverse from the lake, without loss of too much elevation, will lead to good skiing through the trees. There are places all along the canyon where an intermediate can ski down to the stream and then traverse back to the trail, but care should be taken since some of these slopes are quite steep and heavily wooded. Descending too far on the west side may result in a long climb back to the White Pine trailhead.

The final descent route to be described is the ridge between Red Pine and Maybird. The upper section has very large, widely-spaced fir trees and is delightful skiing terrain. About a third of the way down to the highway, it is best to bear right and ski on the east-facing slopes near the ridge. The lower end of this ridge is very steep, so one may want to drop into the bottom of Red Pine at some point.

The tour isn't over at the base of the gulch. There is no bridge, so crossing Little Cottonwood Creek can be a challenging proposition.

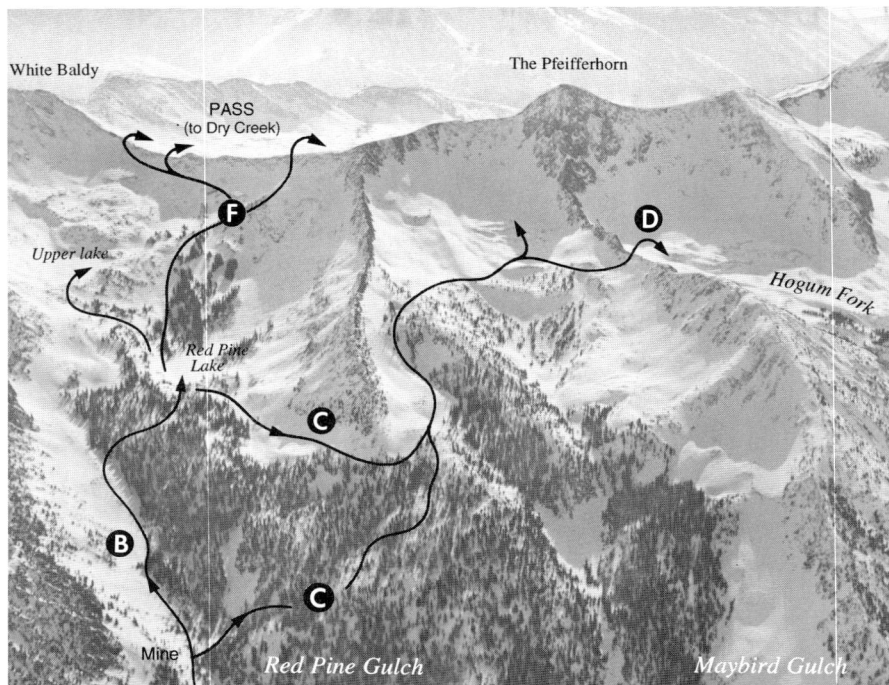

Figure 6.13   The upper basins of Red Pine and Maybird gulches. Three routes (F) ascend to the Red Pine/Dry Creek divide. Routes (C) go from Red Pine to Maybird Gulch, and (D) leads into upper Hogum Fork.

After crossing over (or wading) the stream, a short climb leads to the highway. It may be necessary to walk or hitchhike back to the trailhead; a shuttle car can't be parked at Red Pine because it is in the path of the Tanners Gulch avalanche. Descent from the lower lake to the bottom of Red Pine Gulch is 2400 feet over 2.4 miles.

Maybird Gulch

The canyons west of Red Pine are much less heavily used than the areas already described in this section. Most of them show little effect of man's presence, and for good reason. Their accessibility, slope, complexity of terrain, and potential for avalanches require more stamina, knowledge of terrain, and skiing ability than the others. Their lower sections are steep and narrow gullies, so entry must be from the top. This can involve a long hike. To get to upper Hogum Fork, for example, one must start at the bottom of White Pine, traverse up and across Red Pine and Maybird, and then climb into Hogum.

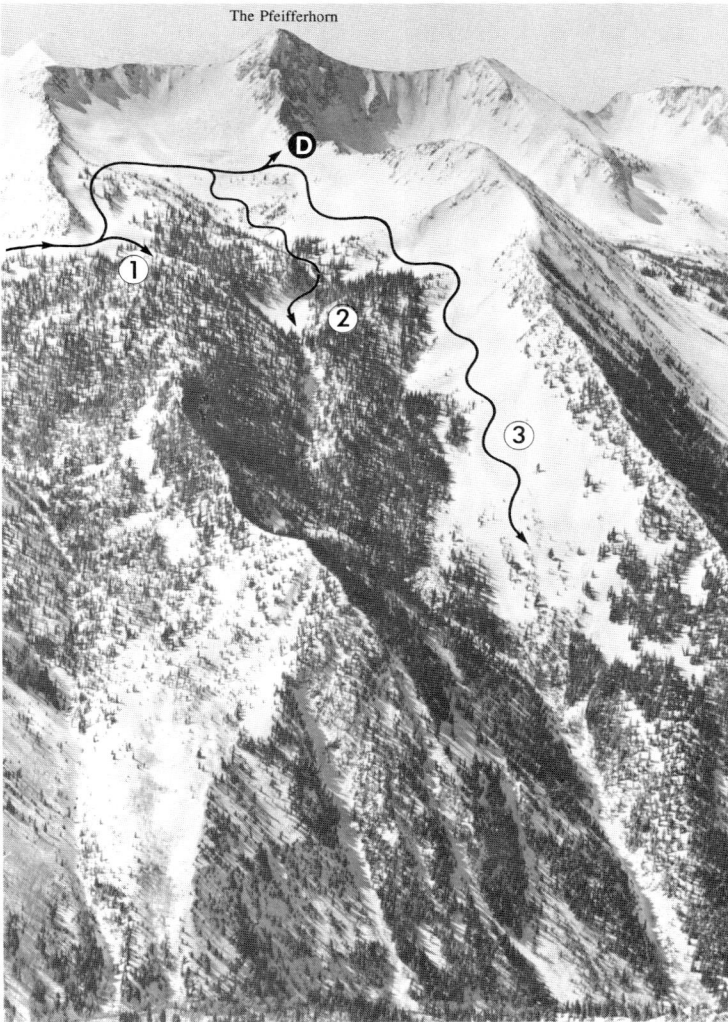

Figure 6.14   The lower part of Maybird Gulch is a narrow, avalanche-prone ravine with wooded and rocky sides. The Maybird stream is known to undercut the snowpack in several places. Extreme care should be exercised in this area at all times of the year.

With the spectacular Pfeifferhorn massif rising at its head, upper Maybird is one of the most scenic areas in the Wasatch. This is an ideal spot for sunshine and camera. The climb into Maybird from Red Pine is easy enough for an intermediate to tour over for picture taking and then return the same way. Only expert skiers should attempt the lower part of the gulch.

Two popular routes, labeled *(C)* in Figure 6.13, lead into Maybird. One possibility is to start ascending the west side of Red Pine Canyon from the mine dump described in the Red Pine section. From the top of the first steep pitch, simply traverse up through the firs into the Maybird drainage. The second route is from Red Pine Lake. Ski down and to the left (west), then round the Red Pine/Maybird spur ridge prominently visible in the photo. From the ridge, a short climb through sparsely wooded terrain takes the tourer to a view that is worth the effort. (See the chapter opening photo.) The distance from the White Pine trailhead is four miles with 2200 feet of elevation gain.

Descent. The upper cirque of Maybird Gulch offers three options for the descent. The first, *(1)* in Figure 6.14, is to ski directly into the main stream bed. Most of the run into Little Cottonwood Canyon is in a deep ravine, bordered on both sides by extremely steep slopes and cliff bands. The ravine is not a good place to be when avalanche conditions are a concern. Another potential danger along the stream bed is the presence of holes in the snow which are created by the water flowing underneath. Descent is 3000 feet over 2.5 miles.

The second and third descent options, *(2)* and *(3)* in the photo, involve traversing higher into the western reaches of the upper basin. The broad open slope directly below the Maybird/Hogum ridge can be skied for nearly the entire length of the gulch. This slope may be safer than some of the others, but it is exposed to wind and may not be as enjoyable for the powder connoisseur. At the end of this area, it becomes necessary to drop into the main Maybird ravine. This is accomplished by descending a very narrow and steep couloir visible, but not identified, in the photo. Tourers should scout the area in summer to determine the best descent route into the bottom gully.

There is no bridge over Little Cottonwood Creek at the bottom of Maybird, so the crossing may prove interesting. (See Figure 3.4 in Volume 1.) If a shuttle car has been arranged, the tour is completed with a short and brushy climb from the creek to the highway.

The Pfeifferhorn

A winter ascent of the Pfeifferhorn is more a mountaineering trip than a ski tour. We include it in this book because it has become such a popular outing. Despite its many spectacular rocky faces and steep snowy couloirs, the peak can be climbed by a strong tourer, even if he has limited mountaineering experience.

Three routes are commonly used to reach the 11,326 foot summit

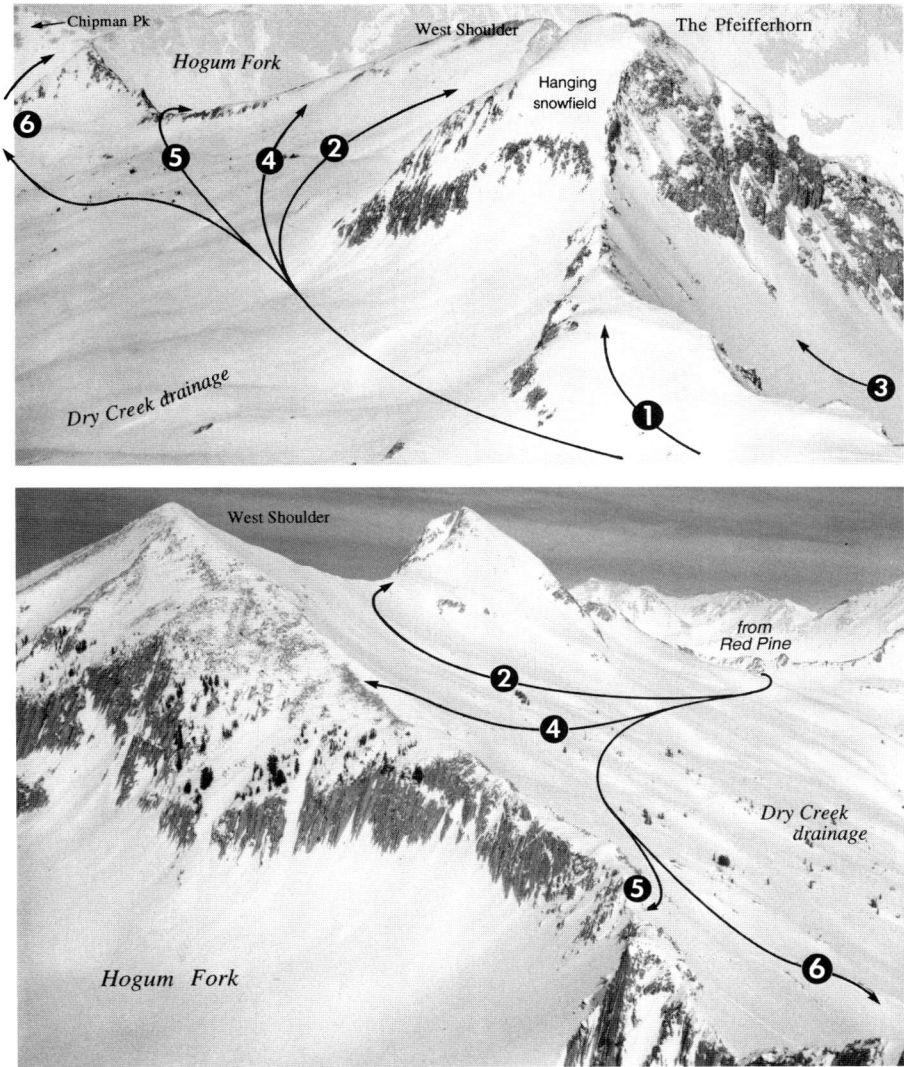

Figure 6.15   The Pfeifferhorn. The steep and rocky east ridge (1), which commences at the Red Pine/Dry Creek divide above Red Pine Lake, is the most commonly used ascent route to the summit. The "hanging snowfield" is avalanche-prone. Route (2) leads to the summit from the south and west, and (3) joins the east ridge from Maybird Gulch. Routes (4) and (5) go to the Dry Creek/Hogum Fork ridge, while route (6) leads to Chipman Peak, Lightning Ridge, and the south summit of Thunder Mountain.

from upper Red Pine Lake. The most direct and most frequently attempted approach is along the east ridge. Less common, but easier and perhaps somewhat safer, is the west ridge. Direct ascents are possible on the headwall of Maybird Gulch. These routes are labeled *(1)*, *(2)*, and *(3)*, respectively, in the upper portion of Figure 6.15. Both ridge alternatives require an ascent to the crest of Red Pine Gulch. This is an extremely exposed climb, as shown in Figure 6.13, and great caution must be exercised. The usual route is the prominent secondary ridge between the upper and lower lakes in Red Pine. Hazardous avalanche paths are found on each side of this ridge, so departure from the route is not advisable. It may be necessary to remove skis in order to negotiate the last few feet to the top, since cornices sometimes form in this area that overhang into Red Pine, and the snow beneath them may be wind packed and icy.

Route 1. The direct route to the top of the Pfeifferhorn is along the east ridge as illustrated in the photograph. Skis are usually removed before attempting the last part of the ridge and the final ascent to the summit. Portions of the summit ridge are narrow and rocky, and can cause some difficulties for someone on skis. Good soles on the ski boots are a requirement for this climb. The snowfield below the summit is an obvious avalanche area and should be skirted along the right flank close to the ridge overlooking Maybird Gulch. Total climb from the bottom of White Pine is 3700 feet and 5.3 miles.

Route 2. The second alternative is for the tourer who is not comfortable climbing the snowfield near the summit. This route drops down into Dry Creek Canyon, which borders the Pfeifferhorn to the south, and makes a wide loop around the base of the peak. Skis should be removed at the ridge overlooking Hogum Fork. The final ascent to the summit is along its west ridge, which is not as steep and imposing as the previously described route. The distance for this climb is six miles.

Route 3. This route originates in Maybird Gulch, ascends the steep headwall to the Pfeifferhorn's east ridge, and continues to the summit as route *(1)*. The steep headwall faces north and northeast and is quite avalanche-prone; it can also be windpacked and ice-crusted.

Descent. The obvious way down after ascending the Pfeifferhorn is to retrace the route followed on the way up. This means skiing (or walking) down into Red Pine. An alternative is to go down the Dry Creek drainage to the town of Alpine. The snow on the south-facing slopes is often less than spectacular, snowmobiles may be encountered at lower elevations, and the car shuttle is horrendous, but the trip has its own subtle rewards. More discussion of touring opportunities in Dry Creek will be found in the third volume of *Wasatch Tours*.

Figure 6.16   Hogum Fork is the largest side canyon in Little Cottonwood Canyon. Two routes access its upper basins. The "basic" route (D) approaches from Maybird Gulch; the "backside" route passes through upper Red Pine Gulch and traverses the Pfeifferhorn's south side.

Hogum Fork

Hogum Fork, one of the largest drainages in Little Cottonwood, has three upper cirques which are headed by the Pfeifferhorn, Lightning Ridge, and Thunder Mountain. Like Maybird, it is open at the top with a steep narrow gully at the lower end. Here the similarity ends. Hogum has more terrain, is less accessible, has greater avalanche hazard, and is steeper and trickier to negotiate at the bottom. Viewed from the Little Cottonwood highway, the bottom part of Hogum appears to be unskiable.

Two routes, both of which start at the White Pine trailhead, access the upper basins of Hogum. The "basic" route starts at White Pine, traverses into Red Pine, then goes into Maybird. (See *(D)* in Figures 6.13 and 6.16.) Just below the Pfeifferhorn there is a depression along the Maybird/Hogum ridge that is easily reached from the Maybird side. Caution is urged in this area; it should not be attempted unless the snow is extremely stable. Descent into Hogum is by way of a rock gully that may or may not be filled with snow. Sometimes it may be filled with ice! The distance from the bottom of White Pine to the Hogum ridge is 4.4 miles and 2700 vertical feet. The "backside" route is described in the Pfeifferhorn section and labeled *(5)* in Figure 6.15.

The open terrain in upper Hogum Fork always appears inviting, but its broad treeless expanse is very exposed to wind and sun. The skiing may vary from delightful powder turns through open cirques and scattered trees, to flailing through breakable crust and wind-packed snow. Whatever delights are found in upper Hogum will be replaced by frustration in the lower section. The steep rocky terrain is very brushy in places, and the snow at the bottom is often marginal due to its low elevation. The crossing of Little Cottonwood Creek can also be traumatic. The descent is 3800 feet over 3.4 miles.

To anyone undertaking this tour, we recommend a careful examination of Figure 6.17 to choose a route down the lower section. Good luck!

Hogum Summits and "Supertours"

The upper cirques of Hogum Fork are ringed by some of the most spectacular summits in the Wasatch. The Pfeifferhorn and its west shoulder stand at the eastern extreme of Hogum. Chipman Peak—offset slightly south of the ridgeline—dominates the central cirque. The south walls of the central and northern cirques constitute Lightning Ridge. The south summit of Thunder Mountain stands at the head of Hogum's northern basin. All the summits and ridgecrests are at or above 11,000 feet in elevation and well above timberline. All the prominences play an important role in a category of ski tours best described as "supertours," which require an extremely high level of physical strength and stamina, as well as advanced skiing and mountaineering skills. Because the supertours involve descents into Bells Canyon, detailed descriptions are in the Bells Canyon section of Chapter 7.

Routes to the high spots around‏Hogum Fork, are described here, although not in great detail. It is assumed that anyone attempting one of these summits will need only a rough outline and some good photographs. Two such photographs, each giving a different perspective of upper Hogum, appear in Figure 6.18.

Thunder Mountain (South Summit). The south summit of Thunder Mountain is the longest *practical* ski tour in the drainages of Little Cottonwood Canyon. Chipman Peak and Lightning Ridge are high spots along its complicated route. The "standard" ski tours to

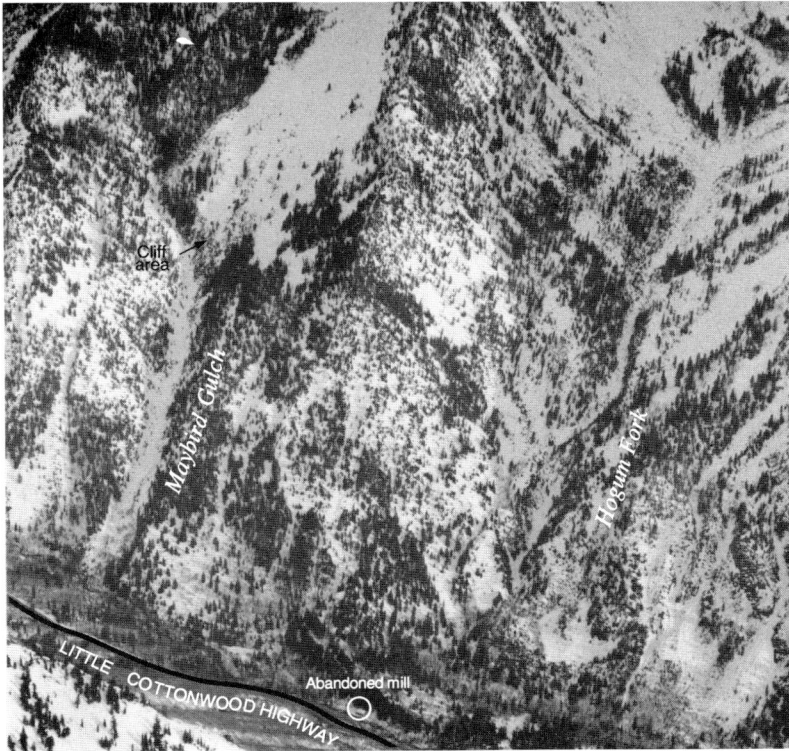

Figure 6.17   Lower Maybird and Hogum gulches. The bottom of Hogum Fork is steep, narrow, brushy, and rocky. With some luck, a route to and across the stream can be found. Maybird is little better.

Thunder Mountain commence from the White Pine trailhead and ascend into upper Red Pine. At that point, tourers have three options. The "northern route" traverses around the north side of the Pfeifferhorn; two "southern routes" go around the other side of the mountain.

The Northern Route. This alternative, labeled *(A)* in Figure 6.18, traverses the Pfeifferhorn along its north side (via the Maybird/Hogum ridge crossing), ascends the south end of Lightning Ridge via a steep, avalanche-prone couloir, and traverses Lightning Ridge to the summit of Thunder Mountain. Ascent of the couloir is the most dangerous part of this option.

From the top of the couloir a several hundred yard traverse along the ridge (sometimes rocky) leads to a low saddle between Lightning Ridge and Chipman Peak. Chipman Peak is easily ascended from here. The remainder of the tour to Thunder Mountain is a gently upward

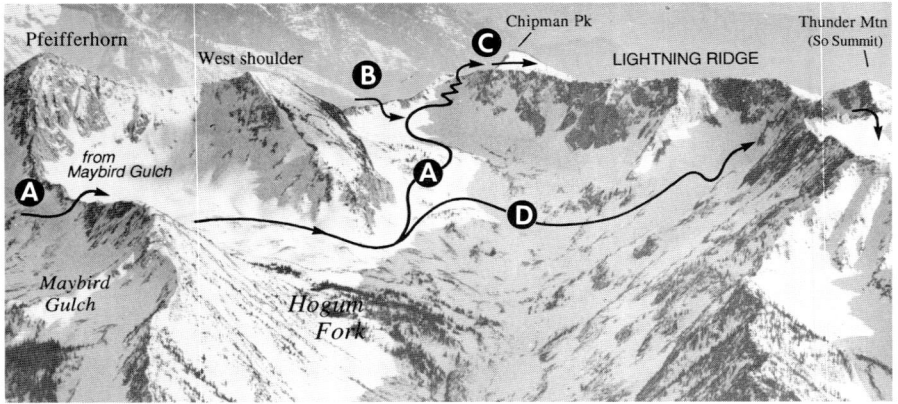

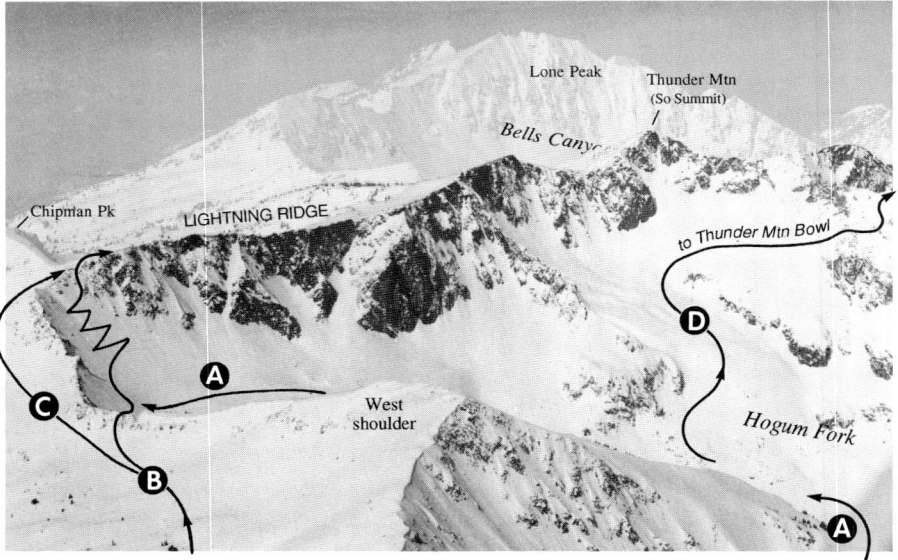

Figure 6.18   Hogum Fork's various summits and ridgelines are used for access to Bells Canyon, to be described in the next chapter. Routes (A), (B), and (C) are variants of the "standard route" to Chipman Peak, Lightning Ridge, south summit of Thunder Mountain, and Bells Canyon. Route (D) is a very steep "direct approach" into Bells Canyon's Thunder Mountain Bowl.

traverse of Lightning Ridge. The temptation to descend (or even to remain level) along this traverse should be avoided, as it will lead to a cul-de-sac created by Lake Hardy. From the highest point reached along Lightning Ridge, it becomes necessary to descend a few hundred feet to a saddle before continuing up the ridge to the summit of Thunder Mountain.

The main disadvantage of this tour is its frequent exposure to Hogum

Fork's avalanche paths. Ascent from the White Pine trailhead to Thunder Mountain is almost eight miles, with over 3000 vertical feet of climbing.

The Southern Route. Two alternatives, *(B)* and *(C)* in Figure 6.18, leave the Red Pine drainage to cross into that of Dry Creek. Both pass the Pfeifferhorn along its south side, as shown in Figure 6.15, before ascending Lightning Ridge and merging with the northern route to the summit. Route variant *(B)* drops into upper Hogum for ascent of Lightning ridge via the adrenalin-pumping avalanche couloir. Route *(C)* swings southward (with a slight descent) around a rocky prominence, then ascends a rocky couloir to the crest of Lightning Ridge near its junction with the branch ridge leading to Chipman Peak. From here, both of these routes to Thunder Mountain are identical to the northern variant.

Thunder Mountain Bowl. The descent of Thunder Mountain Bowl into Bells Canyon is one of the more challenging ski runs in the Wasatch. A number of routes are detailed in the Bells Canyon section in Chapter 7. Two routes of ascent are possible from upper Hogum Fork. The "standard" route follows the one just described to the summit of Thunder Mountain. From there it ridgehops to the top of Thunder Mountain Bowl.

The Direct Approach. One other possibility, route *(D)* in Figure 6.18, is much shorter and less complex, but it is usually more hazardous. The route follows a series of morainal depositions in upper Hogum and ascends directly to the crest of Thunder Mountain Bowl. Depending on where the ridge is intercepted, some downward rock scrambling may be necessary to reach skiable snow. This approach route is only 7.3 miles long.

Coalpit Gulch

Coalpit Gulch (Figure 6.19) is the westernmost, the steepest, and the shortest ravine to descend into Little Cottonwood Canyon.

Neither author of *Wasatch Tours* has ever toured (or descended) Coalpit. And for good reasons! A cursory search of newspapers and avalanche publications reveals that the snowpack along the head and sidewalls of this canyon is a "frequent flyer." Some avalanches that have descended this steep ravine have reached nearly to the highway. Local folklore has several avalanches covering the highway to a depth of 20 or 30 feet.

A *summer* field trip reveals the following: a 45-50 degree headwall

Figure 6.19   Coalpit Gulch is the steepest and shortest side canyon to descend into Little Cottonwood Canyon. The couloirs at each side of the gulch are popular among extreme skiers and snowboarders.

with large mounds of avalanche debris at its base and throughout the upper portions of the canyon; a narrow streambed choked with more debris in the central and lower part; a 30-40 foot waterfall part way up the canyon that would have to be climbed during ascent and downclimbed or rappelled (or jumped!) during descent; and, of course, considerable

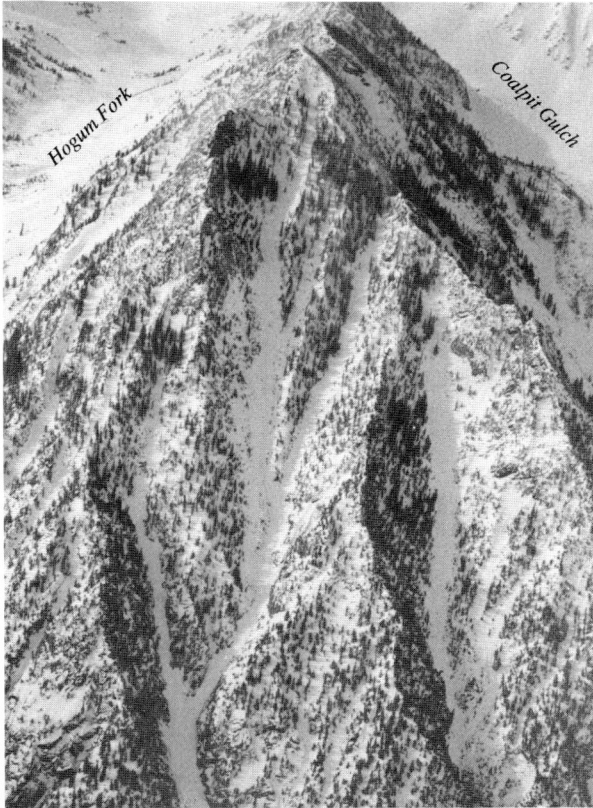

Figure 6.20   The "Y" couloir between Hogum and Coalpit offers challenges to the most competent of extreme skiers.

oak brush at the base of the canyon.

The steep, long, and narrow couloirs on either side of Coalpit are a bit less formidable. A growing number of extreme skiers and snow-boarders ascend these couloirs every weekend to place well-executed linked turns down their sheltered snowfields□

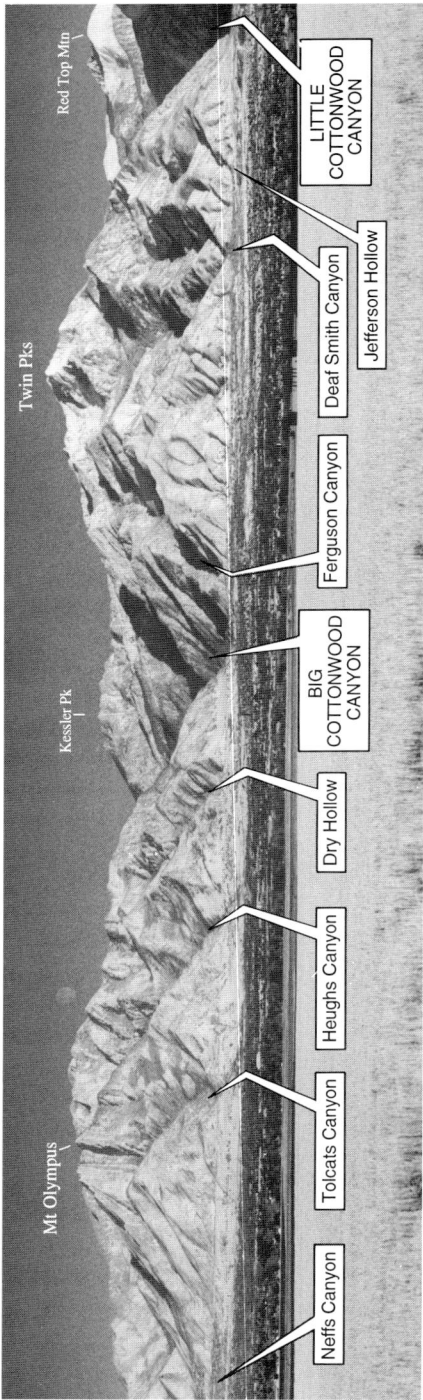

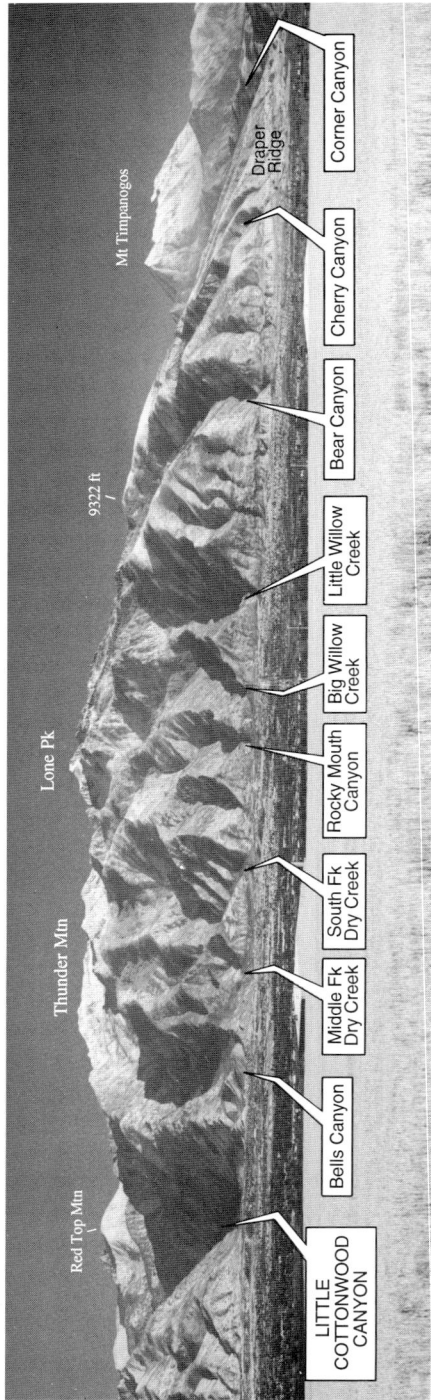

Steps canyons, sometimes impenetrable scrub, and uncertain snow conditions along low-elevation
west-facing slopes characterize many of the canyons found along the east edge of Salt Lake Valley.

Chapter 7

WEST FLANK CANYONS

There is a strange irony in the fact that the canyons and gulches closest to Salt Lake City traditionally have had the least backcountry recreational usage. The "west flank" canyons to be described in this chapter are the ones that descend from the westernmost summits of the Wasatch directly into Salt Lake Valley. The illustration on the opposite page provides an overview of the canyons and summits discussed in this chapter.

All west flank canyons commence at approximately 5000 feet elevation and terminate at elevations of 9500 to 11,000 feet. Their lengths vary between two and six miles. Due to the rapid elevation gain, most of the canyons to be described are fairly rugged. Some are too rocky and constricted to be considered for skiing or hiking. Only about half of them contain foot trails, and just a couple have jeep roads.

Due to their westerly exposure the canyons discussed in this chapter generally have unpredictable and varying snow conditions. The best ski touring is between mid-winter and early spring. Late spring outings can also be delightful, but tourers must be prepared to shoulder their skis while traversing the lower elevations of the routes. Thick scrub oak and other varieties of pace-slowing vegetation are not uncommon along many of the ascent and descent routes.

During the 1960's, 70's, and part of the 80's, access to the west flank canyons was not much of a problem, since most of the approach routes went across unfenced sagebrush-covered fields. Throughout the past three decades, little thought was given by Salt Lake County government to obtaining trailhead and trail right-of-way easements as they

routinely approved subdivisions that crept ever higher up the foothills.[1]
As a result, few convenient trailheads exist for the west flank canyons,
especially in the areas south of Big Cottonwood Canyon. After vigor-
ous urging by backcountry recreationists and conservation organizations
along the Wasatch Front, Forest Service planners included trailhead development as part of their 1985 Forest Plan. Today, working in conjunction with county and municipal planners and knowledgeable hikers
and tourers, the Forest Service is endeavoring to acquire critical private
lands for trailhead development "as funds, resources, and political will
become available."

The canyons to be described start with Neffs Canyon, at the southeast corner of Salt Lake City, and continue southward to Corner Canyon,
the southernmost canyon in Salt Lake Valley. Included in this chapter
are: Neffs, Tolcat, Ferguson, Deaf Smith, Bells, Dry Creek, Big and
Little Willow, and Corner canyons. Due to their touring significance,
Mount Olympus, the Draper Ridge, and Lone Peak are also discussed.

Because of the uncertain status of trailheads and access, most of the
descriptions of the West Flank canyons are intentionally brief. High res-
olution photographs provide an overview of access, terrain, and touring
possibilities.

NEFFS CANYON

Neffs Canyon, unlike its neighbors to the south, has not yet been violated
by civilization. The early pioneers, John Neff in particular, utilized some
of the canyon's timber resources, but the harvesting was done with a
degree of moderation. After only a partial defloration of the virgin
hillsides, the sheep and cattle raisers sought greener pastures elsewhere
in the Wasatch. Several mining incursions have been made, but unlike
Bingham Canyon in the Oquirrhs, they were abandoned before the area
was totally disemboweled.

For many decades, Neffs Canyon has remained relatively untouched.
No cabins or condominiums protrude from its wooded slopes. No summits have been decapitated for ski lift towers. Not a single summer rock
concert has been promoted here, and the helicopter skiing concession

---

[1]As early as the 1970's, the leadership of the Wasatch Mountain Club urged Salt
Lake County planners and commissioners to include trail-related easements through
several subdivisions planned along the foothills. Their projections of future backcountry recreational demands along the Wasatch Front were ignored—and sometimes
ridiculed—by political leaders (who often financed election and re-election campaigns
by funds acquired from land developers).

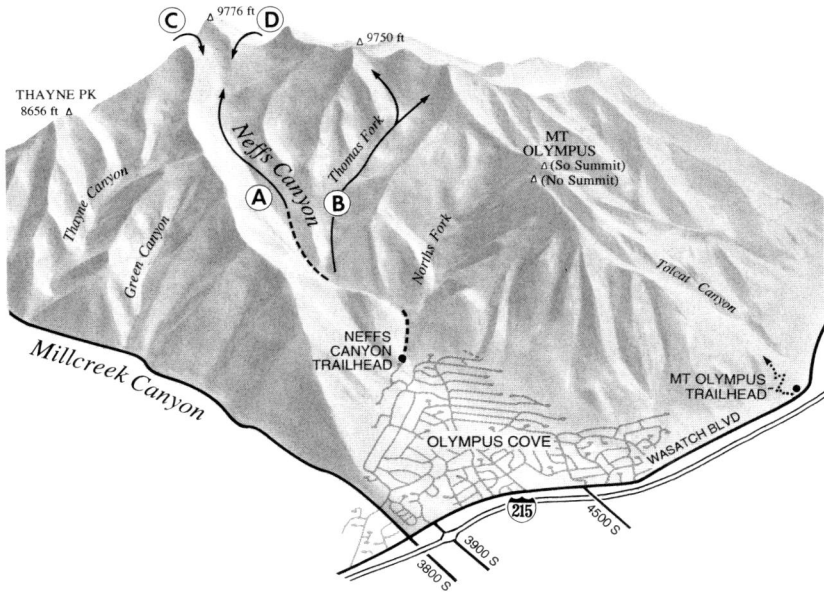

Figure 7.1 All of the tours described in this section involve ascent and/or descent of the Neffs Canyon jeep road. The routes are (A) Standard Neffs Canyon tour, (B) Thomas Fork, (C) Neffs Canyon from Millcreek, and (D) Neffs Canyon from Big Cottonwood.

is forbidden (by wilderness designation of the area) to operate in the canyon.

At four miles in length, Neffs Canyon is one of the shortest drainages to descend into Salt Lake Valley. The canyon's bottom elevation is about 5600 feet; it tops off at a 9776 foot unnamed summit that's common to Neffs, Millcreek, and Big Cottonwood canyons.

The north side of Neffs has no major drainages and is generally covered with thick scrub oak. Two small tributaries join the main canyon from the south. Norths Fork, named after one of the early pioneers who cut timber in the area, lies directly beneath the rocky northeast slopes of Mount Olympus. Thomas Fork, the uppermost side canyon, is longer but not quite as steep. Both are heavily wooded in their lower sections.

Unlike Millcreek and Big Cottonwood, Neffs Canyon does not have a great variety of ski touring possibilities. This canyon contains no routes suitable for a beginner, but does provide opportunities for those with intermediate or advanced capabilities. Routes into this canyon, as well as tours on and about Mount Olympus, are described in the following sections.

The routes illustrated in Figure 7.1 are all quite challenging, since they end on a narrow trail through otherwise impenetrable brush. They have little exposure to severe avalanche hazard, however, and allow the option of turning back at any point. No car shuttle is necessary unless the tour crosses to or from Millcreek or Big Cottonwood Canyon. The tours are generally intermediate in difficulty, but the overall challenge of a Neffs trip depends to a large extent on the snow conditions at low elevations. January, February and March seem to be the best months for skiing in this canyon.

Standard Neffs Canyon Tour

All tours from the bottom of Neffs start at the Neffs Canyon trailhead, which is in White Park at the top of White Way. The most complex part of these trips is the drive from the city to the trailhead through the affluent Olympus Cove neighborhood. Most of this subdivision can be avoided by traveling along Wasatch Boulevard to 3800 South. This street is then followed eastward about 0.3 mile until it intersects Park View Drive (3700 East). Turn right onto Park View Drive, then follow it for about 1.2 miles in a winding southeasterly direction until it intercepts Park Terrace Drive. Turn left (east) on Park Terrace and follow it past a "Dead End" sign to White Way, which branches to the right. White Way is the right way to the trailhead at the pavement's end. This is a popular necking area, but early in the day there should be plenty of room to park the car for ski touring.

The Neffs Canyon trail starts at the northeast corner of the parking area and soon joins the jeep road that leads into the canyon. After 0.5 mile the road turns to the left and crosses the stream. At this point the trail into Norths Fork branches to the right. The road up the main canyon parallels the stream for 1.3 miles, crossing it twice more. About 150 yards past the final stream crossing, the jeep road ends and a hiking trail begins.

The start of the hiking trail is ill-defined, especially during the winter. It traverses a very short distance up a steep slope just to the right of the end of the road.[2] At the top of the slope the trail turns into a deep rut. Follow this section through a dense forest (prominently visible in the lower part of Figure 7.2) for about 0.3 miles until the terrain opens at the bottom of two slopes of moderate steepness. The trail is usually

---

[2]This trail is on the south side of the stream, but the U.S.G.S. quadrangle shows it on the north side. What is indicated on the map is actually the route of an abandoned water pipeline, which is sometimes a good descent route from Neffs' upper meadows.

Figure 7.2 Although snow conditions are frequently marginal at lower elevations, upper Neffs Canyon has some good skiing terrain. An abandoned pipeline on the north side of the canyon may bypass some of the brush in the bottom of the drainage.

lost (or abandoned) here. This is no problem since at this point the timber and brush are reasonably sparse. A gentle traverse to the right leads to the top of a secondary ridge that can be followed for another 0.3 mile. At the end of this ridge, it is possible to angle downward a short distance into the middle of the canyon.

The remainder of the trip to the Neffs/Big Cottonwood divide follows the open slopes near the canyon bottom. From the trailhead to the divide is 3.7 miles and 3600 vertical feet. If you choose to ascend the 9776 foot unnamed peak common to Neffs, Big Cottonwood, and

Millcreek, simply stay to the left and follow a small sub-drainage to the summit. The climb would then be 4.0 miles and 4200 feet of elevation gain.

Descent. Two descent variations are possible from the divide back to the starting point. The first retraces the ascent route through the open slopes to the base of the secondary ridge. Instead of climbing back onto this ridge, one can remain on the north side of the canyon above the stream gully. The old pipeline footnoted earlier will soon be intercepted. It rejoins the jeep road near its end, which is the only reasonable route back to the car.

The second descent possibility follows some well sheltered, semi-open slopes and depressions just west of the Neffs/Big Cottonwood divide. This eventually joins the pipeline near the base of the secondary ridge.

From the top of the 9776 foot peak, it is also possible to ski into Porter Fork in Millcreek Canyon. From the summit, simply ski along the ridge to the north for about 0.7 mile and then into the Porter drainage. This area is described in Chapter 4.

Thomas Fork

Considerably more interesting and picturesque than the standard Neffs Canyon tour is an ascent of Thomas Fork. From the top of the highest point at the head of the fork (Peak 9750 in Figures 7.2 and 7.3) there is a good view of the double snow plumes from the twin summits of Mount Olympus. Farther west one can contemplate the entire panorama of the Salt Lake Valley, with the Oquirrh Mountains and the Great Salt Lake in the distance. Punctuating this magnificent view is the giant smoke stack at the Kennecott Copper smelter in Magna.

Thomas Fork is a little shorter, steeper, and more difficult than the standard tour. The route is shown in Figure 7.3. It is 3.6 miles long and has an elevation gain of 4200 feet. As in the previous tour, one starts at the Neffs Canyon trailhead and follows the jeep road past its junction with Norths Fork at the first crossing of the stream bed. About 0.75 mile beyond this point, to the right of the jeep road, is a seemingly impenetrable oak grove located atop an ancient alluvial fan. Leave the road here and head south almost directly into the grove. No ski area developers have cleared the willows and oak, so considerable ingenuity and determination are required to get through the brush. True cross country touring is, after all, a character developing and strengthening form of recreation.

After about half a mile of bushwhacking, the terrain becomes more

Figure 7.3 Thomas Fork has two good touring routes, but both end up in thick oak brush at the bottom. The better choice for the ascent is the one on the left in the photo.

open and manageable. This area is clearly visible at the extreme bottom of Figure 7.3. From there the preferred climbing route becomes obvious, basically following the left line on the photograph.

There appear to be only two steep areas that require avalanche precautions. The first is the semi-wooded slope at the lower half of the figure. The second steep area (not visible in the photo) is a small bowl just below the summit of the 9750 foot peak which is the destination of the tour. This bowl can be avoided by ascending a steep tree-covered ridge just to the west.

Figure 7.4   Unpersuaded by arguments of "a broadened tax base," "greater employment opportunities for his fellow deities," and "the need to balance economic and environmental considerations," an enraged Zeus banishes two executives of the Winter Olympics Organizing Committee who proposed to carve the five-ring Olympics symbol into the red quartzite face of Mount Olympus.

Descent. Skiing out of Thomas Fork is relatively straightforward. Besides the suggested climbing route, only one simple alternative exists. This is the right line in Figure 7.3. The lower portion on this descent is very steep in spots, so it should be attempted only under the safest snow conditions.

Neffs From Other Canyons

Since the upper regions of Neffs Canyon adjoin Millcreek and Big Cottonwood canyons, it is possible to enter Neffs from either canyon. A good knowledge of hiking trails and the terrain during snowless times is extremely important.

Neffs from Millcreek. The upper part of Neffs Canyon adjoins Porter Fork in the Millcreek drainage. An approach from that direction is at least as good as the standard route up Neffs, so it is a reasonable alternative. Details of the climb to the top are found in Chapter 4 and illustrated in Figure 4.8. Generally, the Porter Fork route follows a ridge that ends at the 9776 foot peak. This variation of the Neffs tour only saves 400 feet of climb (3800 vertical feet instead of 4200) but the snow on the northeast facing slopes of Porter is often much better that that in Neffs, particularly at low elevations. Another advantage of not hiking

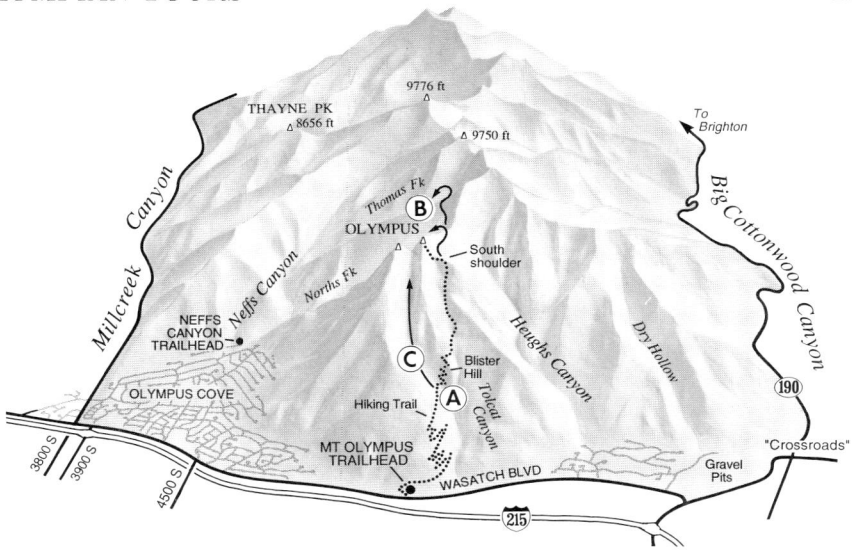

Figure 7.5   All of the "Olympian" tours require ascent high onto the shoulders of Mount Olympus. Route (A) to Norths Fork follows the Mount Olympus hiking trail for most of its length. Route (B) continues beyond the head of Norths Fork to Thomas Fork. Route (C) departs the hiking trail to ascend Tolcat Canyon to a pass between the two summits of Mount Olympus.

up Neffs is that the snow on the trail will be left unpacked, which can help slow skiers down during their descent.

Neffs from Big Cottonwood. The Neffs/Big Cottonwood ridge can be reached from the "S-curve" in the Big Cottonwood highway by ascending either branch of Mill B North Fork. The east branch ends at the divide west of the 9776 foot peak described earlier. The west branch leads to the top of Thomas Fork. Snow conditions on the north side of Big Cottonwood Canyon are usually marginal, often sun crusted, icy, or lacking in snow entirely. Except for the first 0.3 mile, no trail exists and the route goes through alternating sections of rock bands and brush. About two miles and 600 feet of elevation are saved by using this approach, but the overall time required may be greater than on the standard tour.

OLYMPIAN TOURS

The "Olympian" tours involve climbing Mount Olympus and require a greater degree of commitment than most of the advanced outings described in this book. In addition to the usual steepness and avalanche factors, the routes require some hiking and rock scrambling. Tours on

Figure 7.6   The Mount Olympus hiking trail is one of the most popular trails in the Wasatch. It ascends the lower portion of Tolcat Canyon and leads to the south shoulder of Mount Olympus, the departure point for the Norths Fork and Thomas Fork tours. No trail leads to the base of the Tolcat Couloir.

Mount Olympus range from the sublime (such as a descent of Thomas Fork) to the extreme (like the couloirs pictured in Figures 7.8 and 7.9). The Olympian Tours require *extremely precise* skiing ability and nerves of steel.

The three practical tours in the Mount Olympus area are shown in Figure 7.5. These are Mount Olympus/Norths Fork, Mount Olympus/Thomas Fork, and the Mount Olympus couloirs. In addition, a series of "memorial couloirs" along the northeast side of the mountain are described briefly at the end of this section for those carefree tourers who have no mortgages to pay and no mistresses to maintain.

All of the Olympian tours start from the Forest Service's Mount Olympus trailhead on Wasatch Boulevard about 1.5 miles south of the 45th South traffic light. Ample parking space is usually available along the highway.

Mount Olympus to Norths Fork

Almost the entire Mount Olympus hiking trail is visible in Figure 7.6. From the Mount Olympus trailhead on Wasatch Boulevard, the trail zig zags through open, grassy slopes for about the first mile. It then traverses for 0.25 mile directly into Tolcat Canyon, where a stream bed comes down from between the peaks of Mount Olympus. After crossing the stream the trail ascends a steep area (known among hikers as "Blister Hill"), crosses a ridge, and traverses farther southeast toward a second stream channel.

The trail winds upward for the next half mile through a moderately steep, scrub-covered slope following the drainage of the second stream channel. At the top is a broad shoulder with lots of evergreens, visible at the top of Figure 7.6 and the bottom of Figure 7.7. This serves as an excellent picnic spot in the summer. The 9026 foot south summit of Mount Olympus juts 500 feet above to the north. The ascent route to the peak is a series of scrambles among rock outcroppings and narrow gullies. Tourers who make a summit attempt should leave their skis on the flat shoulder and proceed on foot. The outcroppings and gullies have been known to be covered with wind and ice-crusted snow. Extreme care should be exercised in this area.

The top of Norths Fork is about 0.4 mile east of the plateau. It lies at the saddle between Mount Olympus and the next rocky prominence along the ridge. You can traverse slightly upward beneath the south face of the peak, as shown in Figure 7.7, or you can descend about 100 feet, then traverse and climb some moderately steep slopes to the pass. The first alternative has some short rock scrambles, while the latter has some avalanche potential, so take your pick! Wasatch Boulevard to the Norths Fork saddle is about four miles with 3800 feet of elevation gain.

Descent. The ski run down Norths Fork can at times be very diffi-cult. The upper section is steep and avalanche prone. The lower areas are extremely brushy and may contain marginal snow. A good route is along the eastern side until the canyon narrows at the bottom. Here

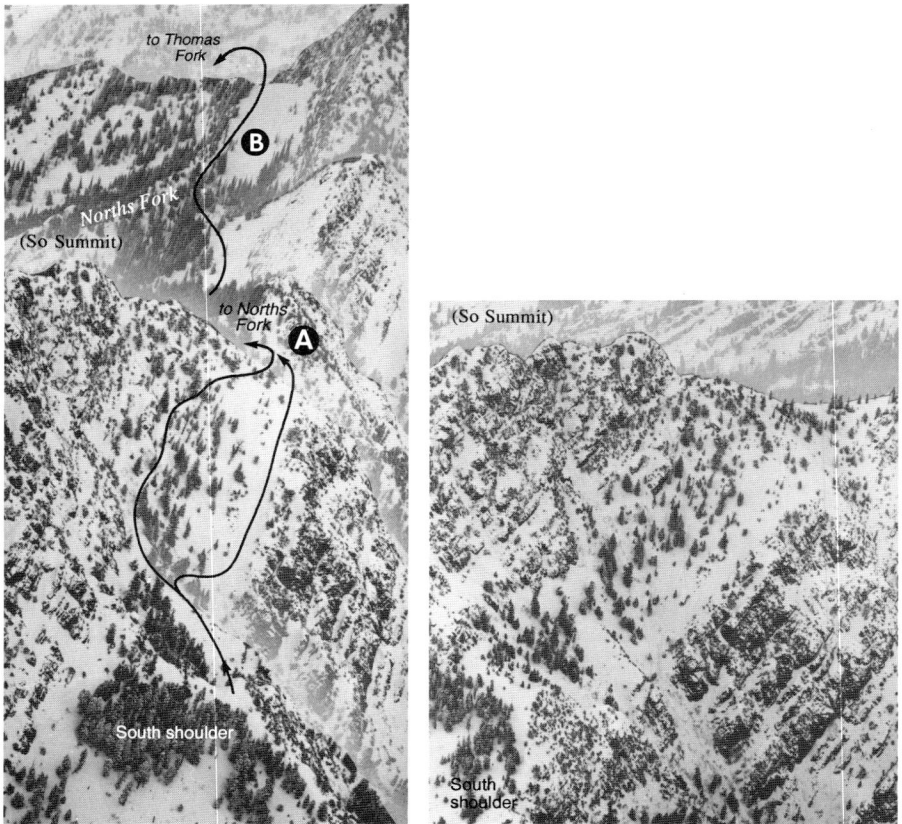

Figure 7.7   Norths Fork can be intercepted from the Mount Olympus south shoulder by traversing eastward to the pass at the head of the fork (A). Two traverse routes are possible; both are exposed to snowslough and rockfall hazards from above. The cliffband beneath the routes adds another element of uncertainty and hazard. A continuation of this route (B) leads to Thomas Fork.

you can cross the stream and intercept a steep, winding foot trail that descends the western side of the fork. This joins the main Neffs Canyon jeep road which returns to the Neffs Canyon trailhead.

Mount Olympus to Thomas Fork

Thomas Fork is just east of Norths, so the climbing route is identical to that just described. From the saddle at the top of Norths Fork, drop down about 200 vertical feet and traverse directly eastward a few hundred yards to the base of a steep cliff band. If the cliff harbors no avalanche slab, proceed under it, staying as close to the trees as

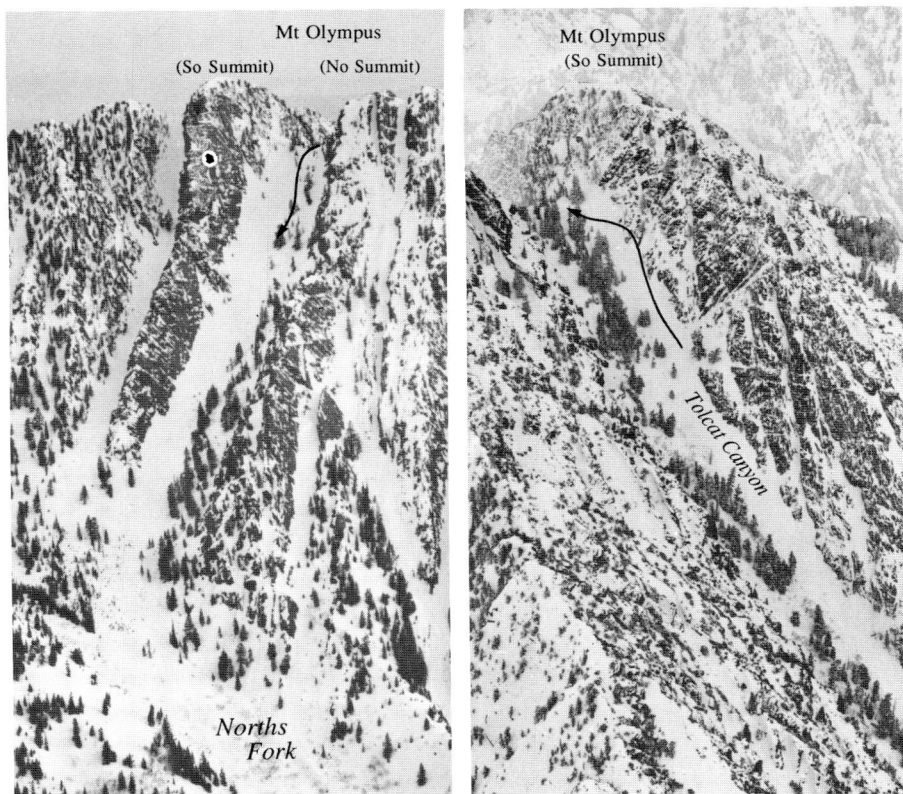

Figure 7.8   *Right:* Upper Tolcat Canyon is the ascent route to the saddle between the two peaks of Mount Olympus. *Left:* The Mount Olympus Couloir, on the northeast side of the saddle in Norths Fork, is an excellent run for a qualified downhill skier.

necessary. Once past this area, continue the traverse several hundred yards farther east to the base of an open slope. Ascent of this slope puts you at the top of Thomas Fork. Both the cliff band and open slope are clearly visible in Figure 7.7, which shows the route *(B)* just described. The top of the fork is at an elevation of 8800 feet, which provides a 3200 foot descent over 2.5 miles into the main canyon.

Mount Olympus Couloir

The Mount Olympus Couloir is one of the steepest and most challenging ski touring runs in the Wasatch. It involves an ascent, via Tolcat Canyon, to the saddle between the north and south summits of Mount Olympus, followed by a descent, via a steep couloir, into Norths Fork.

Figure 7.9   The "Memorial Couloirs," several steep couloirs located adjacent to the Mount Olympus couloir, provide challenging descents for expert skiers. *Inset:* The earliest known descent of a memorial couloir was made by Gary Gruvor and Ron Wilson in the early 1980's.

This tour starts at the Wasatch Boulevard trailhead and follows the Mount Olympus trail until it intersects the first stream bed. From there, rather than crossing the stream and ascending Blister Hill, the stream bed is followed directly up to the 8800 foot saddle between the peaks. It is about a mile and 2500 vertical feet from the trail to the saddle, giving this section of the tour an *average* angle of about 30 degrees. The steep upper section of Tolcat is shown in the right half of Figure 7.8. It can be ascended either by traversing among the trees (better use skins for this one!) or by zig-zagging in the open slopes visible in the photograph. Needless to say, this route should not be attempted under uncertain snow and avalanche conditions.

At the top of the saddle there is ample room to relax and to ponder the descent. (You might also want to question seriously your reasons for being there!) Wasatch Boulevard to the saddle is about three miles and 3900 feet.

Descent. The route into Norths Fork is probably the simplest and least complicated to be described in this book. It is straight. It is narrow. It is short. And it is steep! The initial 1300 vertical feet of the couloir are more that 40 degrees. Its simplicity is illustrated in the left part of Figure 7.8 and in Figure 7.9. After skiing down the couloir, just follow the route described previously for Norths Fork.

The Memorial Couloirs. It is apparent from Figure 7.9 that there are several chutes on either side of the main Olympus couloir that are even straighter, narrower, steeper, and considerably more hazardous than the one just described. At present they are called the "Mount Olympus Memorial Couloirs." Since the first edition of *Wasatch Tours* in 1976, the authors have been informed of only one descent of a memorial couloir. The feat was accomplished by Gary Gruvor and Ron Wilson in the early 1980's. The small photo insert in Figure 7.9 was submitted by one of the participants as an offering of proof.

TWIN PEAKS CANYONS

Three westerly drainages originate at the higher regions of Twin Peaks: Ferguson Canyon, North Fork Deaf Smith Canyon, and Deaf Smith Canyon. At 4 miles, the North Fork of Deaf Smith Canyon is the longest; it is also the only one of the three to crest at Twin Peaks' dual summit.

Unlike drainages deeper in the range, all of the Twin Peaks canyons are constricted at their bases, with access trails frequently encroached by scrub brush and blocked by deadfalls. That's what makes them attractive for the expert tourer in search of complete solitude. The upper basins, on the other hand, are typical of those throughout the

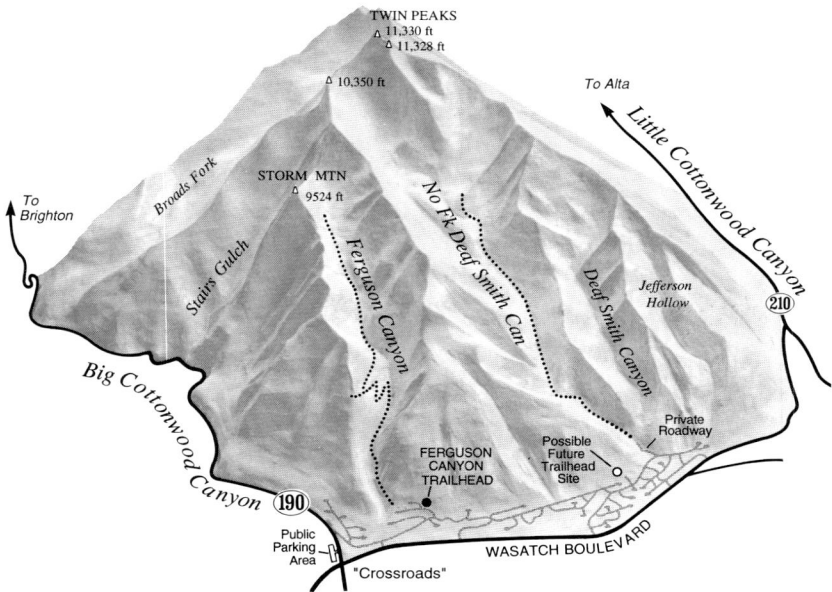

Figure 7.10   Of the three drainages along the west flank of the Twin Peaks massif, only Ferguson and North Fork Deaf Smith canyons contain hiking trails. Ferguson has the only "official" Forest Service trailhead. Access to the public hiking trail in Deaf Smith requires permission to cross private properties. The Forest Service is working to develop a public right-of-way into that canyon.

Wasatch. They're generally quite open, have numerous snowslopes and avalanche paths, and are ringed by steep headwalls.

Ferguson Canyon

During the mid-1890's miners trudged daily into Ferguson Canyon to scratch out precious metal-bearing ores from its various strata. A hundred years later, in the mid-1990's, *minors* have discovered the deep recesses of Ferguson. The canyon is a popular recreation area used by rock climbers, tourers, and hikers. "And unfortunately," Forest Service officials lament, "primarily by juvenile partyers who regularly trash the canyon, vandalize signs, and build and maintain illegal campfires."

Until urban sprawl crept to the canyon's mouth, access to Ferguson Canyon was never a problem. Hikers and tourers would simply follow a 4-wheel drive roadway as far into the mouth of the drainage as practical, park, and commence foot travel into the canyon. Forest Service personnel have recently created a formal Ferguson Canyon Trailhead on the east side of Timberline Drive at 7732 South.

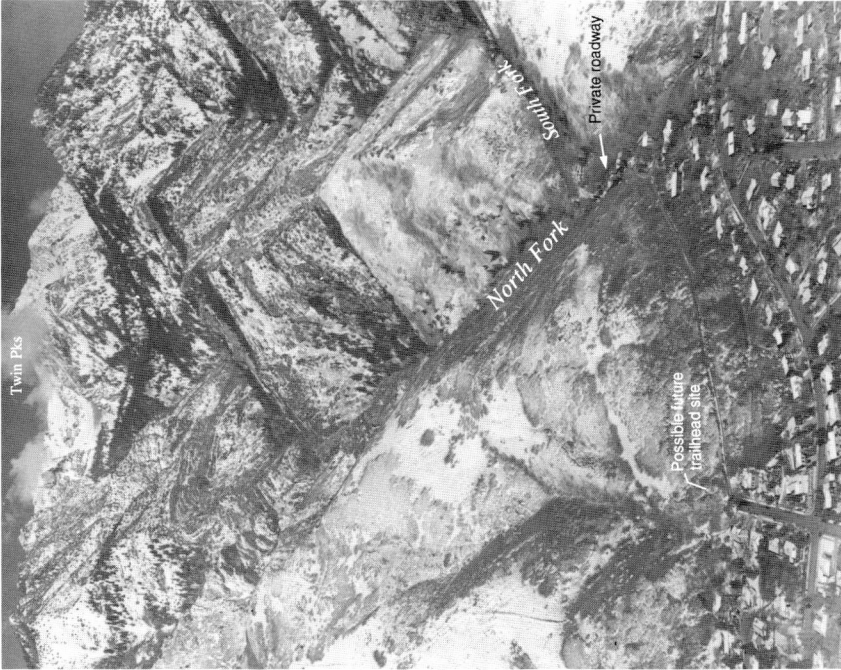

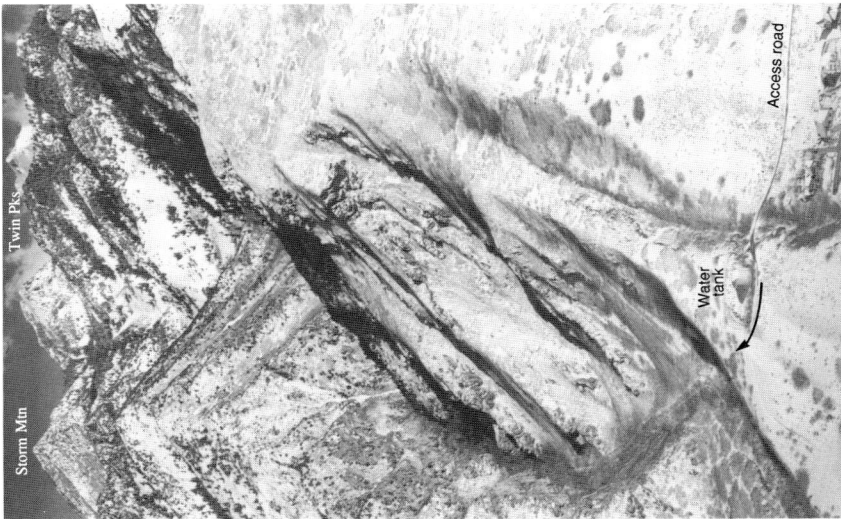

Figure 7.11 *Left*: Ferguson Canyon. *Right*: Deaf Smith Canyon. The North Fork is the larger of Deaf Smith Canyon's two branches. The west ridge of Twin Peaks divides the upper region of the North Fork into two basins.

To locate the trailhead start at the intersection of the Big Cotton-wood Canyon highway (SR-190) and Wasatch Boulevard. From there follow Wasatch Boulevard south 0.25 mile to 7535 South. Turn left (east) there, then immediately right (south) onto Prospector Drive. Follow that southward about 0.4 mile to a left (east) branch, which is Timberline Drive. Just past the turn, Timberline circles northward. The trail is located along the east side of the road as it ends the turn. At present, trailhead parking is limited to the sides of the road. In the future, officials promise, a small parking lot will be constructed just off the roadway.

The first part of the trail is an access road that leads northward to a water storage tank clearly visible in the left part of Figure 7.11. A foot trail goes along the west side of the tank, then angles downward to join the trail leading into the canyon. The canyon bottom is narrow, and the trail crosses the stream several times. About 1.5 miles into the drainage the trail switchbacks three or four times upward along the north side of the canyon. It then forks at the top of the switchbacks. The left (north) fork leads a short distance to a scenic viewpoint on the ridge separating Ferguson Canyon from Big Cottonwood. The right (southeast) fork continues another two miles into Ferguson's upper basin.

Deaf Smith Canyon

Long known as Little Willow Canyon, Deaf Smith Canyon has a history that's "vintage Utah." In the early to mid-1890's some mining was conducted at the Jefferson Mine near the mouth of the canyon. The discovery of small amounts of gold (that soon petered out) attracted additional miners to the area and prompted the owner and promoter of the mine to name the rapidly growing collection of boarding and bunk houses "Gold City." The owner of the mine had come from the east, and had convinced many easterners to become investors.

In his unpublished recollections of Little Willow Canyon, early Union resident Ira Proctor continues the narrative:

> "After mining for several years, they began to build a big concentrate mill with heavy timbers and when it was completed they installed Westinghouse Motors and all other material to run a mill. And they also painted the mill a bright red; it could be seen for miles from the Valley. They built a cement transformer house to furnish electricity for the mill. I (Ira Proctor) and [several others] did the electrical work in the Transformer House. Upon completion of this

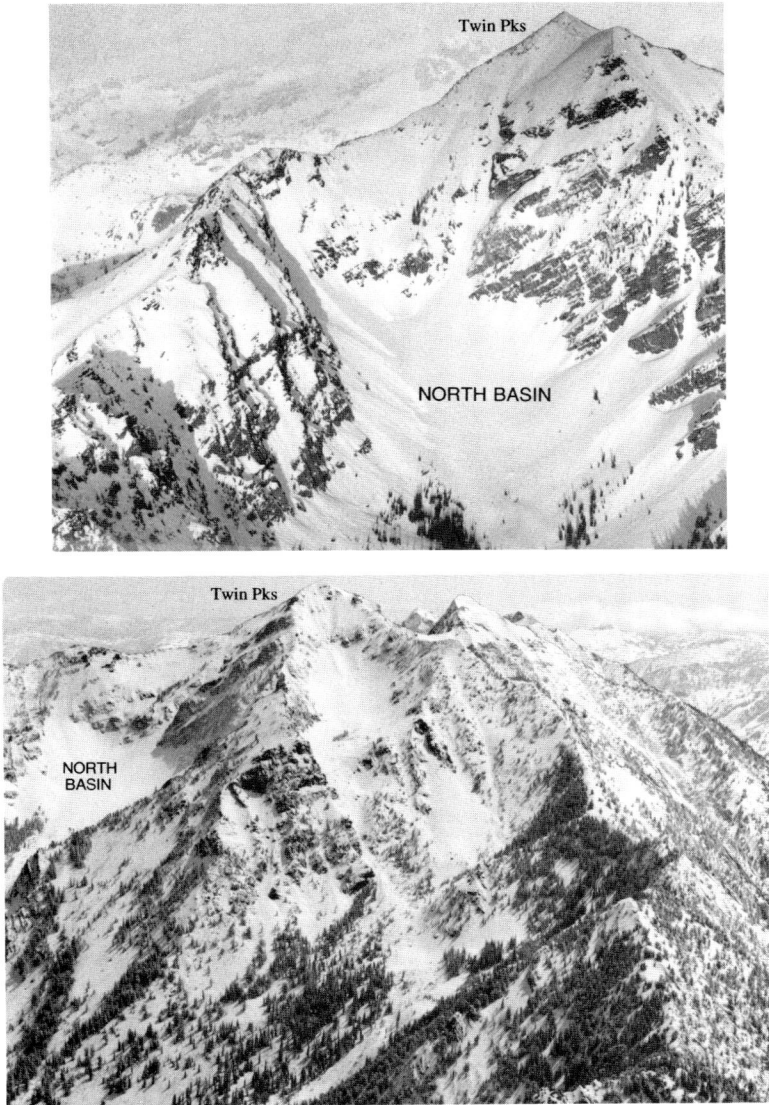

Figure 7.12   Upper region of North Fork Deaf Smith Canyon. *Top:* the north basin; *Bottom:* the south basin.

Concentrate Mill they had a big celebration and a special train brought a large crowd of stockholders and investors from the East for the big event. They had plenty to eat and drink and they all had a good time.

The Mill never turned a wheel! It was a stock promotion

deal! Mr. Schmithroth, the promoter, disappeared and never was seen again."

Deaf Smith Canyon consists of two forks—North Fork and the main fork. North Fork drains directly off Twin Peaks. Its upper region is divided into two basins by the rocky west ridge of Twins. The main fork of Deaf Smith is shorter and does not reach to the crest of Twin Peaks.

Access to Deaf Smith Canyon has always been difficult, and generally illegal. The National Forest boundary, where the "official" trail commences, is quite high and much exclusive private property has to be crossed to gain access. In the past, such crossings have led to encounters best described as "ugly." The Forest Service, county planners, and other interested parties are endeavoring to develop a public right-of-way and trailhead into Deaf Smith Canyon. When they will consummate the deal is anybody's guess.

The right part of Figure 7.11 shows the Deaf Smith drainages and some foothill roadways. The National Forest boundary runs north/south approximately at the confluence of the two forks. Figure 7.12 depicts the upper basins of North Fork beneath Twin Peaks.

BELLS CANYON

Bells Canyon, reportedly the site of Orrin Porter Rockwell's long lost gold mine, is a glacial canyon that empties into Salt Lake Valley just south of Little Cottonwood Canyon. Much like Neffs Canyon, the Bells drainage has escaped the ravages of metal miners. For a period during the late 1800's a small granite quarry was operated near the waterfall in the canyon. Rock for gravestones and house foundations was the quarry's principal product. In 1896 the base for the Brigham Young Monument was cut from the granite outcroppings just north of the creek in Bells Canyon. Just how the extraordinarily massive stone was moved down the canyon is an excellent topic for conjecture while ascending the lower (boring) stretches of the canyon's trail. The first volume of the Daughters of the Utah Pioneers' *Chronicles of Courage* states that it was done for the sum of $10.

Bells Canyon is the largest west flank canyon to be discussed in this chapter. It is approximately six miles in length and accesses the heart of the Lone Peak Wilderness. Bells terminates in two branches, one headed by Lone Peak (elevation 11,253 feet) and the other by Thunder Mountain (11,154 feet). Figure 7.13 is a schematic representation of

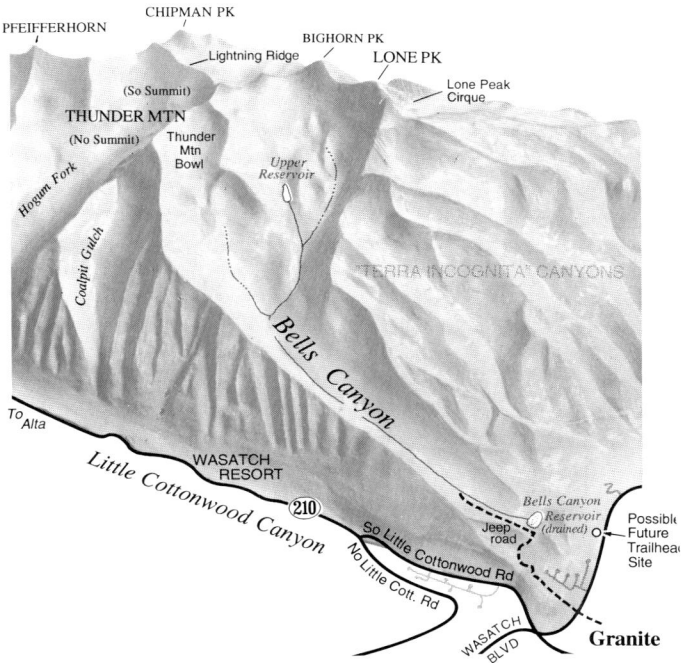

Figure 7.13   Bells Canyon is the longest of the West Flank canyons. It terminates near the community of Granite.

the canyon's topography and various points of interest. Figure 7.14 is a
photographic overview of the canyon and roadways at its base.

Bells Canyon contains two water storage reservoirs. The Upper Bells
Canyon Reservoir is located at 9400 feet elevation about five miles up
the canyon. The lower reservoir is near the outlet of the canyon at an
elevation of 5600 feet. Due to its location over a fault zone and a recent
failure, the lower reservoir has been drained and is now being managed
as a catch basin/stock basin.

Winter access to Bells Canyon is gained from two diametrically opposite directions: from its mouth near the community of Granite, and
from its 11,000 foot crest by way of Dry Creek or the subdrainages of
Little Cottonwood Canyon. With a 5100 foot base elevation, ascents
(or descents) of the canyon can exceed 6000 vertical feet.

Bells Canyon from Granite

The long tradition of public backcountry recreational use in Bells Canyon
stretches back to the early 1900's. Today, according to the Forest Service, the area receives 3000-5000 visitors yearly. Recreational access to

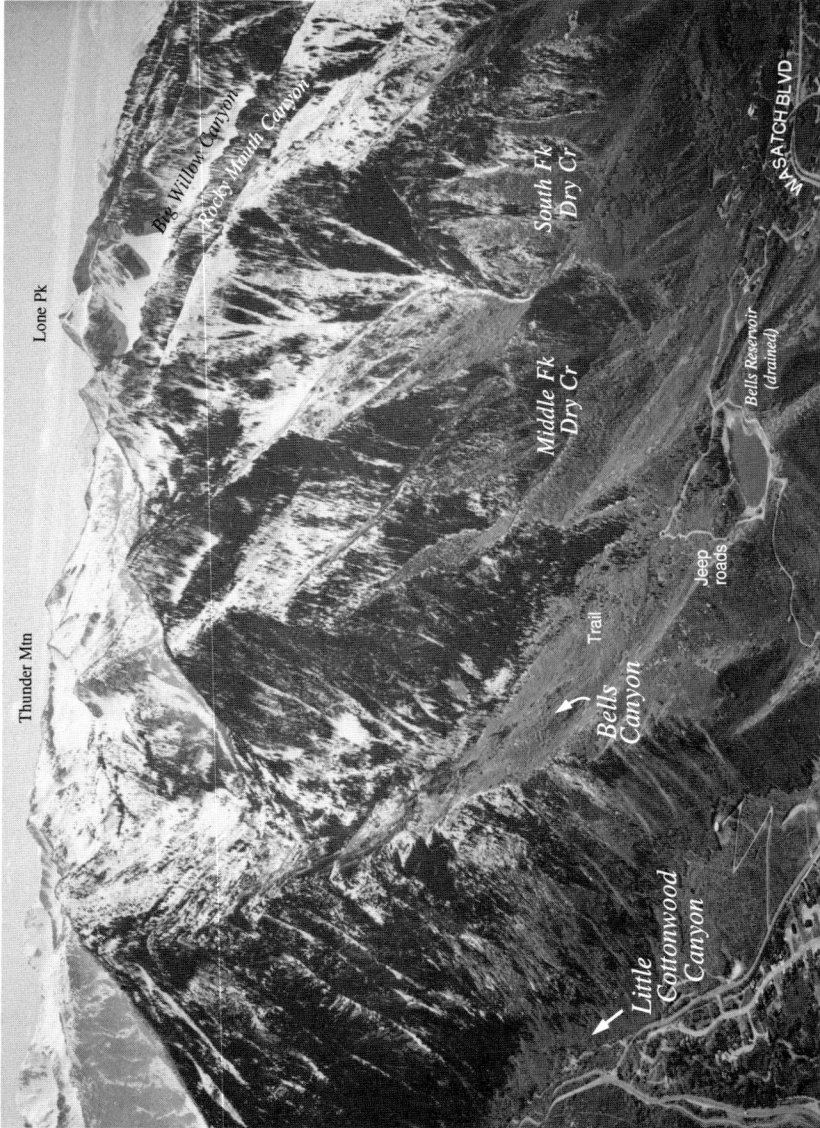

Figure 7.14   Bells Canyon overview. The Bells Canyon Reservoir was recently declared unsafe and has been drained down considerably.

the drainage has always been across private properties or lands managed for watershed protection by a local irrigation company. Several access routes commonly utilized by hikers and climbers are described in the Wasatch Mountain Club's *Hiking the Wasatch* and its companion map; accurate descriptions of the trail within the canyon are found there also.[3]

Assuming one has arrived hassle-free at the Lower Bells Reservoir, two clear-cut choices (and one not so clear-cut) exist for the tourer who wishes to ascend the canyon. Following the hiking trail all the way up the canyon is the simplest choice. Tourers who choose to do so will soon learn that following this route on skis becomes quite cumbersome. The alders often bend over the trail, making travel difficult; in some areas the trail follows a deep and cobbly rut. In shallow snow common to low elevations, the edges of the rut and the cobbles become irritants to be avoided.

The "high traverse" and the "lost gold mine" alternatives are worth considering. Approximately the first two miles of the hiking trail are common to both options.

The High Traverse Route. Late in the season, *after the snowpack has consolidated and all avalanche activity has ceased,* it's possible to avoid the irritants by abandoning the hiking trail about 1.5 miles from the lower reservoir. The departure is southward and upward through the brush to the tongue of a steep avalanche slope that descends from the south wall of the canyon. In hard snow common to spring mornings, the avalanche gully can be walked (or sidestepped) straight up, providing a sizeable gain in elevation.

The avalanche gully, *(A)* in Figure 7.15, is ascended only to the point where it becomes practical (and safe) to enter the sparsely timbered area to its left (east). From there, open, partially timbered, and bouldered slopes are followed eastward and southward into the upper regions of the canyon. *NOTE: the sparse timber, the open slopes, and the abundant snowdepth along this route are a result of frequent avalanching (and rockfalls!) from the steep slopes above; this route should not be attempted under uncertain avalanche conditions, and tourers are warned to remain well clear of rockfall hazards.* The remainder of the high traverse route into the upper basin of Bells Canyon is visible in the lower-right corner of Figure 7.19.

---

[3]The problem of public access may soon be solved by the Forest Service with a proposed land trade that would transfer some 200 acres of private land near the mouth of the canyon into public ownership. Plans for construction of a new trailhead near the edge of a southward extension of Wasatch Boulevard are being considered.

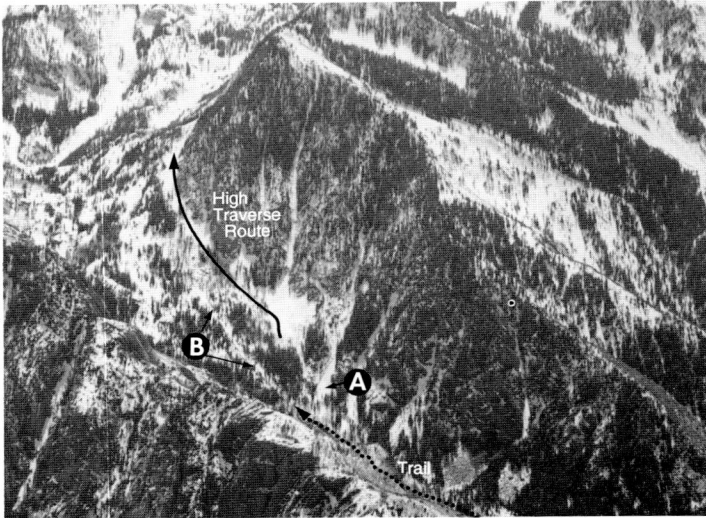

Figure 7.15   The "high traverse" route involves ascending a steep avalanche slope (A) and traversing eastward beneath several other slidepaths. The *hypothetical* "lost gold mine" route (B) would follow a diagonal treeless terrain feature that avoids the major avalanche gullies associated with the high traverse.

The Lost Gold Mine Route. A third route alternative, deduced from study of aerial photographs, *and as yet untested by the authors,* may be a practical means of avoiding problems associated with the hiking trail or the upper traverse. Marked *(B)* in Figure 7.15, the route appears to bypass the worst avalanche gullies by ascending a relatively open diagonal terrain feature we've conjectured to be the road from Orrin Porter Rockwell's long-lost gold mine. The wealth of the Church is immeasurable, and gold is heavy. A stream of wagons hauling it would have left a rut easily visible from space.

Bells Canyon Ski Mountaineering

The upper basins and summits of Bells Canyon (Figure 7.16) provide excellent and innumerable opportunities for advanced touring and winter mountaineering. From the main fork of the canyon it's possible to ascend Lone Peak, Bighorn Peak, Chipman Peak, or Thunder Mountain's south summit. The Thunder Mountain ascents can be done on skis from a variety of approaches. No specific routes need description; advanced tourers who reach the base of the peaks will instinctively know where to go, how to get there, and what to do once there.

Figure 7.16 The upper basins of Bells Canyon provide many opportunities for advanced touring and winter mountaineering. *Top photo:* Main branch of Bells Canyon. *Bottom:* Thunder Mountain and Thunder Bowl.

Descents of Bells Canyon, either by way of the main fork or the Thunder Bowl variation, will be discussed in the "Bells Canyon from Little Cottonwood" section that follows.

Lone Peak. No venture into Bells Canyon would be complete with-

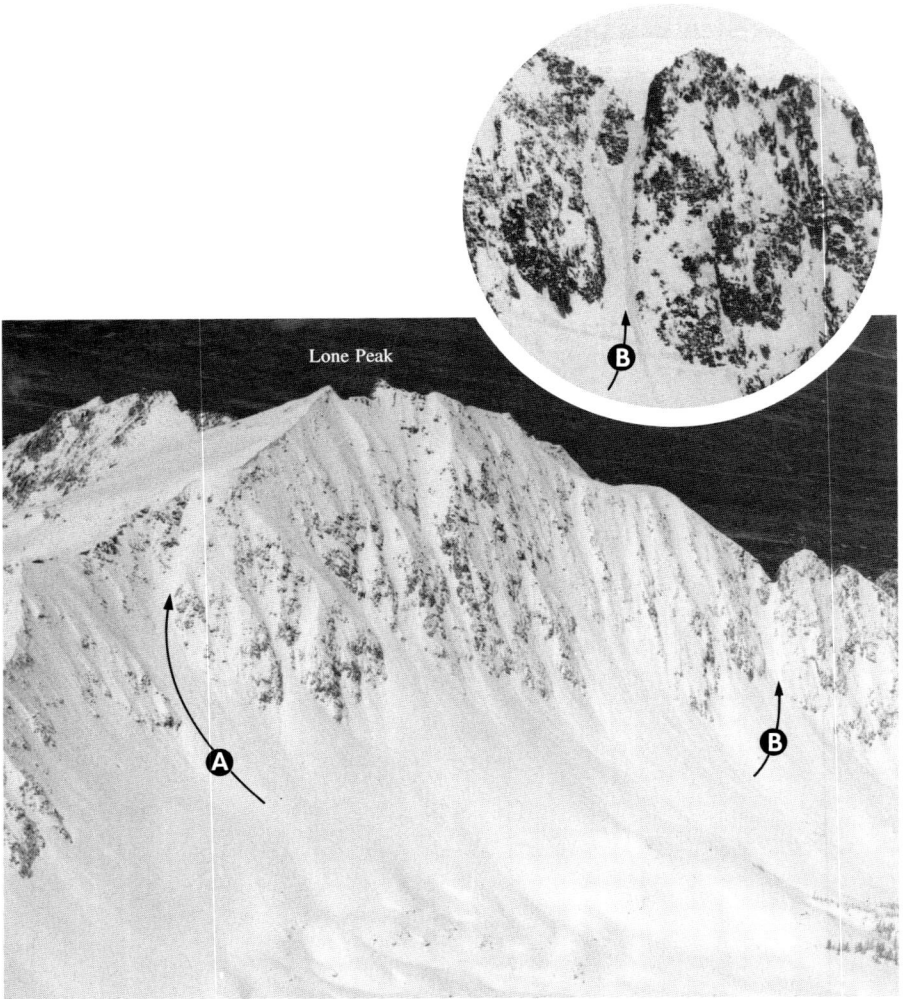

Figure 7.17   The steep couloir (A) leads to the east ridge of Lone Peak and its east summit. Couloir (B) leads to the west ridge and the main (west) summit. The crest of the ridge between the two summits is extremely exposed on both sides of the peak.

out an ascent of Lone Peak, the gemstone of Utah's first wilderness. During summer, such an ascent is generally a simple matter that involves, at worst, a lot of boulder hopping. With boulders encased in ice-hardened rhyme and approach slopes drifted with avalanche-prone wind slabs, winter ascents of Lone Peak become a different matter. A working knowledge of mountaineering skills (involving rope and ice axe) is required for a summit attempt. Very early starts are necessary, and the possibility of a late descent should be anticipated. Some tourers prefer to camp overnight in upper Bells Canyon to allow enough time to get to the summit. The peak can be climbed by way of its east ridge or from the northwest.

The East Ridge. The steep couloir, route *(A)* in Figure 7.17, leads to Lone Peak's very gentle east ridge. The ridge is easily walked to the peak's east summit. The ridge leading to the main (west) summit is extremely exposed along both sides and some serious rock scrambling— with added security provided by a belay—is required to get there. Several other steep slopes, with less avalanche and slip-and-slide hazard, are located east of the couloir and can be ascended to access the east ridge.

The Northwest Ridge. Lone Peak's northwest ridge is considerably more challenging than the eastern approach. The couloir, route *(B)* in the illustration, is steeper and requires a 10-20 foot rock climb to access the ridge crest. A belay is certainly in order for this route. Depending upon snowdepth it may be necessary to bypass the ridge crest along its west side by traversing a narrow ledge along the top of a 300 foot cliff. A rope belay here is more reassuring than relying on protection offered by scruffy trees that grow along the edge of the dropoff.[4]

Little Cottonwood to Bells Canyon Supertours

It's been suggested that a touch of "lunacy" is necessary to undertake any of the Little Cottonwood Canyon to Bells Canyon ski tours. While the need for lunacy may be debatable, a requirement for moonlight is a strong possibility for one of these outings. In addition, the participants should be intimately familiar with the terrain in both summer and winter, be in top physical condition, be expert avalanche analysts, and be prepared for any emergency, including an overnight stay. These supertours are best done in late winter and spring, when the days are long and the snow is most stable.

Tours into Bells Canyon from Little Cottonwood usually start at the White Pine trailhead, although some have been done from Alta. The most popular routes are illustrated schematically in Figure 7.18. All the approach routes to the Little Cottonwood/Bells Canyon divide except the route from Alta, have been described in the preceding chapter and illustrated in Figures 6.12, 6.13, 6.15, and 6.18.

---

[4]This route was *descended* in late March 1965 or 1966 by Milt Hollander, Max Townsend, Cal Giddings, and Alexis Kelner. It was the descent portion of a Draper to Bells Canyon ski tour.

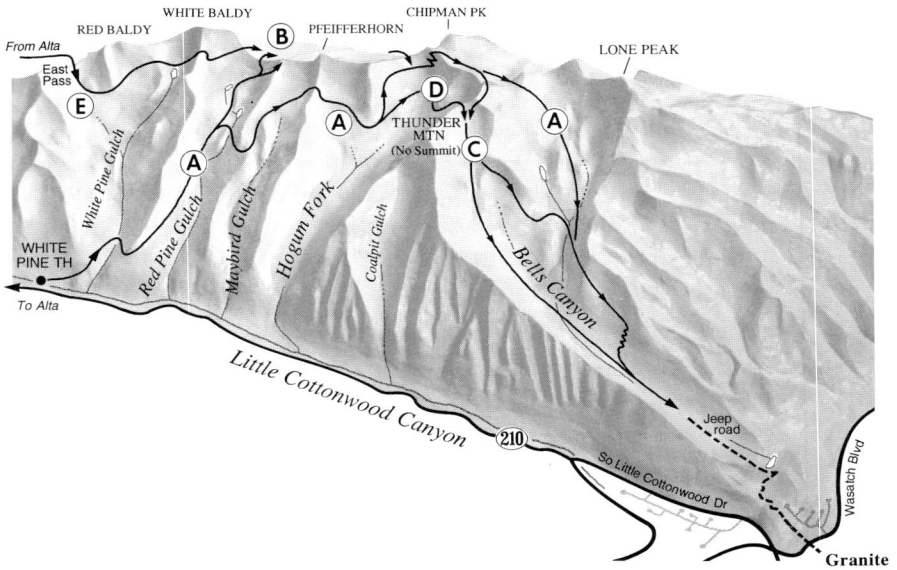

Figure 7.18   The Little Cottonwood to Bells Canyon Supertours. (A) White Pine-Bells, northern route, (B) White Pine-Bells, southern route, (C) White Pine-Thunder Mountain Bowl, (D) White Pine-Thunder Mountain Bowl "shortcut" route, and (E) Alta-Bells Canyon.

Bells Canyon From Alta. One of the most notorious supertours is the trip from Alta to Bells Canyon.[5] A particularly early start is in order to avoid darkness during descent of Bells Canyon.

The tour commences at Alta (either at the base of Albion Basin or Collins Gulch) and ascends the packed ski runs to Germania Pass, the pass between Mount Baldy and Sugarloaf Peak. From Germania Pass the route traverses the top of Mineral Basin to the pass into Mary Ellen Gulch, which is ascended to the summit of American Fork Twin Peaks. From American Fork Twins a gentle downward traverse leads through the "east pass" into the top of White Pine Canyon.[6] A descent from the pass, followed by an upward traverse around the base of Red Baldy leads to White Pine Lake. West of White Pine Lake a steep, gully-like (and avalanche-prone) slope leads to a notch in the White

---

[5]This route was first completed by Bruce Christenson and A. Kelner in May 1969. The tour commenced at 2:00 a.m. and ended nineteen hours later in Granite. An interesting sidelight of this trip was the fact it was done on downhill skis, and climbing skins were not necessary on any part of the route.

[6]Detailed descriptions of these areas will be included in Volume 3 of *Wasatch Tours*.

Pine/Red Pine canyons divide. From the notch, a nearly level traverse (dashed line in Figure 6.12) leads to the Red Pine Canyon/Dry Creek divide. The divide is crossed into the Dry Creek drainage, and the base of the Pfeiferhorn is traversed along its south flank. Rather than entering Hogum Fork, the traverse continues southwestward around a rocky shoulder, followed by a steep ascent to a pass between that shoulder and Chipman Peak. From the pass, a gently ascending traverse of Lightning Ridge leads (eventually) to the "low spot on the ridge" at the base of Thunder Mountain's south summit. (See Figure 7.19.)

This is the place to stop for lunch (or dinner, if the pace has been particularly slow) and to remove climbers and otherwise prepare for a near seven mile, 6000 vertical foot descent of Bells Canyon to the community of Granite.

Thunder Mountain. A strong party can continue the grand tour to the south summit of Thunder Mountain and to Thunder Mountain Bowl just a quarter mile to its north. The south summit is easily ascended by walking (or sidestepping) up a slope near its east ridge. From the summit, a northward descent along the ridge leads to the rim of Thunder Mountain Bowl. Early in the season, or in years of minimal snowfalls, descending into the bowl may require some rock scrambling.

Bells Canyon and Thunder Mountain Descent Routes. Innumerable descent possibilities exist in the main drainage of Bells Canyon and in its northern tributary that originates at Thunder Mountain Bowl. Three routes, pictured in Figure 7.19, represent the most topographically disparate options.

Bells Canyon (Main Fork). Descent of Route *(A)* commences at the "low spot on the ridge" beneath the south summit of Thunder Mountain. From there a short southwestward ski run beneath the south summit puts one at the Dry Creek/Bells Canyon divide. Tourers choosing to ski the open slopes beneath Lone Peak's north wall should expect some flatland traversing before joining the steeper valley leading into the main canyon. A higher route through the timber is a better alternative. A high downward traverse, with one small uphill segment, soon joins the "high traverse" ascent route. The final descent of the first avalanche slope mentioned in the ascent description can be quite disconcerting as the late-afternoon snow hardens on approach of evening.

Thunder Mountain Bowl. Route *(B)* is the Thunder Bowl descent route from the south summit of Thunder Mountain. Except for the steep headwall, the skiing terrain in the bowl consists of gently-sloped morainal mounds. After the bottom of the bowl is reached, two choices for the remainder of the descent become apparent. Variation *(1)* in

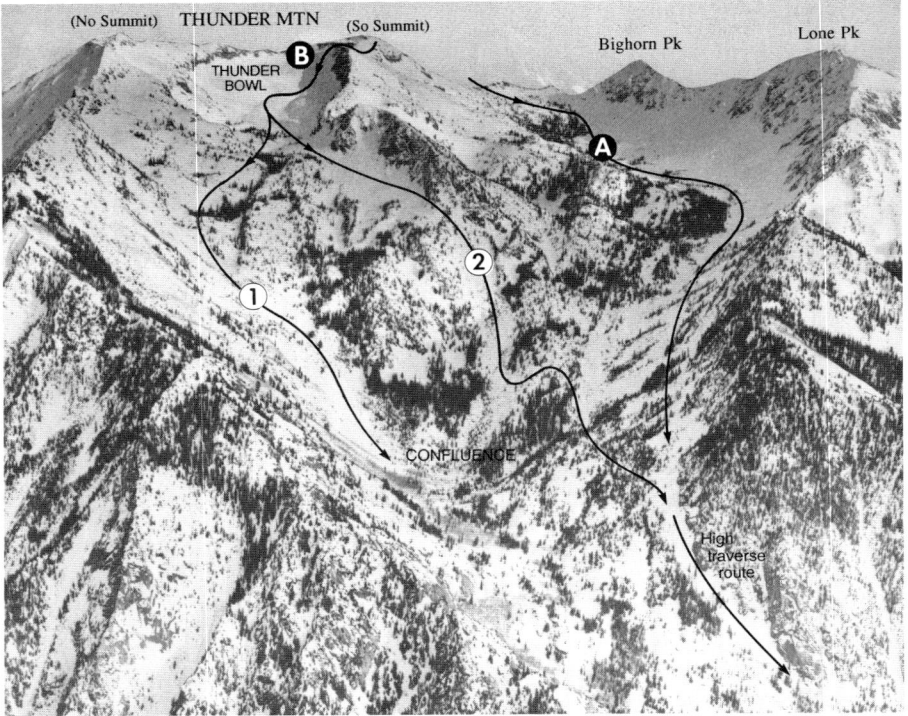

Figure 7.19   Bells Canyon has two very large glacial cirques that offer innumerable descent possibilities. Three of the more common options are illustrated; see text for descriptions.

Figure 7.19 meanders downward through groves of timber toward the confluence of Bells Canyon's two branches. While this route looks most inviting in the photo, tourers should be warned that several significant cliffbands transect the route.

Variation *(2)* in the illustration (the "middle" route) exchanges the several significant cliffbands in the descent just described for *several significant avalanche paths*. Basically, the middle route leads left from the bottom of Thunder Bowl, traverses beneath a rocky prominence, and descends a delightfully steep (and hazardous!) slope toward the confluence of the two drainages. Descending all the way to the confluence of the two Bells Canyon drainages, however, leads to several inconveniences farther down. More flatland traversing will be required below the joining of the forks, and the gullied and cobbly trail described previously will need to be skied.

The best option for all descents is to enjoy skiing the slopes above the confluence, but not quite to it, then taking a gradual upward traverse to intercept the "high traverse" ascent route. The feasibility of the "lost gold mine" feature as a descent route has not been ascertained by the authors.

A Note on Distances. The following table shows the length of each supertour and its elevation changes:

SUPERTOUR	ASCENT		DESCENT	
	dist(mi)	elev(ft)	dist(mi)	elev(ft)
White Pine-Bells	7.4	3200	5.8	5400
White Pine-Thunder Mtn.	7.8	3500	4.4	5700
White Pine-Thunder Mtn. (Hogum shortcut route)	7.3	3500	4.4	5700
Alta-Bells	10.9	3100	5.8	5400
Alta-Thunder Mtn.	11.3	3400	4.4	5700

THE "TERRA INCOGNITA" CANYONS

For nearly three decades, local Lone Peak touring aficionados have speculated about the possibilities of ski touring in the seven canyons and gulches that descend the west flank of the Lone Peak massif between Bells and Corner canyons. In the early to mid-1960's, a series of exploratory tours were made from Draper into the upper regions of Lone Peak. Some of these ventures started from the Corner Canyon jeep road; some commenced from the base of the Draper Ridge. But the areas between the Draper Ridge and Bells canyon remained unexplored. The seven canyons, depicted schematically in Figure 7.20 and pictorially in some preceding and following photographs, became known as "Terra Incognita."

Public access to the seven Incognita canyons formerly consisted of bushwhacking through scrub oak along interminably long foothill approaches. With the southward extension of Wasatch Boulevard into the foothills south of Little Cottonwood Canyon, and with the construction of several Sandy City reservoirs and water collection systems in the mouths of the canyons, the barriers to "easy access" were believed to have been lifted.

Unfortunately the development of the systems and reservoirs brought with it the encroachment of suburban neighborhoods on top of and across access routes into the canyons and the public forest lands within them. In the last couple of years the suburban sprawl has accelerated to the point where public access has been significantly compromised and

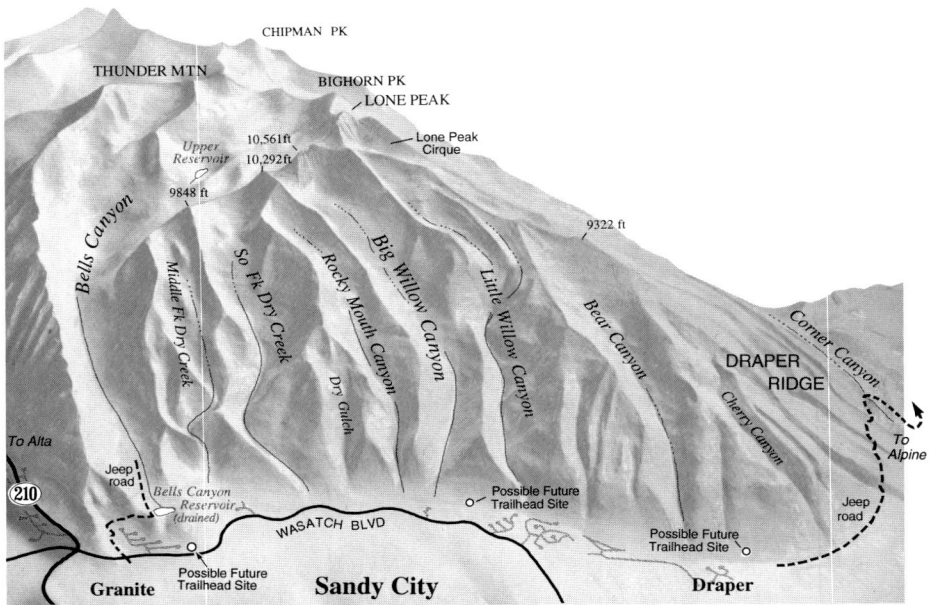

Figure 7.20   The "Terra Incognita" canyons south of Bells Canyon. Quite inaccessible until recently, these canyons are becoming victims of Sandy City's and Draper's urban sprawl.

in some cases shut off completely. Within a few years, the foothill areas east of Wasatch Boulevard (illustrated in Figures 7.14, 7.21, and 7.22) will resemble those of Olympus Cove.

After much urging by backcountry recreationists and several local conservation and user groups, the Forest Service began giving serious— but very belated—consideration to the problem of public access. A "Front Access Team" (FAT) was formed in August 1991 to develop recommendations for access into the National Forest lands along the urban/forest interface. As this volume goes to press in late 1994, the trailhead situation in the Terra Incognita area of the Wasatch is described as being "in a state of flux."

Draper Ridge/Lone Peak

Draper Ridge is the prominent ridge visible along the south edge of Salt Lake Valley that climbs gradually from the Point of the Mountain toward the summit of Lone Peak. The ridge is one of the most heavily abused areas along the Wasatch Front. Lackadaisical management by nearly all levels of government has contributed to proliferation of ORV

Figure 7.21 Dry Creek and Dry Gulch are the northernmost of the "Terra Incognita" drainages.

trails to the level where little unroaded terrain remains. In 1967 the Forest Service permitted a motion picture company filming *The Devil's Brigade* to bulldoze yet another ridge road onto the land mass. Though closed to vehicular use for nearly 30 years, the scar has yet to show signs of recovery.

The Draper Ridge hiking trail system has been described as "an assembly of firebreaks, jeep trails, horse, game, cattle, and foot trails." Three trails are commonly used by hikers to ascend Lone Peak: the "standard hiking trail," the "Firebreak Trail," and a Corner Canyon trail sometimes called "Jacob's Ladder." All trails commence from the Upper Corner Canyon Road that traverses along the base of the Draper Ridge just east of Draper. The three routes converge to a common trail near the 9000 foot level for the remainder of the ascent to Lone Peak. The road/trail system is clearly visible in Figure 7.23.

Because it's the most direct ski touring route to Lone Peak, the Firebreak Trail will be the only one discussed in this section. The standard hiking approach is detailed in John Veranth's *Hiking the Wasatch* and Dale Green's accompanying map. Other cross country skiing routes to

Figure 7.22   Big and Little Willow are two of the canyons whose access has been threatened by subdivision expansion.

Lone Peak will be described in Volume 3 of *Wasatch Tours.*

Lone Peak via the Draper Ridge Firebreak. The authors categorize the Lone Peak ski tour as a supertour. *Tourers who consider ascending the peak should be prepared for a long and arduous day.*

The Firebreak Trail, at the left of Figure 7.23, is probably the steepest stretch of trail in the Wasatch. Because the ridge is frequently exposed to severe winds, it can be free of snow even during winters of exceptional snowdepth.

The base of the Firebreak route is reached by exiting I-15 at Exit 294 (to Draper) and driving east on SR-71 into Draper. Turn right (south) on 700 East Street, proceed 1 block, and turn left (east) on Pioneer

Figure 7.23   The Draper Ridge/Corner Canyon area near Draper is one of the most heavily abused areas in the Wasatch. The "Firebreak" route is the most direct winter route for access to Lone Peak.

Avenue (12400 South). Continue eastward on Pioneer four miles. Turn right on 2000 East Street, and follow that to the end of the pavement. A gravel road, commonly known as the "Upper Corner Canyon Road," continues southward from there.

The gravel road is followed about 1.5 miles until a steep jeep trail ascending southeastward becomes visible on the left (east) side of the roadway. The Upper Corner Canyon Road is sufficiently wide to accommodate several parked cars without obstructing traffic. The parking site—and start of tour—is at an elevation of 5100 feet.

The first leg of the Firebreak Trail follows the steep jeep trail south approximately 0.5 mile, then angles abruptly east and over the next mile ascends 2000 feet to a rocky outcropping overlooking Draper and the south end of Salt Lake Valley. From the outcropping, it's necessary to descend a brush-dominated gully southeasterly 0.25 mile and to intercept a horse/foot trail (the "standard hiking trail") easily visible on the opposite slope. A brief traverse along the foot trail brings one to the lip of a small meadow at an elevation of 7400 feet.

The route ascends the drainage above the meadow toward the base of a rocky ridge, then follows the ridge until it nears a 9322 foot rocky prominence from where Lone Peak's summit becomes visible for the first

Figure 7.24   Lone Peak. *Bottom photo:* Two approaches are possible into
Lone Peak Cirque. Route (A) traverses high at the base of a granitic ridge
and is a direct route to Lone Peak's west shoulder. Route (B) drops into the
valley and follows it to the cirque. *Top photos:* The summit of Lone Peak is
commonly ascended along its west shoulder and ridge. The last few hundred
yards to the summit usually requires ropework to assure safety.

time. The route follows a small depression just south of the prominence,
crosses a ridge, and gently traverses along the south-facing slope toward
a meadow with trees. The route enters the meadow and follows the
streambed eastward about 1 mile toward some granitic outcroppings
visible ahead. Skirting the base of the outcroppings to the right leads to

a ridge separating drainages. The ridge is crossed into the new drainage that originates in Lone Peak Cirque. The outcroppings and the dividing ridge are clearly visible in the bottom portion of Figure 7.24. From here, a high traverse *(A)* along the base of the outcroppings leads to the west shoulder of Lone Peak. Some tourers prefer to descend *(B)* into the valley and follow that to Lone Peak Cirque.

Winter ascents of Lone Peak's summit are relatively rare, as some rope and ice axe work may be required. Most tourers prefer to end their Lone Peak tour at the peak's west shoulder, or somewhere along the summit ridge. (See top photos in Figure 7.24.) The ascent (from parking area to cirque) is about six miles and 6000 vertical feet.

Descents. The authors have experience with four descent options, only three of which are reasonable. Skiing directly into Alpine by following the cirque's streambed is definitely not recommended. The south-facing snow and impenetrable oak brush can make such a descent unforgettably undesirable.

The least troublesome option is to retrace the ascent route. During March or April, when Lone Peak tours become practical, it is possible to ski down to the meadow at the top of the Firebreak Trail. The remainder of the descent, however, is usually on marginal (or absent) snow.

Another pleasant ski descent is possible along the west base of the granitic ridge. Only a minimal traverse is necessary to rejoin the upward route at the meadow.

It is also possible to ski down—*very carefully*—the north ridge of Lone Peak 0.25 mile to the top of a very steep couloir that descends into Bells Canyon. (This route, as an ascent route, was described in the Bells Canyon Ski Mountaineering section.) A rope is essential here, to lower members of the touring party from a 10 foot ledge. The last person down is retrieved by use of a shoulder stand. Good luck!□

ABOUT THE AUTHORS

A native of Maine, Dave Hanscom started skiing at the age of two. After skiing competitively at Middlebury College, specializing in cross country and jumping, he and his wife Mary moved to Utah in 1970. The family enjoys cross country skiing in the Wasatch and Uinta mountains.

Alexis Kelner was born in Latvia, where ski touring is a way of life from birth. World War II displaced him, and he has resided in Utah ever since. Disgusted with the overcommercialization of the resorts, he took up cross country skiing in 1956; he and his friends pioneered a number of the more challenging touring routes in the area.

During the 60's, after writing many articles about ski touring in the Wasatch, Alexis planned to assemble a cross country skiing guide that would have included some of his spectacular photographs of the local mountains. While Ski Touring Director for the Wasatch Mountain Club in the early 70's, Dave observed that Utah tourers needed less crowded alternatives for their winter outings, and that many had little understanding of the hazards associated with the sport.

In 1973 Mel Davis, owner of Wasatch Publishers, proposed that Dave and Alexis collaborate on a touring guide. Published in 1976, *Wasatch Tours* was the product of that proposal.

Since 1976, Dave has taught many classes in avalanche safety and written numerous articles on ski touring. A founder of the Utah Nordic Ski Association, he organizes cross country ski races and works to preserve opportunities for ski touring. Alexis has authored *Skiing in Utah– A History* and *Utah's Olympic Circus*. His avalanche expertise led to a contract by the Forest Service to illustrate their *Avalanche Handbook*. He is an outspoken advocate for preservation of the local canyons.